Applied Computing

Springer

London
Berlin
Heidelberg
New York
Barcelona
Hong Kong
Milan
Paris
Singapore
Tokyo

The Springer-Verlag Series on Applied Computing is an advanced series of innovative textbooks that span the full range of topics in applied computing technology.

Books in the series provide a grounding in theoretical concepts in computer science alongside real-world examples of how those concepts can be applied in the development of effective computer systems.

The series should be essential reading for advanced undergraduate and postgraduate students in computing and information systems.

Books in this series are contributed by international specialist researchers and educators in applied computing who draw together the full range of issues in their specialist area into one concise authoritative textbook.

Titles already available:

Deryn Graham and Anthony Barrett
Knowledge-Based Image processing Systems
3-540-76027-X

Linda Macaulay
Requirements Engineering
3-540-76006-7

Derrick Morris, Gareth Evans, Peter Green, Colin Theaker
Object Orientated Computer Systems Engineering
3-540-76020-2

John Hunt
Java and Object Orientation: An Introduction
3-540-76148-9

David Gray
Introduction to the Formal Design of Real-Time Systems
3-540-76140-3

Mike Holcombe and Florentin Ipate
Correct Systems: Building A Business Process Solution
3-540-76246-9

Jan Noyes and Chris Baber
User-Centred Design of Systems
3-540-76007-5

Available in the Advanced Perspectives in Applied Computing series:

Sarah Douglas and Anant Mithal
The Ergonomics of Computer Pointing Devices
3-540-19986-1

Ulrich Nehmzow

Mobile Robotics:
A Practical Introduction

Springer

Ulrich Nehmzow, Dipl. Ing., PhD, CEng, MIEE
Department of Computer Science, University of Manchester, Manchester M13 9PL, UK

Series Editors

Professor Ray J. Paul, BSc MSc PhD
Department of Information Systems and Computing, Brunel University,
Uxbridge, Middlesex UB8 3PH, UK

Professor Peter J. Thomas, MIEE MBCS CEng FRSA
Centre for Personal Information Management, University of the West of England,
Frenchay Campus, Bristol BS16 1QY, UK

Dr Jasna Kuljis, PhD MS Dipl Ing
Department of Mathematical and Computing Sciences, Goldsmiths College,
University of London, New Cross, London SE14 6NW, UK

ISBN 1-85233-173-9 Springer-Verlag Berlin Heidelberg New York

British Library Cataloguing in Publication Data
Nehmzow, Ulrich
  Mobile robotics : a practical introduction. – (Applied
  Computing)
  1. Mobile robots   2. Robotics
  I. Title
  629.8'92
ISBN 1852331739

Library of Congress Cataloging-in-Publication Data
Nehmzow, Ulrich, 1961-
    Mobile robotics : a practical introduction. / Ulrich Nehmzow.
      p. cm -- (Applied Computing)
    Includes bibliographical references and index.
    ISBN 1-85233-173-9 (alk. paper)
    1. Mobile robots.   I. Title.   II. Series.
  TJ211.415 .N44 1999
  629.8'92 21—dc21
                                                                    99-043763

Typeset by Camera ready by author
Printed and bound at the Athenæum Press Ltd., Gateshead, Tyne & Wear
34/3830-54321   Printed on acid-free paper SPIN 10784389

Foreword

Robotics is a big field which combines many different disciplines. These include computer science, electrical and electronic engineering, mathematics, mechanical engineering, and structural design. Mobile robotics forms one important corner of the field of robotics in general. Mobile robots share some aspects and problems with other kinds of robots, such as industrial robot manipulators, but they also have some important problems that are particular to moving around and doing things in the real world.

Industrial robot manipulators, which are now widely used in car factories, for example, apart from being stationary, work in well structured and closely controlled environments. Very little happens in these environments that is not a direct consequence of the actions of the robot. There is also very little variation in what happens, how it happens, and in where things are or what the robot has to manipulate and how. We call these kinds of robot environments, *well structured controlled environments*. They are necessary for industrial robots to work properly.

The interest in investigating and developing mobile robots is very largely motivated by both a need and a desire to have robots that can work with and for people in their normal work or day-to-day environments: in offices, hospitals, museums and galleries, libraries, supermarkets and shopping centres, sports centres, exhibition centres, airports, railway stations, universities and schools, etc. and, one day, in our homes too. All these are, however, examples of a very different kind of environment from the one industrial robots work in. They *are* structured: they are all designed and built for us to live, work, and play in. This structure of our every day environments is not, however, designed specifically for robots, and nor would we want it to be. It is also generally unacceptable to people to have to control their work or living places so as to make it possible for robots to operate in them.

Mobile robots must be able to operate in our everyday environments, with all the normal variation and uncertainty that are characteristic of the places in which we work, live, and play. Environments in which there are typically other things going on, not just what the robot does. These kinds of environments we call *semi-structured uncontrolled environments*, to distinguish them from the kinds of places industrial robots must operate in.

Getting around and doing things in semi-structured uncontrolled environments is typically not something we find difficult to do. Unless we are confined to a wheelchair, for example, or suffer some other kind of mobility or perceptual impairment. For mobile robots, however, getting around and doing things in real environments remains a big problem in general. It requires a kind of intelligence that industrial robots, and other robots that work in well structured controlled environments, do not have, and do not need.

As soon as we start to need our robots to be in some way intelligent, even only a little bit, the field of robotics opens up even more. We need to bring in concepts and techniques from other fields such as artificial intelligence, cognitive science, psychology, and even animal behaviour. Just like the fields mentioned at the beginning, each of these are in themselves large areas of study, and typically require years of specialised education and practice to master.

So, if investigating and developing mobile robots, requires good knowledge from so many widely different disciplines, how are students of mobile robotics ever to get started? Very few people are able to spend years learning enough of each of these diverse fields before starting on mobile robotics, even if they wanted to. The process might be accelerated by reading one of the various comprehensive textbooks on robotics or mobile robots, but these often assume and require knowledge of concepts and techniques from other related fields, or they only offer rather superficial introductions to the subject.

From my experience, and that of an increasing number of teachers of mobile robotics, by far the best way of starting to learn all that needs to be known and understood to work in mobile robotics, is to build and test your own real robots. For some years now it has been possible to buy, quite cheaply, kits or parts sufficient to put together a small mobile robot. There are also a number of books and Web pages that introduce and describe enough of the electronics, mechanics, and programming to do this. There has not, however, been a good text book that sets out to introduce the basic problems and concepts and techniques of mobile robotics in a way that new students can apply them almost straight away; so that they can start building real mobile robots and start to get direct experience of some of the basic and still important problems of the field. This book does this. It presents a series of chapters that deal with the basic conceptual and technological aspects of mobile robots that are needed to make a start, and it then introduces basic problems of mobile robots. In each of these chapters the ideas and concepts are illustrated by case studies of real robots. These case studies are, of course, particular examples of how the basic problems can be solved. There are other robots that solve the same problems in other ways. However, the most important thing about the case studies presented in this book is that the author is intimately familiar with them, having developed and worked with each of them himself. This means that the presentations contain all the details necessary to understand how each robot was built and tested, and why, and, most important, it means that the presentations contain sufficient detail for students to reuse or re-implement the ideas and techniques involved in their own robots.

This is thus a text with which to start to learn about doing mobile robotics. It, of course, will not, and cannot, teach students everything they will need to know, but it will give them the right kind of start. Direct experience of trying to make real mobile robots move around and do things in the real world is, I would say, a necessary basis for learning more. This book offers this kind of essential start to students of mobile robotics.

Donostia / San Sebastian, July 1999   *Tim Smithers*

Preface

The aims of this book are expressed in its title, *Mobile Robotics: a Practical Introduction*.

Mobile Robotics The book discusses the design of autonomous, mobile robots, i.e. mechanical devices that are equipped with an on-board power source, on-board computational resource, sensors and actuators.

The robots' ability to move autonomously and freely is gain and loss at the same time: gain, in that the robots can be used for tasks that require movement (e.g. transportation, surveillance, inspection and cleaning tasks), and can position themselves optimally for their operation. They are therefore uniquely suited to large-area operation in environments that are inaccessible or dangerous to humans. Loss, on the other hand, in that the autonomous movement in semi-structured environments, i.e. environments that have not been specially prepared for robot operation, can produce unexpected events, fluctuations and uncertainty. Control algorithms for autonomous mobile robots need to take this into account, and deal with noise, unpredictability and variation.

This book addresses these problems, by looking at methods of building adaptable, learning robots, and by introducing navigation methods that do not rely on modifications to the environment, or pre-installation of knowledge (such as maps). The end products are mobile robots that move autonomously in their environment, learn from mistakes and successes, and are able to move to specified places reliably — all without modifications to the environment, or user-supplied maps.

Introduction This book is primarily intended for final year undergraduate students and postgraduate students of mobile robotics. It provides an introduction to the field, and explains the core concepts so that readers with a basic knowledge of engineering mathematics and physics will be able to follow them. It contains numerous examples and exercises that highlight the main points.

However, through its 12 detailed case studies the book provides more challenging material for advanced students and practitioners of mobile robotics. The purpose of the case studies is to demonstrate how problems in mobile robotics can be addressed, how mobile robotics experiments are conducted and documented, and to encourage you to implement mechanisms on your own robot.

Practical Throughout the book, and especially in the case studies, I have tried to give all necessary details to design your own robot. The essence of mobile robotics are robots, and the sooner the student begins to design robots, the better.

The case studies in particular present more challenging examples of mobile robotics research. Besides allowing replication of existing work, they contain pointers to open problems which can be used to start original research.

Acknowledgements Dealing with a research discipline where emergent phenomena and collaborative behaviour are key issues, this book is a proof in point: it is the result of years of fruitful and stimulating co-operation with my colleagues and students, and my main task in writing this book was to structure the work and present it such that the final book could emerge. I am grateful for the stimulating academic environments I could work in, first at the University of Edinburgh, later at Manchester. The University of Manchester in particular has supported much of the work presented in this book, financially and in other ways. Thank you to the Department and to all my colleagues there.

Some of the experiments presented in this book were carried out by my students. Carl Owen's work on route learning is described in section 5.4.3, Tom Duckett's research in robot self localisation is the topic of section 5.4.4, and Ten Min Lee's experiments in robot simulation are discussed in chapter 6. On this latter project, I also acknowledge the inspiring collaboration with my colleague Roger Hubbold. Alan Hinton conducted the experimental work described in section 4.4.3. Andrew Pickering has given the technical advice and support in all of these projects. Their committed work has been a great joy and encouragement to me.

Science is not done in isolation, but depends crucially on the interaction with others. I am grateful for the inspiring friendship with Tim Smithers, and the many stimulating discussions with Jonathan Shapiro, Roger Hubbold, David Brée, Ian Pratt-Hartmann, Mary McGee Wood, Magnus Rattray and John Hallam, to name but a few. Thank you, Tim, for writing the foreword.

Various research groups have provided stimulating environments, and thus contributed to the material presented here. Tom Mitchell kindly invited me to visit his group at Carnegie Mellon University, and co-authored the paper that is the basis of section 4.1. Case study 8 is the result of a sabbatical spent at the Electrotechnical Laboratory in Tsukuba, Japan. This visit was made possible by a fellowship from the Japanese Science and Technology Agency and the Royal Society. Finally, my visits to Bremen University and Bernd Krieg-Brückner's group there, which are due to a research project funded by the British Council and the German Academic Exchange Service, sharpened my focus on many issues discussed in this book. I benefited greatly from all these collaborations, and thank my hosts and sponsors.

I am also indebted to David Brée, Andrew Wilson, Jonathan Shapiro, Claudia Nehmzow and Tim Smithers for their constructive comments on earlier drafts of this book, and to Stephen Marsland for his help in editing the bibliography.

I thank all my family for their unstinting support and love, and my wife Claudia for her help in the final preparations of this book, and for being such a brilliant companion. Finally, I acknowledge the invaluable contributions of Henrietta, aged four, who supplied me with the numerous blueprints of robots that decorate my office and made me marvel at the design of animate and inanimate agents.

Manchester, July 1999   *Ulrich Nehmzow*

Contents

1 Introduction

Summary. This chapter sets the scene. It presents an introduction to the scientific issues in mobile robotics, gives an overview of the contents of each chapter, and encourages you to build your own robot to put this book into action.

Autonomous mobile robotics is a fascinating research topic, for many reasons. First, to change a mobile robot from a computer on wheels that is merely able to sense some physical properties of the environment through its sensors into an intelligent agent, able to identify features, to detect patterns and regularities, to learn from experience, to localise, build maps and to navigate requires the simultaneous application of many research disciplines. In this sense, mobile robotics reverses the trend in science towards more and more specialisation, and demands lateral thinking and the combination of many disciplines.

Engineering and computer science are core elements of mobile robotics, obviously, but when questions of intelligent behaviour arise, artificial intelligence, cognitive science, psychology and philosophy offer hypotheses and answers. Analysis of system components, for example through error calculations, statistical evaluations etc. are the domain of mathematics, and regarding the analysis of whole systems, physics proposes explanations, for example through chaos theory.

Second, autonomous mobile robots are the closest approximation yet of intelligent agents, the age-old dream. For centuries people have been interested in building machines that mimic living beings. From mechanical animals, using clockwork, to the software and physical agents of artificial life — the question of "what is life and can we understand it?" has always motivated research.

Perception and action are tightly coupled in living beings. To see, animals perform specific head and eye movements. To interact with the environment, they anticipate the result of their actions and predict the behaviour of other objects. They alter the environment in order to communicate (so-called stigmergy) — nest building in ants is an example of this.

Because of this tight coupling between perception and action there is a strong argument for investigating intelligent behaviour by means of *situated* agents, i.e. mobile robots. In order to investigate simulations of life and lifelike agents that

1

interact intelligently with their environment, we need to close the loop between perception and action, allowing the agent to determine what it sees. Whether we will have autonomous robots that match human intelligence within 50 years, or whether humans will even be obsolete by then (very fuzzy statements, because the definitions of "intelligent" and "obsolete" are not at all clear), as some writers predict, or whether we will have to wait another 100 years for truly intelligent household robots, as others reply, autonomous mobile robots offer a uniquely suited research platform for investigating intelligent behaviour.

Third, there are commercial applications of mobile robots. Transportation, surveillance, inspection, cleaning or household robots are just some examples. However, autonomous mobile robots have not yet made much impact upon industrial and domestic applications, mainly due to the lack of robust, reliable and flexible navigation and behaviour mechanisms for autonomous mobile robots operating in unmodified, semi-structured environments. Installing markers such as beacons, visual patterns or induction loops (guiding wires buried in the ground) is one way round this problem, but it is expensive, inflexible and sometimes outright impossible. The alternative — navigation in *unmodified* environments — requires sophisticated sensor signal processing techniques which are still in their experimental evaluation phases. Case studies in this book present some of these techniques. So, to let mobile robots work in areas which are inaccessible to humans, or to perform repetitive, difficult or dangerous tasks, is yet another strong motivation for developing intelligent, autonomous robots.

And finally, there is also an aesthetic and artistic element to mobile robotics. Swarms of robots collaborating to achieve a particular task, or moving about avoiding collisions with one another and objects in their environment, beautifully designed mobile robots, like for instance micro-robots, or miniature legged robots, appeal to our sense of aesthetics. It is not surprising that mobile robots and robot arms have been used for artistic performances (e.g. [Stelarc]).

Construct Your Own Working Robot Mobile robotics, by nature, has to be *practised*. There are a range of relatively cheap mobile robots available now, which can be used for student practicals, student projects, or robotics projects at home (robotics as a hobby is rapidly gaining ground). *GRASMOOR* (see figure 1.1), built at the University of Manchester, is one example — it has its own onboard controller, infrared sensors, light sensors, tactile sensors, and a differential drive system[1]. *GRASMOOR* is controlled by a variant of the MIT 6270 controller, a controller with analogue and digital inputs for sensors, and pulse-width-modulated output to drive motors (the different types of sensors that can be used on robots are discussed in chapter 3, and pulse width modulation generates electric pulses of variable length to drive motors at variable speed). Like many robot micro-controllers, the 6270 controller is based on the Motorola 6811 microprocessor.

It is not difficult to get going for a few hundred pounds, using robot kits or technical construction kits based on children's toys, some of which have micro-controllers and the necessary software environment to programme the

---

[1] In a differential drive system the left and right wheel of a robot are driven by independent motors.

FIG. 1.1. THE MOBILE ROBOT *GRASMOOR*

robots. Information about the MIT 6270 robot design competition can be found at http://lcs.www.media.mit.edu/people/fredm/projects/6270/, and a good introduction to building your own robot is [Jones & Flynn 93]. If you are competent at building electronic circuits — and they needn't be very complicated — you can also use commercially available micro-controllers, and interface sensors and motors to them to build your robot. The basic message is: you don't have to invest large sums to build a mobile robot.

Experiments with Mobile Robots This book contains 12 detailed case studies that cover the areas of robot learning, navigation and simulation. Furthermore, there are examples, exercises and pointers to open questions. One of their purposes is to indicate interesting areas of robotics research, identifying open questions and relevant problems.

A fascinating introduction to thought experiments with robots is Valentino Braitenberg's book on "synthetic psychology" ([Braitenberg 84]), which contains many experiments that can be implemented and carried out on real robots.

Organisation of the Book Scientific progress rests on the successes and failures of the past, and is only achieved if the history of a scientific area is understood. This book therefore begins by looking at the history of autonomous mobile robotics research, discussing early examples and their contributions towards our understanding of the complex interaction between robots, the world they operate in, and the tasks they are trying to achieve.

A robot, obviously, is made from hardware, and the functionality of a robot's sensors and actuators influences its behaviour greatly. The second chapter of the book, therefore, looks at hardware issues specifically and discusses the most common robot sensors and actuators.

A truly intelligent robot needs to be able to deal with uncertain, ambiguous, contradictory and noisy data. It needs to learn through its own interaction with the world, being able to assess events with respect to the goal it is trying to achieve, and to alter its behaviour if necessary. Chapter 4 presents mechanisms that can support these fundamental learning competences.

Mobility is (almost) pointless without the ability of goal-directed motion, i.e. navigation. This book will therefore cover the area of mobile robot navigation, taking some inspiration from the most successful navigators on earth: living beings (chapter 5). Five case studies highlight the mechanisms used in successful robot navigation systems: self-organisation, emergent functionality and autonomous mapping of the environment "as the robot perceives it".

Scientific research is not only about matter, it is about method as well. Given the complexity of robot-environment interaction, given the sensitivity of a robot's sensors to slight changes in the environment, to colour and surface structure of objects, etc., to date the proof of a robot control program is still in physical experiments. To know what robot behaviour will result from a specific robot control program, one actually has to run the program on a real robot. Numerical models of the complex interaction between robot and environment interaction are still imprecise approximations, due to the sensitivity of robot sensors to variations in environmental conditions. However, chapter 6 looks at one approach to construct a more faithful model of robot-environment interaction, and at the conditions under which such modelling is achievable.

The purpose of this book is not only to give an introduction to the construction of mobile robots and the design of intelligent controllers, but also to demonstrate methods of evaluation of autonomous mobile robots — the science of mobile robotics. Scientific method involves the analysis of existing knowledge, identification of open questions, the design of an appropriate experimental procedure to investigate the question, and the analysis of the results.

In established natural sciences this procedure has been refined over decades and is now well understood, but in the relatively young science of robotics this is not the case. There are no universally agreed procedures yet, neither for conducting experiments, nor for the interpretation of results. Environments, robots and their tasks cannot yet be described in unambiguous ways that allow independent replication of experiments and independent verification of results. Instead, qualitative descriptions of experiments and results have to be used. Widely accepted standard benchmark tests in the area of mobile robotics do not exist, and existence proofs, i.e. the implementation of one particular algorithm on one particular robot, operating in one particular environment, are the norm.

To develop a science of autonomous mobile robotics, quantitative descriptions of robots, tasks and environments are needed, and independent replication and verification of experiments has to become the standard procedure within the scientific community. Existence proofs alone will not suffice to investigate mobile robots systematically — they serve a purpose in the early stages of the emergence of a scientific field, but have to be supplemented later by rigorous and quantitatively defined experimentation. Chapter 7 therefore discusses mathematical tools that allow such quantitative assessment of robot performance, and gives three case studies of quantitative analysis of mobile robot behaviour.

The book concludes with an analysis of the reasons for successes in mobile robotics research, and identifies technological, control and methodological challenges that lie ahead.

Mobile robotics is a vast research area, with many more facets than this introductory textbook can cover. The purpose of this book is to whet your appetite for mobile robotics research. Each chapter of this book includes pointers to further reading, and world-wide web links, in addition to the references given in the text. Using these, you will hopefully agree that mobile robotics is indeed a fascinating research topic that throws some light on the age-old question:

"What are the fundamental building blocks of intelligent behaviour?"

2 Foundations

Summary. This chapter introduces the technical terms used in this book, gives an overview of early work in artificial intelligence and robotics, and discusses two fundamental approaches to robot control, the functional approach and the behaviour-based approach.

2.1 Definitions

The purpose of this chapter is to give definitions of technical terms that are used in this book, and to give an introduction to the area of autonomous mobile robotics, looking back at early examples of such robots. Knowing where you come from will help to determine where you would like to go!

The "Further Reading" section of this chapter is particularly large, because this textbook aims to look at current issues, rather than historic ones, and the references given ought to plug some of the gaps that this chapter inevitably has to leave.

What is a 'Robot'? The word "robot" stems from a play from 1921 called "R.U.R." ("Rossum's Universal Robots") by the Czech playwright Karel Capek. Capek derived the word "robot" from the Czech "robota", meaning "forced labour". In 1942, the word "robotics" appeared for the first time in a novel called "Runaround" by the American scientist and writer Isaac Asimov.

According to the *Japanese Industrial Robot Association (JIRA)*, robots are divided into the following classes:

Class 1: *manual handling device*: a device with several degrees of freedom actuated by the operator;

Class 2: *fixed sequence robot*: handling device which performs the successive stages of a task according to a predetermined, unchanging method, which is difficult to modify;

Class 3: *variable sequence robot*: the same type of handling device as in class 2, but the stages can be modified easily;

Class 4: *playback robot*: the human operator performs the task manually by leading or controlling the robot, which records the trajectories. This information is recalled when necessary, and the robot can perform the task in the automatic mode;

Class 5: *numerical control robot*: the human operator supplies the robot with a movement program rather than teaching it the task manually;

Class 6: *intelligent robot*: a robot with the means to understand its environment, and the ability to successfully complete a task despite changes in the surrounding conditions under which it is to be performed.

The *Robotics Institute of America (RIA)* considers only the machines which are at least in class 3 as robots:

A robot is a re-programmable, multi-functional manipulator (or device) designed to move material, parts, tools, or specialised devices through variable programmed motions for the performance of a variety of tasks.

Mobile Robot Most robots in industrial use today are manipulators ("assembly robots") that operate within a bounded workspace, and cannot move.

Mobile robots, the topic of this book, are entirely different: they can change their location through locomotion. The most common type of mobile robot is the Automated Guided Vehicle (AGV, see figure 2.1).

FIG. 2.1. AN AUTOMATED GUIDED VEHICLE

AGVs operate in specially modified environments (typically containing induction loops[1], beacons, or other markers), and carry out transportation tasks along fixed routes.

Because AGVs operate in an engineered environment, they are inflexible, and brittle. Altering the route is costly, and any unforeseen changes (such as objects blocking the path) can lead to failure in completing a mission.

The alternative, therefore, to fixed-program mobile robots is to build *autonomous* mobile robots.

---

[1] Guiding wires buried beneath the floor.

Agent *Agere* simply means "to do", and the word agent is used in this book for an entity that produces an effect. In particular, we use "agent" when talking about software entities, for example the simulation of a robot. While a robot, that is a physical machine, also produces an effect, and therefore is an agent, too, we use the term "robot" for physical machines, and "agent" for their numerical computer models.

Autonomy There are two main definitions of autonomy ([Webster 81]): a) undertaken without outside control, and b) having the power of self-government.

Robots that carry on-board controllers and power supplies — as for example AGVs — are autonomous in the former, weaker, meaning of the word autonomy ("weak autonomy").

However, to cope with unforeseen situations and to adapt to changing environments, the power of self-government ("strong autonomy") is needed. Self-government implies that the machine is able to determine its course of action by its own reasoning process, rather than following a fixed, hardwired sequence of externally-supplied instructions. Strong autonomy requires the ability to build internal representations of the world, to plan, and to learn from experience. Chapter 4 presents a learning mechanism for mobile robots that supports these competences.

An autonomous mobile robot, then, has the ability to move in its environment to perform a number of different tasks, is able to adapt to changes in its environment, learn from experience and change its behaviour accordingly, and to build internal representations of its world that can be used for reasoning processes like navigation.

Intelligence We read about "intelligent machines" and "intelligent robots", in popular science textbooks and magazines — but a usable and clear definition of intelligence is elusive. "Intelligence" refers to behaviour, and the yardstick by which we measure it is very dependent on our own education, understanding, and point of view. Alan Turing wrote in 1947:

> "The extent to which we regard something as behaving in an intelligent manner is determined as much by our own state of mind and training as by the properties of the object under consideration. If we are able to explain and predict its behaviour or if there seems to be little underlying plan, we have little temptation to imagine intelligence. With the same object, therefore, it is possible that one man would consider it as intelligent and another would not; the second man would have found out the rules of its behaviour."

Turing's observation portrays "intelligence" as an unreachable goal, because the moment we understand the workings of a machine, or can predict its behaviour, or determine its underlying plan, it is no longer "intelligent". This means that as we progress in our understanding of design and analysis of artificial systems, "intelligence" moves along with us, staying out of our reach.

However we define "intelligence", the definition is tied to human behaviour. We consider ourselves intelligent, and therefore any machine that does what we do has to be considered "intelligent" too. For mobile robotics, this view has interesting consequences. People have always felt that games like chess require intelligence, whereas moving about in the world without any major hiccups is just "ordinary" stuff, not requiring intelligence. If intelligence is "what humans do, pretty much all the time" (Brooks), then this "ordinary" behaviour is the key to intelligent robots! It has proven a lot more difficult to build robots that move around without getting into trouble than it has to build chess playing machines!

For the purpose of this book, I avoid the term "intelligence" if possible. If used, it refers to goal oriented behaviour, that is behaviour that is in an understandable and explainable relationship with the task the robot is trying to achieve at the time.

The Triangle of Agent, Task and Environment Like "intelligence", the behaviour of any robot cannot be evaluated independently from the robot's environment and the task which the robot is performing. Robot, task and environment depend upon each other, and influence each other (see figure 2.2).

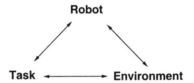

FIG. 2.2. ROBOT, TASK AND ENVIRONMENT ARE INTERLINKED, AND CANNOT BE CONSIDERED INDEPENDENT FROM ONE ANOTHER

Tim Smithers' famous example of this fact is the spider: extremely competent at survival in the countryside, but utterly incompetent in the bathtub! The very same agent appears to be intelligent in one situation, but incompetent in the other.

This means, consequently, that a general purpose robot cannot exist (in the same way that a general-purpose living being does not exist.) A robot's function and operation are defined by the robot's own behaviour within a specific environment, taking into account a specific task. Only the simultaneous description of agent, task and environment describes an agent — alive or machine — completely.

2.2 Applications of Mobile Robots

The ability of mobile robots to move around autonomously in their environment determines the best possible applications of such robots: tasks that involve transportation, exploration, surveillance, guidance, inspection, etc. In particular, mobile robots are used for applications in environments that are inaccessible or hostile to humans. Examples are underwater robots, planetary rovers, or robots operating in contaminated environments.

There is a second broad area of applications of mobile robotics, in the fields of artificial intelligence, cognitive science and psychology. Autonomous mobile robots offer an excellent means of testing hypotheses about intelligent behaviour, perception and cognition.

The control program of an autonomous mobile robot can be analysed in detail, experimental procedures and experimental setup can be controlled carefully, allowing the replication and independent verification of experiments, and individual experimental parameters can be modified in a controlled way. An example of this is case study 4 on p. 107, where the ants' navigation system is modelled on a mobile robot.

2.3 History of Mobile Robotics: Early Implementations

Artificial intelligence and mobile robotics have always been linked. Even before the days of the 1956 Dartmouth College Conference, at which the term "artificial intelligence" was coined, it was known that mobile robots could be made to perform interesting tasks and to learn. William Grey Walter built a couple of mobile robots in the early 1950s which were able to learn tasks like obstacle avoidance and phototaxis by instrumental conditioning, changing charges in a robot's capacitor which controlled the robot's behaviour ([Walter 50]). Early pioneers in artificial intelligence, such as Marvin Minsky and John McCarthy, became interested in robotics almost straightaway after the 1956 Dartmouth Conference. In the late 1950s Minsky, together with Richard Greenblood and William Gosper, attempted to build a Ping-Pong playing robot. Due to technical difficulties with the machine hardware, eventually a robot was built that would catch a ball using a basket instead of the robot's gripper.

At Stanford, Nils Nilsson developed the mobile robot *SHAKEY* in 1969. This robot possessed a visual range finder, a camera and binary tactile sensors, and was connected to a DEC PDP 10 computer via a radio link. *SHAKEY's* tasks included both obstacle avoidance and object movement within a highly structured environment. All obstacles were simple uniformly coloured blocks and wedges. *SHAKEY* maintained a list of formulae representing the objects of its environment and, using a resolution theorem prover called "STRIPS", it determined plans of actions which it then executed.

Again, although the reasoning system worked properly, *SHAKEY* often had problems generating the symbolic information needed for the planner from the raw data obtained from the sensor. The hardware was the difficult part of the robot project. Hans Moravec, then a student at Stanford, recalls ([Crevier 93, p. 115]):

> "An entire run of *SHAKEY* could involve the robot getting into a room, finding a block, being asked to move the block over the top of the platform, pushing a wedge against the platform, rolling up the ramp, and

pushing the block up. *SHAKEY* never did this as one complete sequence. It did it in several independent attempts, which each had a high probability of failure. You were able to put together a movie that had all the pieces in it, but it was really flaky."

Also at Stanford, John McCarthy started a project in the early 1970s to build a robot which would assemble a colour television kit, and again the hardware of the robot – the physical act of inserting components into printed circuit boards with sufficient accuracy – proved to be the difficult part. Many researchers who were interested in robotics in the early days of artificial intelligence, left the hardware aspect of robotics aside and concentrated again on the software and reasoning components of the control system.

The perception at the time was very much that the problem of designing an intelligent robot rested predominantly with the robot's control structure. Once the necessary hardware components were in place to support the intelligent reasoning element of the controller, intelligent behaviour would inevitably follow and much research was therefore focused on control paradigms. Nevertheless, a number of influential robotics projects were carried out in the 1970s.

The *JPL Rover*, developed in the 1970s at the Jet Propulsion Laboratory in Pasadena, was designed for planetary exploration. Using a TV camera, laser range finder and tactile sensors the robot categorised its environment as "traversable", "not traversable" and "unknown". Navigation was performed by dead reckoning using an inertial compass (dead reckoning is discussed on p. 96).

At Stanford, Hans Moravec developed *CART* in the late 1970s. This mobile robot's task was obstacle avoidance using a camera sensor. The robot would take nine pictures at one location to create a two-dimensional world model. It would then move 1 metre ahead and repeat the process. To process those nine images took 15 minutes: 5 minutes to digitise the 9 pictures; 5 minutes to perform a low level visual reduction of the image, in which obstacles were represented as circles; and 5 minutes for the maintenance of the world model and path planning. *Cart* was successful at avoiding obstacles, albeit very slow. It had, however, problems in getting its own position right or to see obstacles which lacked sufficiently high contrast.

In Europe in the late 1970s, *HILARE* was developed at LAAS in Toulouse; it was one of the first European mobile robot projects. *HILARE* used computer vision, laser range finders and ultra-sonic sensors to navigate in its environment. A slow process of scene analysis, which was carried out every 10 seconds, and a faster dynamic vision process, which was carried out every 20 centimetres of movement, were the underlying control principles. Nearby obstacles were avoided using ultrasonic sensors. Navigation and path planning were achieved by using a two-dimensional polygon representation of space and a global co-ordinate system.

2.4 History of Mobile Robotics: Control Paradigms

2.4.1 Cybernetics

In the early days of mobile robotics research, the starting point for building an intelligent machine was in most cases an engineering background. Cybernetics, one predecessor of artificial intelligence, is the best example of this.

Cybernetics is the application of control theory to complex systems. A monitor — which could be either some internal function or a human observer — compares the actual system status x_t at time t with the desired system status τ_t. The error $\epsilon_t = x_t - \tau_t$ is the input signal to a controller, whose goal it is to minimise the error ϵ_t. The controller will take an action y_{t+k} at the next time step $t + k$, and the equation

$$y_{t+k} = f(\epsilon_t) = f(x_t - \tau_t) \tag{2.1}$$

describes the complete control model, with f being an (initially unknown) control function.

The goal of cybernetics is to define the control function f and all control parameters (such as delays, lags, input and output signals, etc.) in such a manner that the system will respond appropriately to sensory stimuli: intelligence is the minimisation of an error function.

There are many related approaches to the design of intelligent agents using control theory as a foundation, for example homeostasis, a self-regulating process that maintains a stable equilibrium of life-governing processes that is optimal for survival. The underlying idea always is that the "intelligence function" is expressed as a control law, and an error is defined and minimised through control theory.

2.4.2 Functional Approach

The sense-think-act cycle (see figure 2.3) is an extension of the cybernetics approach. While in cybernetics the goal is to minimise the control error of a controlled system, in the sense-think-act cycle a more general definition of error is used, and the objective of the cycle is to minimise that error. It works very much like a coffee percolator: sensor signals enter the system at the top, percolate through several layers of control, whose purpose it is to minimise discrepancies between observed and desired behaviour, to emerge transformed into motor actions at the bottom. The cycle is repeated continuously, and provided the layers of control in the middle are chosen correctly, overall intelligent behaviour will result from this process.

In figure 2.3, the control system is decomposed into five functional modules. The first module processes the data received from the robot's sensors (sensor signal preprocessing).

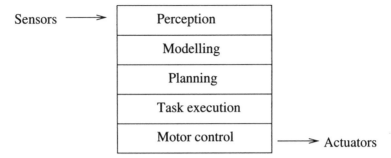

FIG. 2.3. Sense-Think-Act cycle: Functional decomposition of a mobile robot control system. Sensory information is processed in a serial manner, using an internal world model.

The preprocessed data is then used to either construct or update an internal world model, or it is compared with an already existing world model for classification. The world model is the yardstick by which data is evaluated, and the basis for all control decisions.

The third module, the planner, uses the world model and the current perception to decide upon a plan of action. It is important to realise here that this plan is based on the robot's assumed nature of the world (the world model, which is, by its nature, a generalised and abstracted representation of the real world as it is "out there").

Once a set of actions has been generated, the fourth and fifth modules execute the actions by controlling the robot's actuators (e.g. motors). Often these components are also based on some internal world model, describing in an abstract form the results of a particular action.

This sense-think-act process is repeated continuously until the main goal of the robot has been achieved.

Constructing a representation of the world, and devising a list of actions to achieve a goal (planning), are classical AI problems. Thus, according to the functional decomposition of figure 2.3, AI can be seen as a part of robotics. In order to build an intelligently behaving robot, just add sensors and actuators to an AI system: *Intelligent robot = classical AI system + right engineering*.

The Physical Symbol System Hypothesis Most early robots in robotics research are based on the functional approach. The underlying hypothesis that generated this work was the physical symbol system hypothesis of Newell and Simon. In 1976, they defined a physical symbol system as follows:

> "A physical symbol system consists of a set of entities called symbols, which are physical patterns that can occur as components of another type of entity, called an expression or symbol structure. Thus, a symbol structure is composed of a number of instances or tokens of symbols related in some physical way (such as one token being next to another). At any instance of time, the system will contain a collection of these symbol structures. Besides these structures, the system also contains

a collection of processors to operate on expressions to produce other expressions: processors of creation, modification, reproduction and destruction. A physical symbol system is a machine that produces, through time, an evolving collection of symbol structures. Such a system exists in a world of objects wider than just the symbolic expressions themselves."

The physical symbol system hypothesis was formulated as follows:

"A physical symbol system has the necessary and sufficient means for general intelligent action."

Obviously the physical symbol system hypothesis is a hypothesis and cannot be proved or disproved on logical grounds. However it was found to be compelling and generated much of the early robotics research work.

Problems of the Functional Approach Thus, the functional approach was the fundamental paradigm of most of the early work in mobile robotics. However, despite the good results that were achieved using control theory in technical applications, and despite considerable research effort, the success of achieving intelligent robot behaviour were so modest that it led to researchers abandoning the hardware aspects of the work, and focusing on the "intelligent" (software) part instead. As mentioned above, this led to the view that once the engineering aspect of robotics was solved, the intelligent controller could be bolted on to a reliable robot base, and an intelligent robot would result. Until such bases were available, it was more fruitful to concentrate on control issues (i.e. software), rather than to struggle on with building real robots.

However, in the 1980s this view — intelligent robotics as a marriage of the right type of engineering with classical symbolic AI — received more and more critical comments, for the following reasons.

First, a functional system is extremely brittle. If any module fails, then the whole system will fail. The main problem is the interface between the sensors and the representation module, which is responsible for building the world model. The robot must be able to decide what needs to be represented in the model and in what form.

A model is used for a range of different purposes. It is needed to represent the environment in such a way that the robot is able to move around without collision and, since the robot has a particular task to perform, the representation must include all necessary information needed to develop a plan. The crucial point to make here is that the planning module only refers to the world model, it cannot access the sensors. It could easily be the case that the sensors detect an object which would be relevant for the planner, but which is not represented in the world model, and which would therefore be overlooked (think of John Cleese in "A Fish called Wanda", who is so distracted by Jamie Lee Curtis that he drives off with his briefcase on the roof of his car — if he has a world model in operation at the time, it does not contain a symbol for "briefcase on car"). Too much detail, on the other hand, leads to an increase of the time needed to build and maintain the model (recall how long it took *CART* to process the digital images obtained from its camera and to update its world representation).

A fast processing time is necessary in a dynamic environment, since it is not unlikely that the environment changes while the planning programme is devising a plan based on the previously updated world map representation. Keeping a world model up to date is computationally expensive. A large amount of processing is spent simply maintaining the world model. It seems more sensible that the robot should respond immediately to actual changes in the environment and, although a planner could take into account multiple goals, to use different fundamental behaviours that each address specific aspects of the robot's behaviour.

A fast reaction time is particularly important for mobile robots, who are, after all, operating in and interacting with a dynamic world. There are situations where a very fast response is required (e.g. avoiding oncoming obstacles, or avoiding driving down stairwells), and the considerable processing time needed to preprocess sensor signals and maintain a world model is a serious impediment in this respect. Expressed differently, the functional approach does not adequately reflect the robot's need for quick reaction.

Furthermore, it appeared less and less likely that intelligent robot behaviour could actually be achieved by symbol manipulation in a physical symbol system bolted on to an adequately engineered mobile robot base. The question arose whether intelligent behaviour actually is the result of symbol manipulation, or whether some ingredient was missing.

Alternatives to the functional approach appeared, and a number of criticisms of the functional approach were expressed. One of them was the symbol grounding problem.

The Symbol Grounding Problem The symbol grounding problem, expressed by Stevan Harnad ([Harnad 90]), states that behaviour, although interpretable as ruleful, does not have to be governed by symbolic rules, but rather that the mere manipulation of symbols is not sufficient for cognition. Instead, symbols have to be grounded in some meaningful entity. In other words: the symbol alone is meaningless, it is its (physical) effect on the robot that is relevant for the robot's operation (whether I call a seating-implement "chair" or "table" does not really matter — the meaning of either word is defined by its connection with physical objects in the real world).

The symbol grounding problem is a serious challenge to control based on symbolic world models. It states that symbols *per se* are meaningless, and it follows from that that reasoning based on meaningless symbols itself is also meaningless. But what are the alternatives?

2.4.3 Behaviour-Based Robotics

Based on the objections to the functional approach stated above — dependency on potentially meaningless symbols, brittleness due to chained reasoning processes, computational complexity due to elaborate world models — the research community tried to develop robot control paradigms that could operate without symbolic representations, that would have a tighter linking between perception and action, and be computationally cheaper. However, if complexity was reduced at all these various levels, the "intelligent bit" had to come from somewhere else. This "somewhere else" lay in the way of interaction between the various processes, leading to so-called "emergent phenomena" and "synergetic effects".

We discuss the various aspects of the new robot control paradigm in turn.

No Symbols, No World Models One argument of behaviour-based robotics is that symbolic representations are an unnecessary burden. They are hard to obtain, hard to maintain, and unreliable. As Brooks states it ([Brooks 90]):

> "Our experience is that . . . once the commitment [to physical grounding] is made, the need for traditional symbolic representations soon fades entirely. The key observation is that the world is its own best model. It is always exactly up to date. It always contains every detail there is to be known. The trick is to sense it appropriately and often enough."

Behavioural Decomposition, Emergent Functionality Secondly, the "percolator effect" of functional decomposition is avoided by using a parallel structure of control system, rather than a serial one (see figure 2.4). Here, the overall control task is decomposed into "task-achieving behaviours" which operate in parallel. Each behaviour module implements a complete and functional robot behaviour, rather than one single aspect of an overall control task, and has immediate access to the sensors and actuators.

The fundamental idea is that task-achieving behaviours — behaviour modules — operate independently of one another, and that the overall behaviour of the robot *emerges* through this concurrent operation: emergent functionality. This idea is related to automata theory. Here, complex behaviour is observed in assemblies of machines (automata), that each obey very simple and tractable rules. Despite the individual automaton's simplicity, the interaction between the automata produces complex, often intractable behaviour in the entire assembly. This shows that complex behaviour does not require complex rules. The parallel to this phenomenon in the living world are societies. Here also complex and unpredictable behaviour emerges through the interaction of agents following local rules.

The fundamental idea is that intelligent behaviour is not achieved by designing one complex, monolithic control structure (functional decomposition), but by bringing together the "right" type of simple behaviours, which will generate overall intelligent behaviour through their interaction, without any one agent "knowing" that it is contributing to some explicit task, but merely following its own rules. (The link to social insects is obvious here. There is no indication that an individual ant has a concept of the entire ant colony. Instead, it appears to be following simple, local rules. The overall behaviour of the ant colony emerges from the behaviour of the individual ant, and the interaction between ants).

Subsumption Architecture The "subsumption architecture" ([Brooks 85]) is one example of this approach to robot control. Figure 2.4 gives an example of a behaviour-based decomposition of a mobile robot control system in this subsumption architecture.

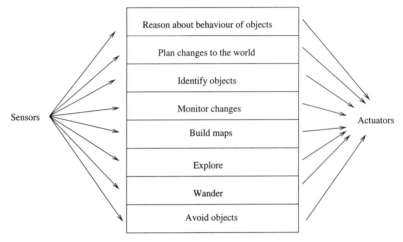

FIG. 2.4. BEHAVIOUR-BASED DECOMPOSITION OF A MOBILE ROBOT CONTROL SYSTEM (AFTER [BROOKS 85])

The concept of the subsumption architecture is that each behaviour of the behaviour-based controller is implemented completely independently from any other behaviour. In the early days of subsumption architecture, this even meant that each behaviour was implemented on its own electronic controller card. The conceptual divisions between behaviours were manifested physically.

Communication between behaviours is limited to the absolute minimum: a wire between a higher level behaviour and a lower level one is used to inhibit (or "subsume") the lower level behaviour. The design concept was that once finished, a behaviour would never be altered again, and that new behaviours could be added to the system *ad infinitum*, using the subsumption wire as the only interface between behaviours[2].

Here is a concrete example of layers of behaviour in a subsumption architecture. In [Brooks 85] Brooks proposes the following eight levels of competence (see also figure 2.4):

1. Avoid contact with objects, whether the objects move or are stationary;
2. Wander aimlessly around without hitting things;
3. Explore the world by seeing places in the distance that look reachable and head for them;
4. Build a map of the environment and plan routes from one place to another;

---

[2] In practice this did not quite work out like that, but here we are more concerned with the concept of behaviour-based control. Practical aspects are considered on p. 19.

5. Notice changes in the static environment;
6. Reason about the world in terms of identifiable objects and perform tasks related to certain objects;
7. Formulate and execute plans that involve changing the state of the world in some desirable way;
8. Reason about the behaviour of objects in the world and modify plans accordingly.

Tight Coupling Between Sensing and Acting In the behavioural decomposition of a control task, each (simple and low level) behaviour has direct access to raw sensor readings, and can control the robot's motors directly. In the functional decomposition this was not the case. Here, the raw sensor signal slowly percolated through a series of processing modules, until a motor command emerged at the end. Tight coupling between sensing and acting dominates the behaviour-based approach, while that coupling is loose in the functional approach.

Advantages of Behaviour-Based Control As said earlier, there were good reasons to abandon the functional approach to intelligent behaviour, and to seek alternative solutions. The behaviour-based approach is one attempt to achieve this, and it has a number of advantages.

- The system supports multiple goals and is more efficient. There is no functional hierarchy between the different layers: one layer does not call another. Each layer can work on different goals individually. The layers run in parallel. The communication between different layers is achieved via message passing, which is not synchronised. It may well be the case that a layer produces several messages which are not read by any other layer. This has the advantage that each layer can directly respond to changes in the environment; there is no central planning module which has to take account of all sub-goals. In other words, no conflict resolution strategy is needed.
- The system is easier to design, to debug and to extend. The control system is built by first implementing the lowest level of competence (that is obstacle avoidance). This layer is then tested. If the layer shows the correct behaviour further levels can be added. Higher layers can process data from lower layers, but they cannot influence the behaviour of lower layers.
- The system is robust. Whilst in the functional approach, the failure of one module leads to the failure of the whole system, in the behaviour-based approach, the failure of one layer has only a minor influence on the performance of the whole system, because the behaviour of the robot is the result of a concurrent operation of several layers of control.

Limitations of Behaviour-Based Control The strongest argument levelled against behaviour-based control is that within a behaviour-based controller it is extremely difficult to see how plans could be expressed. A behaviour-based robot responds directly to sensory stimuli, it has no internal state memory and is therefore unable to follow externally specified sequences of actions.

The question is: which competences require plans (and are therefore beyond a purely behaviour-based approach), and which don't? Many fundamental sensor-motor competences, such as obstacle avoidance or trajectory following do not require internal state. Others, such as sequences of actions where actions depend on each other do require memory and planning. Where the dividing line lies is as yet unclear.

Behaviour based robotics leads to robots that "behave" in a specific environment. They respond to environmental stimuli in meaningful ways, and will achieve tasks through this agent-environment interaction. The problem is that behaviour-based control makes it very hard — impossible so far — to express plans as we know it. We don't know what the translation of "Go there, fetch this, take it over there and then sweep the floor" into task-achieving behaviours is, or even, whether such a translation exists. As we are used to expressing robot tasks in such terms, this is a problem, at least if behaviour-based robots are to be used in a tightly defined environment, executing tightly defined tasks.

2.5   Further Reading

Early Mobile Robots

- SHAKEY (Stanford Research Institute):
  - N.J. Nilsson, A Mobile Automation: An Application of Artificial Intelligence Techniques, *Proc. IJCAI*, Washington DC, 1969.
  - N.J. Nilsson (ed.), SHAKEY the Robot, *Technical Note 323*, Artificial Intelligence Center Menlo Park, SRI International, 1984.
- JPL-ROVER (Jet Propulsion Laboratory, Pasadena):
  - A.M. Thompson, The Navigation System of the JPL Robot, *Proceedings Fifth IJCAI*, Cambridge MA, 1977.
- CART/CMU Rover (Stanford University, Carnegie Mellon University)
  - Hans Moravec, Visual Mapping by a Robot Rover, *Proc. 6th IJCAI*, Tokyo, 1979.
  - Hans Moravec, *Robot Rover Visual Navigation*, UMI Research Press, Ann Arbor, Michigan, 1981.
  - Hans Moravec, The CMU Rover, *Proceedings AAAI 82*, Pittsburgh, 1982.
  - Hans Moravec, The Stanford Cart and the CMU Rover, *Proceedings of the IEEE*, Vol. 71, No. 7, pp. 872–884, 1983.
- HILARE / HILARE II (LAAS, CNRS, Toulouse):
  - G. Giralt, R.P. Sobek and R. Chatila, A Multi-Level Planning and Navigation System for a Mobile Robot — A First Approach to HILARE, *Proc. 6th IJCAI*, Tokyo, 1979.
  - G. Giralt, Mobile Robots, in *Robotics and Artificial Intelligence*, NASA ASI, Serie F(1), 1984.

- G. Giralt, R. Alami, R. Chatila and P. Freedman, Remote Operated Autonomous Robots, *Proceedings of the SPIE — The International Society for Optical Engineering*, Vol. 1571, pp. 416-427, 1991.
- NAVLAB / AMBLER (Carnegie Mellon Univ.)
  - S. Shafer, A. Stenz and C. Thorpe, An Architecture for Sensor Fusion in a Mobile Robot, *Proc. IEEE International Conference on Robotics and Automation*, 1986.
  - Chuck Thorpe, Outdoor Visual Navigation for Autonomous Robots, *Proc. International Conference on Intelligent Autonomous Systems 2*, Vol. 2, Amsterdam, 1989.
  - Chuck Thorpe, *et al.*, Vision and Navigation for the Carnegie-Mellon Navlab, in: S.S. Iyengar and A. Elfes (eds.), *Autonomous Mobile Robots: Central Planning and Architecture*, Vol. 2, Los Alamitos CA, 1991.
  - Chuck Thorpe, Outdoor Visual Navigation for Autonomous Robots, *J. Robotics and Autonomous Systems*, Vol. 7, Issue 2-3, pp. 85-98, 1991.
- FLAKEY (SRI International):
  - M.P. Georgeff *et al.*, Reasoning and Planning in Dynamic Domains: An experiment with a Mobile Robot, *TR 380*, Artificial Intelligence Center, SRI International, Menlo Park CA, 1987.
- YAMABICO (Univ. Tsukuba, Japan):
  - T. Tsubouchy and S. Yuta, Map Assisted Vision System of Mobile Robots for Reckoning in a Building Environment, *Proc. IEEE International Conference on Robotics and Automation*, Raleigh NC, 1987.
  - T. Tsubouchy and S. Yuta, The Map Assisted Mobile Robot's Vision System — An Experiment on Real Time Environment Recognition, *Proc. IEEE RSJ International Workshop on Intelligent Robots and Systems*, Japan, 1988.
- KAMRO (Univ. Karlsruhe):
  - Ulrich Rembold, The Karlsruhe Autonomous Mobile Assembly Robot, *Proc. IEEE International Conference on Robotics and Automation*, Philadelphia PA, 1988.

Control Paradigms

- General Discussion: C. Malcolm, T. Smithers & J. Hallam, An Emerging Paradigm in Robot Architecture, *Proc. International Conference on Intelligent Autonomous Systems 2*, Amsterdam, 1989.
- CMU Rover: A. Elfes and S.N. Talukdar, A Distributed Control System for the CMU Rover, *Proceedings Eighth IJCAI*, Karlsruhe, 1983.
- MOBOT-1 (MIT Artificial Intelligence Lab): Rodney Brooks, A Robust Layered Control System for a Mobile Robot, *IEEE Journal of Robotics and Automation*, RA-2, No. 1, April 1986.
- MOBOT-2 (MIT Artificial Intelligence Lab): Rodney Brooks *et al.*, A Mobile Robot with Onboard Parallel Processor and Large Workspace Arm, *Proc. AAAI 86*, Philadelphia PA, 1986.

- YAMABICO (Univ. Tsukuba, Japan): M.K. Habib, S. Suzuki, S. Yuta and J. Iijima, A New Programming Approach to Describe the Sensor Based Real Time Action of Autonomous Robots, Robots: Coming of Age, *Proceedings of the International Symposium and Exposition on Robots* (designated the 19th ISIR by the International Federation of Robotics) pp. 1010-21, 1988.
- KAMRO (Univ. Karlsruhe, Germany): A. Hörmann, W. Meier and J. Schloen, A Control Architecture for an Advanced Fault-Tolerant Robot System, *J. Robotics and Autonomous Systems*, Vol. 7, Issue 2-3, pp. 211-25, 1991.

3 Robot Hardware

Summary. This chapter discusses the most common sensors and actuators used in mobile robots, their strengths, limitations and common applications.

Robot, task and environment are tightly linked. The overall behaviour of a robot is the result of the interaction of these three components.

Later in this book (chapter 6) we will address the question of identifying the underlying laws governing robot-environment interaction. But before this problem can be tackled, it is necessary to understand the fundamental makeup of the robot itself. What kind of information can be obtained from the various sensors? What type of actuator is suitable for which type of task? These are the questions we look at in this chapter.

3.1 Robot Sensors

Sensors are devices that can sense and measure physical properties of the environment, such as temperature, luminance, resistance to touch, weight, size, etc. They deliver *low level* information about the environment the robot is working in. This information is noisy (i.e. imprecise), often contradictory and ambiguous.

The previous chapter discussed the contrast between a classical, symbolic and functional approach to robot control on the one hand, and a distributed, subsymbolic, behaviour-based approach on the other hand. Sensors do not produce symbols that can immediately be used by a reasoning system. If a symbolic approach is to be adopted, sensor signals need to be translated into symbols first — and it is perhaps for this reason, more than for any other, that the subsymbolic approach to robot control looks so promising.

This chapter will describe the most common sensor and actuator types used in indoor mobile robots to date, giving examples of the kind of reading that can be obtained from them, and their most common applications.

3.1.1   Sensor Characteristics

All sensors are designed to sense or to measure a particular physical property, which "usually" has a meaningful relationship with a property of the environment that one "really" wants to know.

Example: a sonar range finder measures the time it takes for a sonar pulse to be heard again by a receiver placed next to the transmitter. The assumption is that the pulse was reflected by an object in front of the sensor. Using the time for the pulse to travel to the object and back, given the speed of sound, one can compute the distance to the object. So a sonar range finder does not measure range, it measures time of flight. This time of flight is in some way related to range, but the two are not identical (more about this in section 3.1.4).

All sensors are characterised by a number of properties that describe their capabilities. The most important are:

- Sensitivity: ratio of change of output to change of input.
- Linearity: measure for the constancy of ratio of input to output.
- Measurement range: difference between minimum and maximum values measurable.
- Response time: time required for a change in input to be observable in the output.
- Accuracy: the difference between actual and measured values.
- Repeatability: the difference between successive measurements of the same entity.
- Resolution: smallest observable increment in input.
- Type of output.

3.1.2   Tactile Sensors

Tactile sensors detect physical contact with an object. More precisely, they measure a physical property (like the closing of a switch), that is usually caused by physical contact with an object (but could equally well be caused by a faulty sensor, vibration, or other causes).

The simplest tactile sensors are microswitches, or whisker sensors. When a bumper is in contact with an object, a microswitch is closed and gives an electrical signal that can be sensed by the controller. Likewise, when a metal whisker is bent (see figure 3.1), it makes contact with a metal ring, closing the circuit and generating a detectable signal.

Other methods of building simple touch sensors include using strain gauges, or piezoelectric transducers. Strain gauges are thin layers of resistive material based on a flexible substrate. As the substrate is being bent by external force, the layer of resistive material is either stretched (resistance goes up), or compressed (resistance goes down). This change in resistance can be used to detect deformation, and also the degree of deformation. Strain gauges therefore give more information than binary microswitch sensors.

Piezoelectric transducers are crystals (e.g. quartz or tourmaline) that generate charges when being deformed along their one sensitive ("polar") axis. These

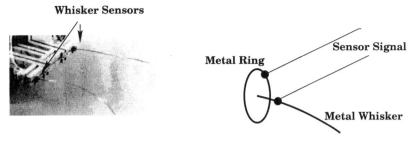

FIG. 3.1. PRINCIPAL DESIGN AND PHYSICAL IMPLEMENTATION OF A WHISKER SENSOR

charges can be measured as short voltage bursts, whose amplitude is an indication of the strength of deformation.

Contact sensors such as strain gauges can be arranged in 2D arrays to form tactile pads, which detect the presence of an object, as well as measuring the object's shape and size.

3.1.3 Infrared Sensors

Infrared (IR) sensors are probably the simplest type of non-contact sensors; they are widely used in mobile robots to detect obstacles.

They operate by emitting an infrared light, and detecting any reflections off surfaces in front of the robot. To differentiate the emitted IR from ambient IR stemming from fluorescent tubes or the sun, the emitted signal is usually modulated with a low frequency (e.g. 100 Hz).

Provided all objects in the robot's environment have a uniform colour and surface structure, IR sensors can be calibrated to measure distance from the objects: the intensity of the reflected light is inversely proportional to the square of the distance.

However, in realistic scenarios surfaces of objects have different colours, which reflect a larger or smaller amount of light. Black surfaces, for instance, are practically invisible to IR. For this reason, IR sensors can effectively only be used for object detection, but not for range measurements.

Problems with IR Sensors If reflected IR is detected, it is safe to assume that an object is present. It is rare that a phantom IR signal is perceived.

On the other hand, the absence of reflected IR does not mean that no object is present! Certain darkly coloured objects are invisible to IR. IR sensors are therefore not absolutely safe for obstacle detection.

Also, because the amount of reflected IR is not only a function of range, but also a function of surface colour, no information is available to the robot regarding the proximity of an object. It is usually best to start avoiding an object as soon as it is detected!

Because the intensity of the IR signal is proportional to d^{-2}, i.e. falls rapidly as the distance d increases, IR sensors are inherently short range sensors. Typical maximum ranges are 50 to 100 cm.

3.1.4 Sonar Sensors

The fundamental principle of robot sonar sensors is the same that is used by bats: a chirp, that is a short (e.g. 1.2 milliseconds), powerful pulse of a range of frequencies, is emitted, and its reflection off objects ahead of the sensor is detected by a receiver. The sensitivity of a sonar receiver is not uniform, but consists of a main lobe and side lobes, each of which have a shape resembling a baseball bat. An example of this so-called beam pattern is shown in figure 3.2, it shows that within a cone of 20 degrees along the centre axis of transmission sensitivity drops by 10 dB (i.e. by factor 10).

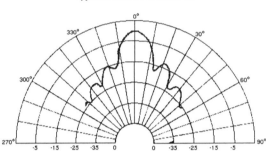

Typical Beam Pattern At 50 kHz

FIG. 3.2. SONAR BEAM PATTERN OF THE POLAROID 600 SERIES ELECTROSTATIC TRANSDUCER AT 50 KHZ

As the speed of sound is known, the distance to the object that reflected the chirp can be computed from the time that elapsed between emission and reception, using equation 3.1 .

$$d = \frac{1}{2}vt \; , \qquad (3.1)$$

with d being the distance to the nearest object within the sonar cone, v the speed of the emitted signal in the medium ($344ms^{-1}$ for sound in air of $20^{\circ}C$), and t the time elapsed between emission of a chirp and the reception of its echo.

The minimum distance d_{min} that can be measured is given by equation 3.2, where v is the travelling speed of sound in the medium, and t_{burst} is the duration of the transmitted burst in seconds. At $t_{burst} = 1.2$ milliseconds, this distance is just under 21 cm.

$$d_{min} = \frac{1}{2}vt_{burst} \; . \qquad (3.2)$$

The maximum distance d_{max} that can be measured is a function of the time t_{wait} between bursts, and is given by equation 3.3 .

$$d_{max} = \frac{1}{2}vt_{wait} \; . \qquad (3.3)$$

Finally, the resolution d_{res} of the sonar sensor is a function of the number of quantisation steps q that are available for the range encoding, and the maximum range of the sensor:

$$d_{res} = \frac{d_{max}}{q} . \tag{3.4}$$

Problems of Sonar Sensors There are a number of uncertainties associated with readings from sonar sensors. First of all, the exact position of the detected object is unknown. As the sensitivity of a sonar sensor is cone-shaped (see figure 3.2) an object detected at distance d could be anywhere within the sonar cone, on an arc with distance d from the robot. The accuracy of object position measurement is a function of the width of the sonar beam pattern.

Secondly, so-called *specular reflections* give rise to erroneous readings. Specular reflections occur when the sonar beam hits a smooth surface at a shallow angle, and is therefore not reflected back to the robot, but outwards. Only when an object further away reflects the beam is a reading obtained, indicating a bigger free space than actually exists.

Methods have been developed to eliminate specular reflections. For example, "Regions of constant depth" ([Leonard *et al.* 90]) can be used to interpret sonar readings showing such specular reflections. In each 360-degree sonar scan there are angular regions for which the sonar range readings are constant over, say, 10 degrees of arc or more. Leonard, Durrant-Whyte and Cox refer to these angular regions as regions of constant depth (RCD). An example is shown in figure 3.3.

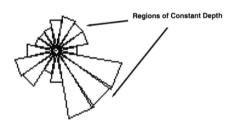

Regions of Constant Depth

FIG. 3.3. SONAR READING, WITH TWO REGIONS OF CONSTANT DEPTH INDICATED

Regions of constant depth can be used to differentiate between readings indicating walls from those indicating corners by obtaining at least two sonar scans from different locations, and discarding all readings other than the regions of constant depth. As explained in figure 3.4, arcs resulting from corners will intersect, whilst those resulting from walls will be tangential to the wall.

There is a third problem that can occur when *arrays* of sonar sensors are used. Unless sonar sensors use coded emissions so-called *crosstalk* can occur, where

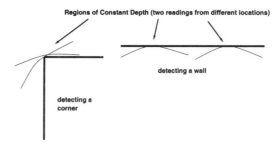

FIG. 3.4. REGIONS OF CONSTANT DEPTH CAN BE USED TO DIFFERENTIATE BETWEEN CORNERS
AND WALLS IN SPECULAR ENVIRONMENTS (AFTER [LEONARD ET AL. 90])

one sensor detects the reflected beam of another sensor, again giving rise to
wrong distance measurements (both too short and too long readings are possible,
depending on the scenario).

The assumed speed of the sound determines the range measured. Unfortunately, the speed of sound is so dependent on air temperature and humidity, that
a change of temperature of 16° C will result in a range error of 30 cm when measuring over a 10 m range! Such an error would not affect simple sensor-motor
behaviours such as obstacle avoidance, but would, for example, result in very
imprecise mappings of the robot's environment in mapping applications.

Exercise 1: Sonar Sensors A mobile robot equipped with sonar range finding
sensors was driven down a corridor having doors at regular intervals, and walls
in between. Two sonar sensor readings obtained are shown in figure 3.5, the
top one from a front-facing sensor, the bottom one from a side-looking sensor.
Which observations can be made from the sonar readings? (Answer on p. 219).

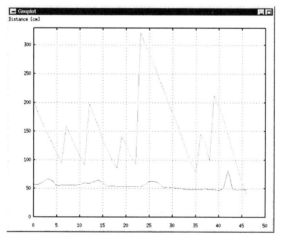

FIG. 3.5. EXAMPLE SONAR READINGS OBTAINED WHILE TRAVERSING A CORRIDOR. THE TOP
LINE SHOWS THE READINGS OF THE FRONT-FACING SENSOR, THE BOTTOM LINE THOSE OF THE
SIDE-FACING SENSOR. THE x-AXIS GIVES DISTANCE IN UNITS OF APPROX. 20 CM.

3.1.5 Laser Range Finders

Laser range finders (also known as *laser radar* or *lidar*) are common now in mobile robot applications to measure the distance, velocity and acceleration of perceived objects. The operating principle of laser range finders is the same as for sonar: instead of a short sound pulse, here a short pulse of light is emitted, and the time elapsed between emission and detection of the return pulse is used to determine range (equation 3.1 applies, with v being the speed of light in this case).

The difference is in the nature of the pulse emitted. The wavelength of near infrared light, which is often used for laser range finders, is very much shorter than that of a sonar pulse. This shorter wavelength reduces the probability of total reflection off a smooth surface, so that the problem of specular reflections is less pronounced.

Typical maximum ranges for commercially available laser range finders may be several hundred metres. Depending on the application, however, one may chose a shorter maximum range. Whilst several hundred metres maximum range is useful for outdoor robot applications, several tens of metres is usually adequate for indoor applications.

The accuracy of commercially available laser range finders is typically in the millimetre range (e.g. 50 mm for a single scan, 16 mm for the average of nine scans[1]), the scan time for a 180 degree scan being 40 milliseconds.

Phase Shift Measurement Instead of using the time-of-flight principle, range can also be determined by the phase difference between an emitted signal and its echo. To do this, the laser signal's intensity is modulated (varied over time). Because of the time of flight of the beam between emission and return to the emitter, a phase difference between transmitted and received laser radiation results.

The phase difference is proportional to range and modulation frequency, and can therefore be used to determine the distance to objects. Figure 3.6 shows the grey-level image and range output of such a laser range finder.

3.1.6 Other Time-of-Flight Range Sensors

The underlying principle for both sonar and lidar sensors is to emit a pulse, and to measure the time of flight of the pulse until it is detected back at the transmitter. Given the speed of the emitted wave (which is known), the time of flight indicates the distance to the object that reflected the pulse.

All time-of-flight range sensors are based on this principle, the difference being the frequency of the transmitted wave. RADAR (**RA**dio **D**etection **A**nd **R**anging) is one example. Here, a radio frequency pulse is emitted (typically in the GHz range), and used for object detection and ranging.

---

[1] Sensus 550 laser range finder of Nomadic Technologies.

FIG. 3.6. RANGE OUTPUT (TOP) AND INTENSITY IMAGE (BOTTOM) OF THE LARA-52000 LASER RANGE FINDER. BLACK OBJECTS IN THE RANGE IMAGE ARE CLOSE, WHITE ONES FAR AWAY (USED WITH PERMISSION BY ZOLLER+FRÖHLICH GMBH).

3.1.7   Other Non-Contact Sensors

A large range of sensors are available for different applications in mobile robots, and for a detailed discussion of the properties of these sensors please refer to [Borenstein *et al.* 96]. For the purpose of this book, a discussion of the most common sensors and their main characteristics is sufficient.

Hall Effect   When a current carrying solid material, for instance a semiconductor, is placed in a magnetic field, an electric field develops that is transverse to the magnetic field and the current. This so-called Hall effect (discovered in 1879 by Edwin Herbert Hall) can be used to detect a magnetic field.

Typical applications in mobile robotics include motion sensors, or Hall effect compasses (see below). A simple wheel revolution counter can be built by placing a permanent magnet in the wheel, and a Hall sensor on the robot. The passing of the magnet can be detected by the Hall sensor, because it induces a change in the magnetic field. To detect both speed and direction of rotation, two Hall sensors can be used: the temporal pattern of their signals indicates the direction of rotation, the frequency of their signals indicates the speed of the wheel.

Eddy Currents   Changes in a magnetic or electric field induce eddy currents in conductors. These can be detected, and used for sensing a changing magnetic field, as in the case of the Hall effect sensor.

3.1.8   Compass Sensors

Compass sensors are very important for navigation applications, and widely used. Compass mechanism used for sensors on mobile robots measure the horizontal component of the earth's natural magnetic field, just as an ordinary hiking compass does (there is a vertical component of the earth's magnetic field as well, which birds, for example, use in their navigation).

Fluxgate Compasses The most common compass principle used in mobile robot compasses is that of a fluxgate compass, which measures the magnetic field strength by changing the properties of an electromagnet in a controlled way.

The functioning principle of a fluxgate compass is as follows. A drive and a sensing coil are wound on a common core (see figure 3.7).

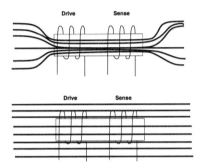

FIG. 3.7. PRINCIPLE OF A FLUXGATE COMPASS. THE CORE IS DRIVEN INTO (BOTTOM) AND OUT OF SATURATION (TOP) BY A CURRENT APPLIED TO THE DRIVE COIL. THE RESULTING CHANGE IN THE MAGNETIC FLUX LINES INDUCES A NEGATIVE ELECTROMAGNETIC FORCE IN THE SENSE COIL, WHICH IS DEPENDENT ON THE AMBIENT MAGNETIC FIELD (AFTER [BOREN-STEIN ET AL. 96]).

When a highly permeable, unsaturated core is introduced into a magnetic field, the magnetic flux lines will be drawn into the core (see figure 3.7). However, if the core is saturated, the flux lines remain unaffected.

By alternately saturating and de-saturating the core, and therefore altering the magnetic flux through the core, a voltage is induced in the sensing coil. This voltage is dependent on the ambient magnetic field, and therefore a measure of its strength.

To measure the direction of magnetic North, two coils at right angles are needed, the current steering angle Θ is given by two voltages V_x and V_y sensed in the two sensing coils:

$$\Theta = arctan\frac{V_x}{V_y} \ . \tag{3.5}$$

Hall Effect Compasses Two orthogonally arranged Hall sensors can also be used as a magnetic compass. Here, the heading Θ is computed, using the two components B_x and B_y of the magnetic field:

$$\Theta = arctan\frac{B_x}{B_y} \ . \tag{3.6}$$

Other Mechanisms There are a range of other mechanisms that can be used to measure the earth's magnetic field, such as mechanical magnetic compasses, magnetoresistive compasses, or magnetoelastic compasses. A discussion of these can be found in [Borenstein *et al.* 96].

Using Magnetic Compass Sensors Indoors All magnetic compass sensors, irrespective of the underlying principle, sense the earth's (very weak) magnetic field. Indoors, distortions due to metal objects (such as steel pillars, steel-reinforced concrete or metal doors), or artificial magnetic fields from power lines, electric motors etc. are unavoidable.

This means that the compass will not always provide a true absolute reference. However, it can still be used to provide a local reference in all situations where the external influences are constant over time (such as a metal pillar that remains in its position constantly). Whatever the reading of the compass, at the same location it will be (approximately) the same every time, and can therefore be used as a local reference. For navigation applications using topological maps, such as the one described in section 5.4.4, a magnetic compass is still very useful.

3.1.9   Shaft Encoders

In mobile robots it is often necessary to measure rotation, for example the rotation of the robot's axles to perform path integration (see chapter 5.1).

Potentiometers (mechanically variable resistors) or, more commonly, shaft encoders can be used for that purpose. Shaft encoders are devices mounted on the rotating shaft; they generate a binary representation of the shaft's position.

There are two major types of shaft encoders: absolute and incremental. In absolute shaft encoders, a disc showing a *Gray code* (a binary code in which only one bit changes between successive words) is read by an optical sensor and indicates the shaft's position.

Absolute encoders will give the current position of the shaft, but are not well suited for integrating (i.e. adding up) movement over time. Incremental encoders are used for that purpose. Here, the disc is read by two photoreceptors, A and B. Track A always precedes track B if the disc is turning in one direction, and lags behind if the disc turns in the other direction. The sequence in which both photocells are triggered, therefore, indicates the direction of rotation, and the number of on/off traversals of each receptor indicates the angle turned. Combinatorial logic is used to add up the movement of the shaft correctly.

Besides rotating shafts, robots may also use shafts that have a sideways movement, for example in manipulators (robot arms). To measure lateral displacement, linear variable differential transformers (LVDTs) can be used. The basic circuit diagram is given in figure 3.8. The output voltage indicates the direction and extent of the lateral displacement of the coil.

Using Shaft Encoders as Odometry Sensors Shaft encoders, as discussed above, can be used to measure the movement of the robot's motors, for both

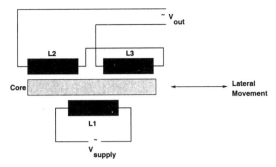

FIG. 3.8. CIRCUIT DIAGRAM OF A LINEAR VARIABLE DIFFERENTIAL TRANSFORMER. L1 IS THE PRIMARY COIL, L2 AND L3 ARE SECONDARY COILS. V_{out} IS THE OUTPUT VOLTAGE INDICATING DIRECTION AND EXTENT OF LATERAL MOVEMENT.

translational and rotational movement (the integrated turns of the robot's axles yields translation, the integrated turn of the robot's steering axles yields rotation). Theoretically, the integration of their output provides the robot's current position. This method is called path integration or dead reckoning (see also p. 96). In practice, however, dead reckoning is very unreliable over all but very short distances. The reason is that the robot regularly performs motions in its environment that are not due to wheel motion, for example skidding or slipping.

Figure 3.9 shows a robot's position as estimated by the on-board dead reckoning system for three consecutive runs through the same environment. It shows clearly the two components to dead reckoning error: translational and rotational error.

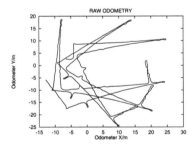

FIG. 3.9. DEAD RECKONING ERROR INTRODUCED BY WHEEL SLIPPAGE AND, MORE IMPORTANTLY, ROTATIONAL ERROR

Dealing with Odometry Error One way of dealing with odometry error is to correct it with further sensor signals, or through post-hoc processing.

Figure 3.10 shows the same data, with the rotational error removed by means of a magnetic compass. Still visible is the translational error component. Provided clearly identifiable landmarks are available, this error can be removed post-hoc by "stretching" or "shrinking" the individual legs of the journey by an appropriate factor ([Duckett & Nehmzow 98]). This is done by manually identifying prominent way-points such as corners in the different laps, and computing the best stretching factor to fit two instances of the same leg of the journey. The result of this procedure is shown in figure 3.11.

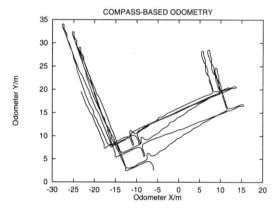

FIG. 3.10. THE SAME DATA AS SHOWN IN FIGURE 3.9, WITH THE ROTATIONAL ERROR BEING REMOVED THROUGH USING A MAGNETIC COMPASS

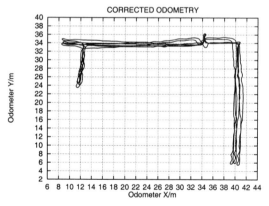

FIG. 3.11. THE REMAINING TRANSLATIONAL ERROR CORRECTED POST-HOC, OFF-LINE

This method is obviously not suitable for real time robot navigation. For analysis of robot behaviour, however, it is suitable. An example for this is given in case study 12 on p. 197.

3.1.10 Motion Sensors

It is obviously important for a moving agent to measure its own speed, for example for navigation by dead reckoning.

Some methods already mentioned in this chapter, such as shaft encoders (p. 32) or revolution counters (p. 30) can be used for this, but there are more.

Time-of-flight range sensors can be extended to measure relative speed between the emitter and the object reflecting the emitted pulse, by exploiting the Doppler effect. Equation 3.7 gives the relationship between the frequency of the transmitted pulse f_{trans}, the frequency of the received pulse f_{rec}, the speed v_t of the transmitter and the speed v_r of the receiver (positive speeds are movements towards the sound source); c is the speed of light.

$$f_{rec} = f_{trans} \frac{c - v_r}{c - v_t} \, . \tag{3.7}$$

It is clear from equation 3.7 that the relative speed between transmitter and receiver $v_r = v_t - v_r$ can be calculated if f_{trans} and f_{rec} can be measured.

Finally, micromechanical accelerometers can be used to measure acceleration (and therefore, by integration, speed and distance — a so-called *inertial navigation system*). The underlying principle of accelerometers is simple: along each of the three cardinal axes, the force F generated by a movement of a suspended mass m is measured to determine the acceleration a according to Newton's law $a = Fm^{-1}$. Double integration of a yields the current position. In practice, it is hard to build accurate accelerometers for mobile robots, because the accelerations to be measured are small, and errors accordingly large. For almost all mobile robot applications accelerometers of sufficient precision are too expensive to be a viable option (accuracies as high as 0.1% of distance travelled are achievable, but at very high cost).

3.1.11 Vision Sensors and Image Processing

CCD Cameras CCD cameras use **C**harge **C**oupled **D**evices to generate matrices of numbers that correspond to the grey-level distribution in an image.

Arrays of photodiodes detect the light intensity values at individual points of the image (so-called picture cells, or pixels). The two-dimensional array of grey-level images constitutes the eventual image. Figure 3.12 shows an actual grey-level image and its numerical representation.

CCD cameras are available for grey-level and colour image acquisition, with a range of image resolutions (i.e. pixels per image) and frame rates (the speed at which one image, or "frame", is acquired). 800 x 600 pixels is a typical image size, and about 30 Hz a typical frame rate. There are variants of CCD cameras for specific purposes, such as the omnidirectional cameras shown in figure 5.46, used for robot navigation.

255	255	200	200	100	100	0	0
255	255	200	200	100	100	0	0
255	255	200	200	100	100	0	0
255	255	200	200	100	100	0	0
255	255	200	200	100	100	0	0
255	255	200	200	100	100	0	0
255	255	200	200	100	100	0	0
255	255	200	200	100	100	0	0

FIG. 3.12. GREY-LEVEL IMAGE AND ITS NUMERICAL REPRESENTATION

Simple Image Processing An image is a huge array of grey-level (brightness) values of individual pixels. Taken individually, these numbers are almost meaningless, because they contain very little information about the scene. A robot needs information like "object ahead", "table to the left", or "person approaching" to perform its tasks, yet receives only 480,000 or more 8 bit numbers every thirtieth of a second.

The conversion of this huge amount of low level information into usable high level information is the subject of computer vision, and is beyond the scope of this book. [Sonka *et al.* 93] provide a useful introduction.

However, there are some simple low level image processing mechanisms available which allow fast and effective image-preprocessing. Typically, they consist of the repeated application of simple procedures, and detect edges, or remove noise. These methods are discussed here because they are used in the robot applications described later in this book.

The fundamental principle of so-called image operators is to modify an individual pixel according to the pixel's own value, as well as those of its neighbours. Often a 3x3 operator is used, but larger operators are also sometimes applied. A generic operator is shown in figure 3.13. Element e is the pixel that will be modified by the operator, the other eight elements are e's neighbours.

a	b	c
d	e	f
g	h	i

FIG. 3.13. A GENERIC IMAGE PROCESSING OPERATOR

Here are some examples of commonly used image operators:

- Median filter. The median filter, an operator that replaces pixel e by the median value of all nine pixel values (that is by the fifth value of an ordered list of nine values) will remove "spikes" from the image, i.e. pixel values that differ dramatically from those of its neighbours.

- High pass filter. This enhances changes in grey-level value (e.g. edges), and removes areas of uniform grey-level distribution. Using equations 3.8 and 3.9, a value Δ is defined as $\Delta = (\delta x)^2 + (\delta y)^2$. If Δ exceeds a preset threshold, pixels are retained (set to '1'), otherwise discarded (set to '0').

$$\delta x = c + f + i - (a + d + g) , \tag{3.8}$$

$$\delta y = g + h + i - (a + b + c) , \tag{3.9}$$

with a to i as shown in figure 3.13.
The angle α of the detected edge is given by

$$\alpha = arctan \frac{\delta x}{\delta y}. \tag{3.10}$$

- Sobel operator. The Sobel operator performs a similar function as the high pass filter, but is defined slightly differently:

$$\delta x = c + 2f + i - (a + 2d + g) , \tag{3.11}$$

and

$$\delta y = g + 2h + i - (a + 2b + c) . \tag{3.12}$$

- Discrete Laplace operator. The disadvantage of the former two edge detectors is, of course, that a threshold for edge detection has to be set *a priori*. This problem can be avoided. Considering the grey-level distribution of an image as a function, the function's first derivative indicates the change grey-levels across the image. The second derivative indicates whether this change is positive and negative, and the points where this second derivative is zero ("zero crossings") is obviously an edge in the image, because here grey-level values change abruptly. The discrete Laplace operator shown in figure 3.14 determines the second derivative of the grey-level distribution and can be used to detect edges.

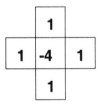

FIG. 3.14. THE DISCRETE LAPLACE EDGE-DETECTING OPERATOR. EVERY PIXEL VALUE IS REPLACED BY THE SUM OF THE FOUR NEIGHBOURING VALUES MINUS FOUR TIMES THE PIXEL'S OWN VALUE.

There are numerous other operators for different purposes, but the general principle is the same: Apply the operator to all pixels and compute new pixel values, then update the whole image accordingly.

3.1.12 Sensor Fusion

Even for tasks of medium complexity it is not sufficient to use one sensor alone. For example, in random exploration and obstacle avoidance some obstacles can only be detected by IRs, some only by sonar sensors, some by both. *Sensor fusion* is the technical term used to describe the process of using information from several sensor modalities (i.e. types of sensors) to form one image of the world.

Because sensors have different characteristics, different strengths and different weaknesses, sensor fusion is an extremely difficult task. Information coming from the various sensor modalities is not consistent at all times. Assumptions have to be made in order to form a global view of the world, and results have to be amended in the light of new evidence.

One method of sensor fusion is to use artificial neural networks that learn to associate perception with some kind of output (e.g. an action, or classification). An example application of sensor fusion using artificial neural networks is given in case study 2 on p. 74.

3.2 Robot Actuators

3.2.1 Electric, Pneumatic, Hydraulic

The most common type of actuator used in mobile robots is the electric motor, usually a DC motor or a stepper motor. The former is the easiest to control — applying DC power operates the motor. The latter's stator coils are sectioned, so that the rotor movement can be determined by applying a voltage to the desired section of the coil. This generates a rotation by a known angle (the angle between coil segments). Stepper motors can therefore be used for fine and precise motion. Electric motors are clean and easy to operate, provide moderate torques (rotational forces) and fine control.

The simplest and cheapest of all drives are pneumatic actuators, which typically operate between fixed positions ("bang bang control") by pumping compressed air between air chambers, and thus moving a piston. While they are cheap and simple to control, they are not capable of high precision.

Hydraulic actuators use pressurised oil to generate motion. They are capable of generating both high powers and high precision movements, but are usually too heavy, dirty and expensive to be used on mobile robots.

3.2.2 Shape Memory Alloys

Shape memory alloys (SMA) are metallic materials such as Nickel Titanium alloys or copper base alloys (such as CuZnAl or CuAlNi), that can, after deformation, return to a previous shape by heating. This effect can be used to create "artificial muscles" for mobile robot applications.

The fundamental principle of creating a force in SMAs is a phase transformation in the alloy between the stronger, high temperature form (*Austenite*) and the weaker, low temperature form (*Martensite*). This phase transformation is achieved through heating (typically by conducting a current through a SMA wire) and cooling (typically through switching off the current, and air cooling). The principle is shown in figure 3.15.

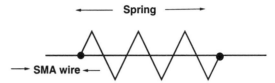

FIG. 3.15. OPERATING PRINCIPLE OF AN "ARTIFICIAL MUSCLE", USING A SHAPE MEMORY ALLOY. THE PHASE TRANSITION BETWEEN AUSTENITE AND MARTENSITE IS ACHIEVED BY HEATING AND COOLING THE ALLOY, RESULTING IN A CONTRACTION OF THE SMA WIRE, AND SUBSEQUENT EXPANSION BY THE SPRING.

The artificial muscle in figure 3.15 works as follows. In the "cool" state the spring expands the artificial muscle. If the SMA wire is heated by an electric current, it contracts and thereby generates a lateral movement.

Further Reading on Shape Memory Alloys

- http://www.sma-inc.com/SMAPaper.html

3.2.3   Non-Holonomic and Holonomic Motion

Robot motion can be characterised by the constraints that restrict that motion. Non-holonomic systems are subject to constraints that involve velocities, while holonomic constraints do not involve velocities.

An example of a non-holonomic constraint is the movement of a wheel on an axle. The velocity of the contact point between wheel and ground in the direction of the axle is constrained to zero, the motion of the wheel is therefore subject to a non-holonomic constraint.

3.3   Example: The Mobile Robot *FortyTwo*

Many experiments discussed in this book have been conducted with *FortyTwo*, a Nomad 200 mobile robot (see figure 3.16). *FortyTwo* is completely autonomous, it has an on-board PC to control the robot's perception and action, and carries its own power supply (lead acid batteries).

This 16-sided robot is equipped with 16 ultrasonic range finding sensors (range up to 6.5 m), 16 infrared (IR) sensors (range up to 60 cm), 20 tactile sensors and a monochrome CCD camera (492 x 512 pixels, focal length of 12.5 mm).

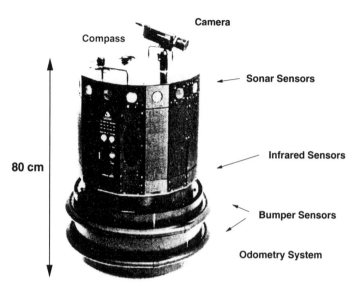

FIG. 3.16. THE NOMAD 200 MOBILE ROBOT *FortyTwo*

The robot is driven by three independent DC motors for translation, steering and turret rotation. A 486 PC is the main controller with several slave processors (Motorola 68HC11) handling the robot's sensors.

A numerical model of this robot, a simulator, can be used to develop initial versions of its control programs. A screen shot of the simulator interface is shown in figure 6.1 on p. 157. This simulator incorporates simplified models of the sensor characteristics of *FortyTwo's* sonar, infrared and bumper sensors.

An optional radio link between *FortyTwo* and a workstation can be used to control the robot remotely.

Software for *FortyTwo*, therefore, can be developed in three different ways:

1. In simulation only, i.e. run and executed on a remote computer;
2. Control software run on a remote computer, but executed on the robot;
3. Control software run and executed on the robot.

The first method is the easiest and quickest way to develop software. No freak sensory perceptions affect the behaviour of the robot, instead a deterministic environment facilitates repeatable experiments very easily. The disadvantage of this method is the inherent inadequacy of the underlying numerical models used, and the inability to model the freak perceptions that ultimately the robot will have to deal with. Only for very basic tasks is it possible to run control code that was developed under simulation unaltered on the robot.

The second method allows fairly quick development of software without the pitfalls of using oversimplified simulations. The only artefacts introduced by this method are differences in program execution due to transmission delays between robot and workstation, which do not occur if code is run on the robot directly. If the ultimate objective is to run the control program directly on the robot, another possible pitfall is that workstations are far more powerful than *FortyTwo's* on-board PC, so that code will run a lot slower on the robot than it will on the external computer.

The third method obviously generates code that works on the robot. It is also the slowest method of the three.

3.4   The Need for Sensor Signal Interpretation

From the description of the various sensors and actuators available for mobile robots, it is clear that what sensors actually sense is some physical property of the environment that is related to something the robot needs to know. There are no "obstacle sensors", merely microswitches, sonar sensors, infrared sensors etc., whose signal corresponds to the presence or absence of an object. But a microswitch might trigger because the robot went over a bump, a sonar sensor might indicate an obstacle because of crosstalk, and an infrared sensor might not detect an object because the object is black.

With this caveat in mind, in chapter 4 we turn to look at the task of eliciting meaningful information from raw sensor readings. One feasible way to achieve this is to let the robot learn from experience, through trial and error.

3.5   Further Reading

- On robot sensors: Johann Borenstein, H.R. Everett and Liqiang Feng, *Navigating Mobile Robots*, AK Peters, Wellesley MA, 1996.
- On robot sensors and robot actuators: Arthur Critchlow, *Introduction to Robotics*, Macmillan, New York, 1985.
- For specific information on sonar sensors see [Lee 95], [Leonard *et al.* 90].
- For information regarding laser range finders see http://www.zf-usa.com.

4 Robot Learning: Making Sense of Raw Sensor Data

Summary. This chapter introduces fundamental concepts of robot learning and machine learning, discusses commonly used mechanisms such as reinforcement learning and connectionist approaches, and presents three case studies of mobile robots that can learn.

4.1 Introduction

Section 4.1 of this chapter discusses the fundamental principles that constitute the robot learning problem, and relates the robot learning problem to the machine learning problem. This section is fairly abstract, and introduces general definitions only.

Section 4.2 is more practical, and explains some commonly used mechanisms of reinforcement learning in mobile robots. This section also gives references, where more detailed information about the discussed algorithms can be found.

The chapter concludes with three case studies of learning robots and an exercise. The case studies give examples of self-supervised learning, supervised learning and unsupervised learning. The exercise is for your own enjoyment — see whether you can do it!

4.1.1 Motivation

Learning establishes in an agent a procedure, a capability or knowledge that was not available before, at the design stage. Learning is unnecessary for implementing capabilities that are completely understood, and can be implemented using a fixed, "hardwired" structure. However, if such a fixed structure cannot be identified at the design stage, learning is a way to establish the desired competence later, through interaction with the environment.

There are many reasons why it may be impossible to implement a competence at the design stage. There may be incomplete knowledge of task, agent or environment. We may not know the environment the agent is to operate in, or the task it is to perform. We may also not know the precise properties of the agent's sensors and actuators, any slight defects or idiosyncrasies.

43

Another reason for not being able to implement a competence at the design stage would be that environment, task or agent are known to change over time, in unpredictable ways. In environments inhabited by humans, for instance, objects can change their position at any time (moving furniture), object properties may change (painting the walls), or general environmental conditions may change (switching light on and off). The task may change as the agent is pursuing a high level goal that involves achieving various different subgoals. And finally, the agent may change in unpredictable ways, too — sensor and actuator characteristics of robots, for instance, change with decreasing battery charge, or changes in temperature and humidity. *ALDER* (see figure 4.14) had the irritating habit of curving slightly left when instructed to move straight, only to start curving right once the batteries ran low. It was impossible therefore to compensate for its inability to move straight, using a hardwired control strategy.

Finally, we (that is the human designers) may be unable to implement a suitable fixed control structure at the design stage, because we perceive the world differently to a robot. We refer to this as the *problem of perceptual discrepancy*. We sometimes simply don't know what the best control strategy would be.

Here is an example for the problem of perceptual discrepancy. Most people would think that good landmarks for a mobile robot navigating in an office-type environment would be doors. Doors are highly visible from long distances, and at varying angles. They are designed to be detected easily. However, they are designed to be detected easily *by humans* — experiments show that for a robot it is far easier to detect the slightly protruding door *frames*, rather than the doors themselves. The frames reflect sonar bursts very well, and shine like beacons in the darkness; and yet for a human door *frames* are completely inconspicuous.

Nothing ever looks exactly the same the second time. Some objects change their appearance over time (like living beings), sometimes environmental conditions are different (e.g. lighting), or the viewing perspective is different. *Generalisation* — a form of learning — can help to identify the salient features of an object, whilst ignoring the changeable ones.

It is for these reasons that we are interested in adding a learning capability to a mobile robot. Learning will enable robots to acquire competences that cannot be implemented by the human designer at the design stage, for any of the reasons given above.

4.1.2   Robot Learning versus Machine Learning

The Metal Skin Metaphor   Consider a mobile robot like *FortyTwo*, shown in figure 3.16. This 16-sided robot possesses a metal skin which separates the interior of the robot from the "world out there", the "real world" (referred to simply as the "world" from now on). Embedded in this metal skin are the robot's sensors, for example the sonars and IR sensors.

Some properties of the world are perceived by the robot's sensors, and made available to the inside — that was lies inside the metal skin of the robot — as electrical signals. For example, some property of the world that made a sonar burst return to the robot after 4 milliseconds arrives at the inside in the form of a signal saying "66 *cm*". The latter signal is not equivalent to the former, it is merely *one* of many possible sensations arising from the state of the world.

The metal skin separates the world from the inside of the robot, and the metal skin metaphor allows us to distinguish between the robot learning problem and the machine learning problem.

The *robot learning problem* addresses the question of making a robot perform certain tasks in the world successfully. The *machine learning problem*, on the other hand, addresses the problem of how to obtain one well defined goal state from the current well defined system state. The machine learning problem is what goes on *inside* the metal skin, whereas the robot learning problem sees robot, environment and task as one inseparable entity (see figure 4.1).

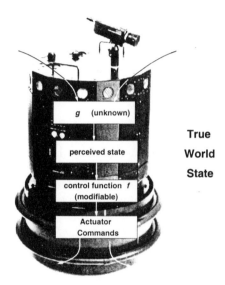

FIG. 4.1. THE ROBOT LEARNING PROBLEM. THE TRUE STATE OF THE WORLD IS INACCESSIBLE TO THE ROBOT - ONLY THE PERCEIVED STATE IS AVAILABLE TO THE LEARNING PROCESS

The true state of the world is transformed, by some unknown function g, into the perceived state of the world. This perceived state of the world can be associated with actions through a control function f, which is modifiable through learning. Changing f is the machine learning problem, which is the subject of the following discussion.

A More Formal Description of Machine Learning   Every learning process has some "goal", and the first consideration is how to define that goal.

Because we only have access to the perceived state of the world, rather than the true state of the world "out there", the most precise definition for goals is in terms of perceived states, i.e. sensor states.

However, it is not always possible to do so, because often there is no one-to-one mapping between some desired behaviour of the robot in the world and the perceived state of the world. Typically, during the execution of actions the same perceived states may occur many times, so that it is impossible to detect the goal behaviour by detecting a goal perceived state of the world. In those cases, qualitative descriptions of the goal have to suffice, which makes the analysis of the learning system more difficult.

Assuming that G is an identifiable goal state, and X and Y are two different perceived states of the world, the machine learning problem can be formally described by

$$G : X \to Y; R , \tag{4.1}$$

interpreted as "if the robot finds itself in a state satisfying condition X, then the goal of reaching a state satisfying condition Y becomes active, for which a reward R is received."

For example, the goal of recharging a low battery can be represented in this way, by setting

X = "Battery level low",
Y = "Robot is connected to battery charger", and
R = 100.

Given a set of such goals, we can define a quantitative measure of robot performance such as the proportion of times that the robot successfully achieves condition Y given that condition X has been encountered, or the sum of the rewards it receives over time. If we wish, we might further elaborate our measure to include the cost or delay of the actions leading from condition X to condition Y.

Given this definition of *robot performance* relative to some set of goals G, we can say that the robot learning problem is to improve robot performance through experience. Thus, robot learning is also relative to the particular goals and performance measure. A robot learning algorithm that is successful relative to one set of goals might be unsuccessful with respect to another. Of course we are most interested in general-purpose learning algorithms that enable the robot to become increasingly successful with respect to a wide variety of goal sets.

Characterisation of the Machine Learning Problem by Target Function

We said above that the machine learning problem can be described as the problem of acquiring the policy that will yield the maximum cumulative reward, as the agent moves from system state to system state. Using the descriptors s for the system's current state ($s \in S$, with S being the finite set of all possible states), a the action selected ($a \in A$, with A being the finite set of all possible actions) and V being the expected discounted future reward, different machine learning scenarios can be described as follows.

The simplest situation would be to learn a control function f directly, from training examples corresponding to input-output pairs of f (equation 4.2).

$$f : S \to A. \tag{4.2}$$

One example of a system that learns f directly is Pomerleau's ALVINN system ([Pomerleau 93]). It learns the control function f for steering a vehicle. The system learns from training data obtained by watching a human driver steer the vehicle for a few minutes. Each training example consists of a perceived state (a camera image of the road ahead), along with a steering action (obtained by observing the human driver). A neural network is trained to fit these examples. The system has successfully learned to drive on a variety of public roads.

Another example of this situation is given in case study 2 on p. 74, where *FortyTwo* learns several sensor-motor competences by observing the actions of a human trainer.

In other cases, training examples of the function f might not be directly available. Consider for example a robot with no human trainer, with only the ability to determine when the goals in its set G are satisfied and what reward is associated with achieving that goal. For example, in a navigation task in which an initially invisible goal location is to be reached, and in which the robot cannot exploit any guiding information present in the environment for navigation, a sequence of many actions is needed before the task is accomplished. However, if it has no external trainer to suggest the correct action at each intermediate state, its only training information will be the delayed reward it eventually achieves when the goal is satisfied through trial and error. In this case, it is not possible to learn the function f directly because no input-output pairs of f are available.

One common way to address this problem is to define an auxiliary function $Q : S \times A \rightarrow V$, an evaluation function of the expected future reward V, that takes into account system state s and the action taken (a). This method, Q-learning, is discussed in detail in section 4.2 of this chapter.

Using Q, the immediate feedback (which is unavailable) is replaced by the internal predictions of how well the agent is going to do.

There are further general categories of the machine learning problem: The robot could learn to predict the next perceived state s' of the world, given it takes an specific action a in state s: $NextState : s \times a \rightarrow s'$, where s' is the state resulting from applying action a to state s. One very useful property of $NextState$ is that it is task-independent and can support any learning process. An example where prediction is successfully applied is given in [O'Sullivan *et al.* 95].

Finally, the robot could learn to map from raw sensory input and actions to a useful representation of the robot's state, $Perceive : Sensor^* \times a^* \rightarrow s$. This corresponds to learning a useful state representation, where the state s is computed from possibly the entire history of raw sensor inputs $Sensor^*$, as well as the history of actions performed a^*. Again, $Perceive$ is task-independent and can be used to support any learning application.

Characterisation of the Machine Learning Problem

by Training Information There are three major classes of training information that can be used to control the learning process: supervised, self-supervised and unsupervised.

In *supervised learning*, training information about values of the target control function are presented to the learning mechanism externally. A prototypical example is the supervised training data obtained from the human trainer for the ALVINN system described above. The *backpropagation algorithm* for training artificial neural networks (see p. 63) is one common technique for supervised learning. The training information provided in supervised control is usually an example of the action to be performed, as in ALVINN or case study 2 (p. 74).

In *self-supervised* learning, the actual learning mechanism is the same as in supervised learning. However, the *external* feedback given by the trainer in the supervised case is replaced by *internal* feedback, supplied from an independent, internal control structure. In reinforcement learning, discussed in section 4.2 below, this is the "critic". In case study 1 (p. 69) this is the "monitor".

Finally, *unsupervised learning* clusters incoming information without using input-output pairs for training, but instead exploiting the underlying structure of the input data. Kohonen's self-organising feature map is a well known example of an unsupervised learning mechanism ([Kohonen 88]). Unsupervised learning, i.e. cluster analysis, has an important role in optimising the robot's organisation of sensory (training) data. For example, unsupervised learning can identify clusters of similar data points, enabling the data to be represented in terms of orthogonal (highly characteristic) features, without the user knowing nor specifying what those features are. This reduces the effective dimensionality of the data, enabling more concise data representation and supporting more accurate supervised learning. An example of such an application is case study 3 on p. 80.

4.1.3 Further Reading on the Robot Learning Problem

- Ulrich Nehmzow and Tom Mitchell, The Prospective Student's Introduction to the Robot Learning Problem, *Technical Report UMCS-95-12-6*, Manchester University, Department of Computer Science, Manchester, 1995 (available at `ftp://ftp.cs.man.ac.uk/pub/TR/UMCS-95-12-6.ps.Z`.

4.2 Learning Methods in Detail

4.2.1 Reinforcement Learning

Introduction

"[The term reinforcement learning covers techniques of] learning by trial and error through performance feedback, i.e. from feedback that evaluates the behaviour, ... but does not indicate correct behaviour" ([Sutton 91]).
"Examples of optimal solutions are not provided during training" ([Barto 95]).

Usually, the form this performance feedback takes is a simple "good/bad" signal at the end of a sequence of actions, for example after finally having reached a goal location, grasped an object, etc. This type of situation is common in robotics, and reinforcement learning can therefore be applied to many robotics tasks.

Reinforcement learning can be viewed as an optimisation problem, whose goal it is to establish a control policy that obtains maximum reinforcement, from whatever state the robot might be in. This is shown in figure 4.2.

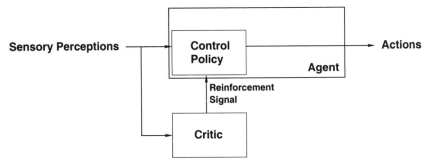

FIG. 4.2. THE REINFORCEMENT LEARNING SCENARIO. PERFORMING ACTIONS IN THE WORLD, THE AGENT SEEKS TO MAXIMISE CUMULATIVE REWARD.

Reinforcement learning techniques are particularly suitable for robotic applications in which mistakes of the robot are not immediately fatal and where some sort of evaluation function of the robot's performance exists. Reinforcement learning uses an overall performance measure (the reinforcement) to control the learning process ([Barto 90] and [Torras 91]), in this it differs from supervised learning schemes (for example certain kinds of connectionist computing architectures), which use specific target values for individual units. This property can be particularly useful for robotics, where often only the overall desired behaviour of the robot is known; however at the same time this can also be a problem, as it can be difficult to establish which parameter within the controller to alter in order to increase the reinforcement.

It is through this performance feedback that a mapping from state (the representation of a particular situation) to action is learned.

[Sutton 91] gives the following overview of reinforcement learning architectures for intelligent agents:

- *Policy only* architecture, which is the simplest architecture. Here, the policy of the agent is the only modifiable structure. These architectures work well only if the rewards are distributed around a baseline of zero (that is positive reinforcement is a positive number, negative reinforcement a negative number, they can't both be positive, with the former being bigger than the latter).
- *Reinforcement comparison techniques* use a prediction of the reward as the baseline and are thus able to cope with rewards distributed around a non-zero baseline.

- The *Adaptive Heuristic Critic* architecture (see below for a detailed discussion) uses a predictor of return (the long-term cumulative reward), not reward, to take non-immediate rewards into account. Neither of the previous two architectures can do this.
- In *Q-learning* (again, see below) the predicted return is a function not only of state, but also of the action selected. Finally,
- *Dyna architectures* are reinforcement learning architectures that contain an internal world model. For each single step of selecting an action and performing it in the real world, Dyna architectures perform another k learning steps using the world model (k is an integer number).

Reinforcement Learning Can Be Slow [Sutton 91] reports that in a simulation on path finding where start and goal location are 16 squares in a 9 x 6 grid apart, it takes a Dyna-adaptive heuristic critic four steps in the simulated world and another 100 steps ($k = 100$) per each of those four steps to find the path. If a new obstacle is placed in the way, the new path is found in a "very slow" process. He also presents a simulation of a Dyna-Q system that has to find a path of length 10 (squares). This takes 1000 time steps, and another 800 after an obstacle is moved in the way. At $k = 10$ this means 100 steps in the simulated environment, and another 80 to find a new path. For a real robot this can be too slow a learning rate. The only cost to be paid in simulation is that of computing time; in robotics however the cost function is a different one: apart from the fact that due to their battery capacity robots only operate for a certain length of time, certain competences such as obstacle avoidance *have* to be acquired very quickly in order to ensure safe operation of the robot. The conclusion is: for mobile robotics it is crucial that the learning algorithm is fast (on the slow speed of reinforcement learning see also [Brooks 91a]).

The fact that reinforcement learning can be extremely slow is shown by other researchers, too. [Prescott & Mayhew 92] simulate the *AIVRU* mobile robot and use a reinforcement learning algorithm similar to the one described by Watkins ([Watkins 89]). The sensor input space of the simulated agent is a continuous function, simulating a sensor that gives distance and angle to the nearest obstacle. The simulated world is 5 m x 5 m in area, the simulated robot 30 cm x 30 cm. Without learning, the agent runs into obstacles in 26.5% of all simulation steps, and only after 50,000 learning steps this rate drops to 3.25%.

[Kaelbling 90] compares several algorithms and their performances in a simulated robot domain. The agent has to stay away from obstacles (negative reinforcement is applied if it hits an obstacle), it receives positive reinforcement if it moves near a light source. Kaelbling reports that all reinforcement learning algorithms investigated (Q-learning, interval estimation plus Q-learning and adaptive heuristic critic plus interval estimation) suffered from the fact that the agent often acquired an appropriate strategy only very late in the run, because it did not come near the light source in the early stages of the learning process and thus did not receive positive reinforcement. After 10,000 runs, the different algorithms obtained average reinforcement values of 0.16 (Q-learning), 0.18 (interval estimation plus Q-learning) and 0.37 (adaptive heuristic critic plus interval estimation). A hand-coded "optimal" controller obtained 0.83. As in the case mentioned earlier ([Prescott & Mayhew 92]), learning took a long time, and the achieved performance was far below optimal performance.

Slow learning rates, finding the appropriate critic for the reinforcement learning architecture and determining how to alter controller outputs in order to improve performance are the main problems when implementing reinforcement learning on robots ([Barto 90]). Another "problem that has prevented these architectures from being applied to more complex control tasks has been the inability of reinforcement learning algorithms to deal with limited sensory input. That is, these learning algorithms depend on having complete access to the state of the task environment" ([Whitehead & Ballard 90]). For robotics applications this is unrealistic and extremely limiting, and there are far more simulations of reinforcement learning architectures than there are implementations on real robots. Two examples of robots using reinforcement learning are given below.

Two Examples of Robots Using Reinforcement Learning   The mobile robot *OBELIX* [Mahadevan & Connell 91] uses reinforcement learning (Q-learning) to acquire a box-pushing skill. In order to overcome the credit assignment problem[1], the overall task of box-pushing is divided into three subtasks: box-finding, box-pushing and unwedging. These three tasks are implemented as independent behaviours within a subsumption architecture, box-finding being the lowest level and unwedging being the highest level. Obelix has eight ultrasonic sensors and one infrared sensor, in addition to that the robot can monitor the motor supply current (which gives an indication whether the robot is pushing against a fixed obstacle). Instead of using the raw data, Mahadevan and Connell quantise it into an 18-bit-long vector which is then reduced to nine bits by combining several bits. This 9-bit input vector is used as an input to the Q-learning algorithm. The possible motor actions of Obelix are restricted to five: forward, left turn, right turn, sharp left turn and sharp right turn. Input information to *OBELIX'* learning controller is small, and uses preprocessed range data, where sonar scans are coded into "range bins".

Their experimental results confirm that Q-learning may require a large number of learning steps: After a relatively long training time of 2000 learning steps, the find-box behaviour obtained an average value of reward of 0.16, whereas a hand-coded box-finder obtained ca. 0.25.

The second example is that of the walking robot *GENGHIS* that learns to coordinate its leg movements so that a walking behaviour is achieved ([Maes & Brooks 90]).   Unlike [Brooks 86a], who determines the arbitration between behaviours by hand, in *GENGHIS* the "relevance" of a particular behaviour is determined through a statistical learning process. The stronger the correlation between a particular behaviour and positive feedback, the more relevant it is. The more relevant a behaviour is in a particular context, the more likely it is to be invoked. In *GENGHIS'* case positive feedback signals are received from a trailing wheel that serves as a forward motion detector, and nega-

---

[1] How does one correctly assign credit or blame to an action when its consequences unfold over time and interact with the consequences of other actions ([Barto 90])?

tive feedback is received from two switches mounted on the bottom of the robot (the switches detect when the robot is not lifted from the ground).

The speed of learning is strongly influenced by the size of the search space (in this case the space of possible motor actions), that is the amount of search that is required before the first positive reinforcement is obtained. [Kaelbling 90] writes that in experiments with the mobile robot *SPANKY*, whose task it was to move towards a light source, the robot only learned to do this successfully if it was helped in the beginning, so that some positive feedback was received. Similarly, in *GENGHIS'* case the search space is small enough to give the robot positive feedback at an early stage. This is equally true for the robot learning example given later in case study 1.

Reinforcement Learning Architectures

Q-Learning In many learning applications the goal is to establish a control policy that maps a *discrete* input space onto a *discrete* output space such that maximum cumulative reinforcement (reward) is obtained. Q-learning is one mechanism that is applicable to such learning situations.

Assuming that we have a set of discrete states $s \in S$ ("state" here refers to a specific constellation of relevant parameters that affect the robot's operation, e.g. sensor readings, battery charge, physical location, etc., with S being the finite set of all possible states), and a discrete set of actions $a \in A$ (A is the finite space of all possible actions) that the robot might perform ("action" here refers to possible responses of the robot, e.g. movement, acoustic output, visual output, etc), it can be shown that Q-learning converges to an optimal control procedure ([Watkins 89]).

The basic idea behind Q-learning is that the learning algorithm learns the optimal evaluation function over the entire state-action space $S \times A$. The Q function provides a mapping of the form $Q : S \times A \rightarrow V$, where V is the value, the "future reward" of performing action a in state s. Provided the optimal Q function is learned, and provided the partitioning of action space and robot state space does not introduce artefacts or omits relevant information, the robot then knows precisely which action will yield the highest future reward in a particular situation s.

The function $Q(s, a)$ of the expected future reward, obtained after taking action a in state s is learned through trial and error according to equation 4.3.

$$Q_{t+1}(s, a) \leftarrow Q_t(s, a) + \beta(r + \lambda E(s) - Q_t(s, a) , \qquad (4.3)$$

where β is the learning rate, r is the reward or punishment resulting from the action a taken in state s, λ is a discount factor ($0 < \lambda < 1$) which reduces the influence of expected future rewards, and $E(s) = max(Q(s, a))$ the utility of state s resulting from action a, using the Q function that has been learned so far.

One example of the application of Q-learning to robot learning has been given above (*OBELIX*). Further examples can be found in [Arkin 98].

Adaptive Heuristic Critic One fundamental problem of reinforcement learning is the *temporal credit assignment problem*: because reinforcement is only received once the final goal state has been reached, it is hard to apportion credit to the actions that preceded the final, successful action.

The way this problem is often addressed is by learning an internal evaluation function which predicts the long-term reward of taking action a in state s. Systems that learn such internal evaluation function are called *adaptive critics* ([Sutton 91]).

Temporal Difference Learning One major drawback of Q-learning is that actions taken early on in the exploration process do not contribute anything towards the learning process – only when finally, by chance, a goal state is reached can the learning rule be applied. This makes Q-learning so time-consuming.

One way of dealing with this problem would be to make predictions of the outcome of actions as the robot explores its world, and to estimate the value of each action a in state s through these predictions. This kind of learning is called *Temporal Difference Learning* or *TD Learning*.

In effect, the learning system predicts reward, and uses this predicted reward for the learning system, until actual external reward is received. A discussion of this method can be found in [Sutton 88].

Further Reading on Reinforcement Learning

- Andrew Barto, *Reinforcement Learning* and *Reinforcement Learning in Motor Control*, in [Arbib 95, pp. 804-813].
- [Ballard 97, ch. 11].
- [Mitchell 97, ch. 13].
- [Kaelbling 90].

4.2.2 Probabilistic Reasoning

We discussed earlier the difference between the machine learning problem and the robot learning problem: the former attempts to find an optimal function with regard to some reward criterion, that maps a fully known input state on to a fully known goal state, while the latter has the additional complication that the true state of the world is unknown.

Uncertainty is a major issue in the interaction between a robot and the environment it is operating in. Sensor signals do not signify the presence of objects, for instance. They merely indicate that the environment is such that a sonar pulse returns to the robot after such and such a time, which indicates with some probability that there is an object out there, reflecting sonar bursts.

Likewise, a robot never knows precisely where it is (the problem of localisation is discussed in detail in chapter 5), and can only estimate its current position with some probability.

In some situations these probabilities are known, or can be estimated to sufficient accuracy to allow mathematical modelling. Markov processes are the most widely used instantiation of such probabilistic models.

Markov Processes A Markov process is a sequence of (possibly dependent) random variables $(x_1, x_2, \ldots x_n)$ with the property that any prediction of x_n may be based on the knowledge of x_{n-1} alone. In other words, any future value of a variable depends only on the current value of the variable, and not on the sequence of past values.

An example is the Markov process shown in figure 4.3, which determines whether a bit string has odd or even parity, i.e. whether it contains an odd or an even number of '1's.

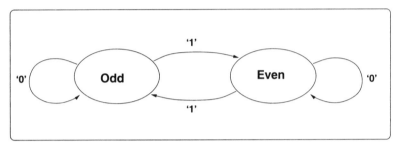

FIG. 4.3. A MARKOV PROCESS TO DETERMINE ODD OR EVEN PARITY OF A BIT STRING

If you start in position 'even' before processing the first bit, and then follow the transitions between the two states according to whether the current bit in the bit string is a '0' or a '1', the final state you end up in indicates whether the bit string has odd or even parity. All transitions are merely dependent on the currently processed bit, not on the sequence of previously processed bits. There is no counting of '1's at all.

Markov Decision Processes One can expand the definition of a Markov process (which was dependent only on the current state s and the transition process a — in the parity example the fact whether a '0' or a '1' was being processed) by adding a state transition model of the environment, and a reward function that assesses the agent's performance.

A Markov decision process is defined by a tuple $< S, A, T, R >$, where S is a finite set of system states, A a finite set of actions, T a state transition model that maps state-action pairs onto a probability distribution over S (indicating the probability of reaching state s' if action a is performed in state s), and R a reward function that specifies the reward the robot receives for taking an action $a \in A$ in state $s \in S$. As this is a Markovian process, knowledge of s and a is sufficient to determine the new state s', and to compute the reward r obtained by moving to state s'.

The value $V(s)$ is the expected sum of future rewards, discounted by a discount factor $0 < \lambda < 1$ that increases as the expected rewards are further away in the future.

It is possible to determine the optimal policy with respect to V in a Markov decision process, and therefore to determine how the agent should act in order to obtain that maximal value V ([Puterman 94]).

Partially Observable Markov Decision Processes A common problem in robotic applications is that usually the state is not fully observable, i.e. it is not always known what the current system state is. In this case, a model of observations must be added. This model specifies the probability of making observation o after having taken action a in state s.

The *belief state* then is a probability distribution over S (the set of all possible states), representing for each state $s \in S$ the belief that the robot is currently in state s.

The procedure for the Markov decision process discussed above can now be modified to partially observable environments, by estimating the robot's current state s, and by applying a policy that maps belief states onto actions. Again, the objective is to determine the policy that will maximise the discounted future reward.

Further Reading on Markov Decision Processes

- Leslie Pack Kaelbling, Michael Littman and Anthony Cassandra, Planning and Acting in Partially Observable Stochastic Domains, *Artificial Intelligence*, Vol. 101, 1998.

4.2.3 Connectionism

Connectionist computing architectures (also called "artificial neural networks") are mathematical algorithms that are able to learn mappings between input and output states through supervised learning, or to cluster incoming information in an unsupervised manner. Their characteristic feature is that many independent processing units work simultaneously, and that the overall behaviour of the network is not caused by any one component of the architecture, but is emergent from the concurrent working of all units. Because of their ability to learn mappings between an input and an output space, to generalise incoming data, to interpret (cluster) input information without supervision (i.e. without teaching signal), their resistance to noise and their robustness (the term *graceful degradation* describes the fact that the performance of such networks is not solely dependent on the individual unit — losing one unit will merely mean a degradation, not a total loss of performance), connectionist computing architectures can be used well in robotics. [Torras 91] gives an overview of (largely simulation) work that has been done in the field: supervised learning schemes have been applied to the generation of sequences, both supervised and unsupervised learning schemes have been used to learn non-linear mappings such as inverse kinematics, inverse dynamics and sensorimotor integration, and reinforcement learning has largely been used for tasks involving optimisation, such as path planning.

Artificial neural networks can be used in a number of applications in mobile robotics. For instance, they can be used to learn associations between input signals (e.g. sensor signals) and output signals (e.g. motor responses). Case studies 1 and 2 (p. 69 and p. 74) are examples of such applications.

They can also be used to determine the underlying (unknown) structure of data, which is useful to develop internal representations, or for data compression applications. In case study 3 (p. 80) *FortyTwo* uses a self-organising artificial neural network to determine the underlying structure of visual perceptions of its environments, and applies this structure to detecting target objects in the image.

The following sections and case studies give a brief overview of common artificial neural networks, and their applications to mobile robotics.

McCulloch and Pitts Neurons The inspiration for artificial neural networks is given by biological neurons, which perform complicated tasks such as pattern recognition, learning, focusing attention, motion control, etc. extremely reliably and robustly. A simplified biological neuron — the model for the artificial neuron — consists of a cell body, the *soma* which performs the computation, a number of inputs (the *dendrites*), and one or more outputs (the *axon*) which connect to other neurons. Signals in the simplified biological neuron model are encoded in electric spikes, whose frequency encodes the signal.

The connections between dendrites and soma, the *synapses*, are modifiable by so-called neurotransmitters, meaning that incoming signals can be amplified, or attenuated.

The simplified model assumes that the firing rate (i.e. the frequency of output spikes) of a neuron is proportional to the neuron's activity. In artificial neural networks, the output of the artificial neuron is sometimes kept analogue, sometimes thresholded to produce binary output. This is dependent on the application.

In 1943 McCulloch and Pitts proposed a simple computational model of biological neurons. In this model, the input spikes of biological neurons were replaced by a continuous, single-valued input signal, the "chemical encoding" of synaptic strength was replaced by a multiplicative weight, the threshold function of a biological neuron was modelled using a comparator, and the spiking output signal of a biological neuron was replaced by a binary value.

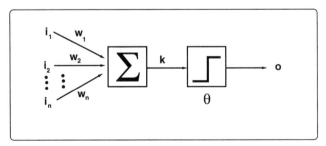

FIG. 4.4. THE MCCULLOCH AND PITTS NEURON

The McCulloch and Pitts neuron is shown in figure 4.4. Its functionality is as follows. The neuron computes the weighted sum k of all n inputs $\imath$, according to equation 4.4.

$$k = \sum_{j=1}^{n} \imath_j w_j \qquad (4.4)$$

This weighted sum is then compared with a fixed threshold Θ to produce the final output o. If k exceeds Θ, the neuron is "on" (usually defined as '$o = 1$'), if k is below the threshold, the neuron is "off" (usually defined as either '$o = 0$' or '$o = -1$').

McCulloch and Pitts ([McCulloch & Pitts 43])   proved that, given suitably chosen weights, a synchronous assembly of such simple neurons is capable in principle of universal computation — any computable function can be implemented using McCulloch and Pitts neurons. The problem, of course, is to choose the weights "suitably". How this can be achieved is discussed later in this section.

Example: Obstacle Avoidance Using McCulloch and Pitts Neurons A robot as shown in figure 4.5 is to avoid obstacles when one or both of the whiskers trigger, and move forward otherwise. Whiskers LW and RW signal '1' when they are triggered, '0' otherwise. The motors LM and RM move forward when they receive a '1' signal, and backwards when they receive a '-1' signal.

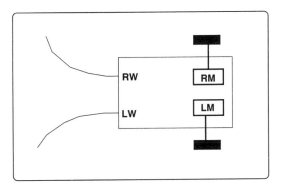

FIG. 4.5. A SIMPLE VEHICLE

The truth table for this obstacle avoidance behaviour is shown in table 4.1.

We can implement this function using one McCulloch and Pitts neuron for each motor, using neurons whose output is either "-1" or "+1". In this example, we will determine the necessary weights w_{RW} and w_{LW} for the *left* motor neuron only. The weights for the right neuron are determined in a similar fashion. We choose a threshold Θ of just below zero, -0.01 say.

The first line of truth table 4.1 stipulates that both motor neurons must be '+1' if neither LW nor RW fire. As we have chosen a threshold of $\Theta = -0.01$ this is fulfilled.

LW	RW	LM	RM
0	0	1	1
0	1	-1	1
1	0	1	-1
1	1	don't care	don't care

Table 4.1. TRUTH TABLE FOR OBSTACLE AVOIDANCE

Line two of table 4.1 indicates that w_{RW} must be smaller than Θ for the left motor neuron. We choose, say, $w_{RW} = -0.3$.

Line three of the truth table, then, indicates that w_{LW} must be greater than Θ. We choose, say, $w_{LW} = 0.3$.

As a quick check with table 4.1 shows, these weights already implement the obstacle avoidance function for the left motor neuron! The functioning network is shown in figure 4.6.

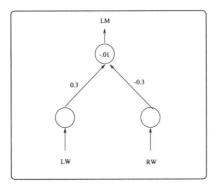

FIG. 4.6. LEFT-MOTOR NODE FOR OBSTACLE AVOIDANCE

The way we determined the weights here was by "common sense". Looking at the relatively simple truth table of the obstacle avoidance function, it is a straightforward exercise to determine weights that will give the desired output function.

However, for more complicated functions, determining weights by "common sense" is very hard, and it is desirable to have a learning mechanism that would determine those required weights automatically. There is a second reason why we want such a learning rule: it would allow us to build robots that learn. The *Perceptron* is a network consisting of McCulloch and Pitts neurons that fulfils this requirement.

Exercise 2: Full Obstacle Avoidance Using McCulloch and Pitts Neurons What will the robot do if *both* whiskers are touched simultaneously? Which artificial neural network, based on McCulloch and Pitts neurons, would implement the function indicated in truth table 4.1, *and* make the robot move backwards if both whiskers are touched? The answer is given in appendix 2.1 on page 220.

Perceptron and Pattern Associator The Perceptron ([Rosenblatt 62]) is a "single-layer" artificial neural network that is easy to implement, low in computational cost and fast in learning. It consists of two layers of units: the input layer (which simply passes signals on) and the output layer of McCulloch and Pitts neurons (which performs the actual computation, hence "single layer network" — see figure 4.7, right).

The function of input and output units is as follows: input units simply pass the received input signals $\vec{i}$ on to all output units, the output o_j of output unit j is determined by

$$o_j = f(\sum_{k=1}^{M} w_{jk} i_k) = f(\vec{w}_j \cdot \vec{i}), \qquad (4.5)$$

where $\vec{w}_j$ is the individual weight vector of output unit j, M the number of input units, and f the so-called transfer function.

The transfer function f of the Perceptron is defined as a step function:

$$f(x) = \begin{cases} 1 & \forall\, x > \Theta \\ 0\, (or - 1) & \text{else.} \end{cases}$$

Θ again is a threshold value.

The Pattern Associator (see figure 4.7, left) is a variant of the Perceptron, with the only difference that here $f(x) = x$. The main difference between Perceptron and Pattern Associator, therefore, is that the Perceptron generates binary output, while the Pattern Associator's output is continuous-valued. Otherwise, these two networks are very similar ([Kohonen 88] and [Rumelhart & McClelland 86]).

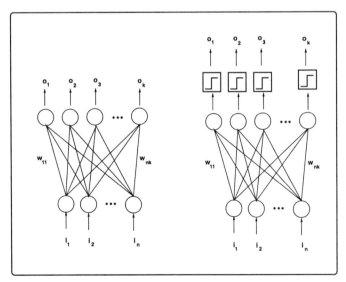

FIG. 4.7. PATTERN ASSOCIATOR (LEFT) AND PERCEPTRON (RIGHT)

The Perceptron Learning Rule In the case of the McCulloch and Pitts neuron, we determined the suitable weights by applying our common sense. For complex networks and complex input-output mappings, this method is not suitable. Furthermore, we would like to have a learning rule so that we can use it for autonomous robot learning.

The rule for determining the necessary weights is very simple[2], it is given in equation 4.6.

$$\Delta \vec{w}_k(t) = \eta(t)(\tau_k - o_k)\vec{\imath}, \qquad (4.6)$$

$$\vec{w}_k(t+1) = \vec{w}_k(t) + \Delta \vec{w}_k, \qquad (4.7)$$

with τ_k being the target value for unit k, i.e. the desired output of output unit k, and o_k the actually obtained output of unit k. The speed of learning is determined by the learning rate $\eta(t)$. A big η (for example 0.8) will result in a network that adjusts very quickly to changes, but which will also be "neurotic" (it will forget all it has learned and learn something new as soon as a couple of freak signals occur). A small η (for example 0.1), on the other hand, will result in a "lethargic" network that takes a long time before it learns a function. The learning rate η is usually chosen to be constant, but may be variable over time.

Example: Obstacle Avoidance Using a Perceptron We'll consider the the same example we have considered before: obstacle avoidance (see p. 57). The difference this time is that we use a Perceptron, and that we *determine* the required weights, using the Perceptron learning rule given in equations 4.6 and 4.7.

Let η be 0.3, and Θ again just below zero, say -0.01. The two weights of the left-motor node are also zero to start with. This initial configuration is shown in figure 4.8.

We now go line by line through the truth table 4.1, applying equations 4.6 and 4.7.

Line one of the truth table yields:

$$w_{LWLM} = 0 + 0.3(1-1)0 = 0$$
$$w_{LWRM} = 0 + 0.3(1-1)0 = 0$$

Likewise, the other two weights also remain zero.

Line two of table 4.1 results in the following updates:

$$w_{LWLM} = 0 + 0.3(-1-1)0 = 0$$
$$w_{LWRM} = 0 + 0.3(1-1)0 = 0$$
$$w_{RWLM} = 0 + 0.3(-1-1)1 = -0.6$$
$$w_{RWRM} = 0 + 0.3(1-1)1 = 0$$

Line three of the truth table gives:

---

[2] The derivation of this rule can be found in [Hertz *et al.* 91].

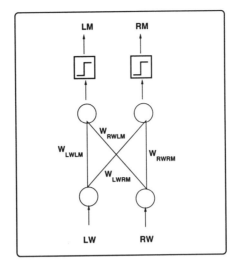

FIG. 4.8. LAYOUT OF A PERCEPTRON FOR OBSTACLE AVOIDANCE

$$w_{LWLM} = 0 + 0.3\,(1 - 1)\,1 = 0$$
$$w_{LWRM} = 0 + 0.3\,(-1 - 1)\,1 = -0.6$$
$$w_{RWLM} = -0.6 + 0.3\,(1 - 1)\,0 = -0.6$$
$$w_{RWRM} = 0 + 0.3\,(-1 - 1)\,0 = 0$$

A quick calculation shows that this network already performs the obstacle avoidance function stipulated by table 4.1 perfectly! The final network is shown in figure 4.9. It is essentially the same network as the one obtained by hand earlier (shown in figure 4.6).

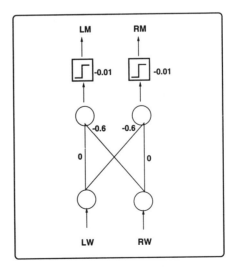

FIG. 4.9. COMPLETE PERCEPTRON FOR OBSTACLE AVOIDANCE

Limitations of the Perceptron Consider a network like the one shown in figure 4.6, and the truth table 4.2 (the exclusive-or function).

A	B	Out
0	0	0
0	1	1
1	0	1
1	1	0

Table 4.2. EXCLUSIVE OR (XOR) FUNCTION

If the network shown in figure 4.6 was to perform this function correctly, the following inequalities would have to be true:

$$w_{LW} > \Theta$$
$$w_{RW} > \Theta$$
$$w_{LW} + w_{RW} < \Theta.$$

The first two expressions add up to $w_{LW} + w_{RW} > 2\Theta$, which contradicts the third inequality. It can't be done. In general Perceptrons are unable to learn functions that are not linearly separable, i.e. functions where two classes cannot be separated by a line, plane or hyperplane in the general case.

This means, of course, that a robot learning by using a Perceptron or a Pattern Associator can only learn functions that are linearly separable. Here is an example of a function the robot could not learn using a Perceptron: suppose we wanted the robot to escape from a dead end by turning left whenever either of two front whiskers is on, and by reversing whenever both whiskers are on simultaneously. For the 'turn-left output node' of the Perceptron this means that it has to be on if either of the two whiskers fires, and to be off in the other two cases. This is the *exclusive or* function, a function that cannot be separated linearly and is therefore unlearnable by a Perceptron output node.

Fortunately, many functions robots have to learn are linearly separable, which means that the very fast learning Perceptron can be used for robot learning (an example is given in case study 1 in section 4.4.1).

In fact, its speed is the major advantage of the Perceptron over networks such as the Multilayer Perceptron or Backpropagation Network (p. 63). A very small number of teaching experiences suffices to produce the correct associations between stimulus and response. A backpropagation network may typically require several hundred teaching experiences before a function is learned. Re-learning (for example when adjusting to new circumstances) then again takes typically several hundred training steps whereas the pattern associator re-learns as quickly as it learned in the first place. This property is important in robotics — certain competences, such as for example obstacle avoidance, have to be learned very quickly, because the robot's ability to stay operational crucially depends on them.

Further Reading on Perceptrons

- [Beale & Jackson 90, pp. 48-53].
- [Hertz *et al.* 91, ch. 5].

Multilayer Perceptron   So far, we have seen that a network consisting of McCulloch and Pitts neurons is capable of universal computation, provided one knows how to set the weights suitably. We have also seen that a single layer network consisting of McCulloch and Pitts neurons, the Perceptron, can be trained by the Perceptron learning rule. However, we also realised that the Perceptron can only learn linearly separable functions.

The explanation for this fact is that each layer of a network consisting of McCulloch and Pitts neurons establishes one hyperplane to separate the two classes the network has to learn (the '1's and the '0's). If the separation between the two classes cannot be achieved with one hyperplane — as is the case in the XOR problem — a single layer network will not be able to learn the function.

A Perceptron with not only one layer of output units, but with one or more additional layers of hidden units (see figure 4.10), however, might be able to do just that! Indeed, it can be shown that the Multilayer Perceptron can implement any computable function. The problem is, as before, to determine the suitable weights.

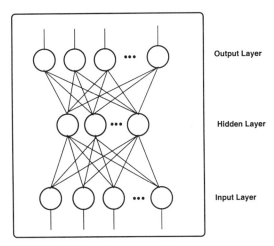

FIG. 4.10. MULTI-LAYER PERCEPTRON

The so-called *backpropagation algorithm* (so called because the update rule uses the backpropagation of output error to determine the required changes in the network's weights) can be used to determine these weights ([Rumelhart *et al.* 86] and [Hertz *et al.* 91]).

To begin with, all network weights are initialised to random values. The thresholds Θ are replaced by weights to an input that is always set to $+1$. This makes threshold updates a part of weight updates, which is computationally simpler.

Once the network is initialised, training commences by presenting input-target (desired output) pairs to the network. These training patterns are then used to adapt the weights.

The output o_j of each unit j in the network is now computed according to equation 4.8.

$$o_j = f(\vec{w}_j \cdot \vec{i}), \tag{4.8}$$

where $\vec{w}$ is the weight vector of that unit j, and $\vec{i}$ is the input vector to unit j. The function f is the so-called activation function. In the case of the Perceptron, this was a binary threshold function, but in the case of the Multilayer Perceptron it has to be a differentiable function, and is usually chosen to be the sigmoid function given in equation 4.9.

$$f(z) = \frac{1}{1 + e^{-kz}}, \tag{4.9}$$

where k is a positive constant that controls the slope of the sigmoid. For $k \to \infty$ the sigmoid function becomes the binary threshold function that was used earlier in the McCulloch and Pitts neurons.

Now that the outputs of all units — hidden units and output layer units — are computed, the network is trained. All weights w_{ij} from unit i to unit j are trained according to equation 4.10.

$$w_{ij}(t + 1) = w_{ij}(t) + \eta \delta_{pj} o_{pi}, \tag{4.10}$$

where η is the learning rate (usually a value of around 0.3), δ_{pj} is the error signal for unit j (for output units, this is given by equation 4.11, for hidden units it is given by equation 4.12); o_{pi} is the input to unit j, coming from unit p.

Error signals are determined for output units first, then for the hidden units. Consequently, training starts with the output layer of the net, and then proceeds backwards through the hidden layer.

For each unit j of the output layer, the error signal δ_{pj}^{out} is determined by equation 4.11.

$$\delta_{pj}^{out} = (t_{pj} - o_{pj})o_{pj}(1 - o_{pj}), \tag{4.11}$$

where t_{pj} is the target signal (the desired output) for the output unit being updated, and o_{pj} the output actually obtained from the output unit being updated.

Once the error signals for the output units have been determined, the penultimate layer of the network — the final hidden layer — is updated by propagating the output errors backwards, according to equation 4.12.

$$\delta_{pj}^{hid} = o_{pj}(1 - o_{pj}) \sum_k \delta_{pk} w_{kj}, \tag{4.12}$$

where o_{pj} is the output of the hidden layer unit currently being updated, δ_{pk} the error of unit k in the subsequent layer of the network, and w_{kj} the weight between hidden unit j and the subsequent unit k on the next higher layer.

This training process is repeated until, for example, the output error of the network drops below a user-defined threshold. For a detailed discussion of the Multilayer Perceptron see, for instance, [Rumelhart *et al.* 86], [Hertz *et al.* 91] [Beale & Jackson 90] and [Bishop 95].

Advantages and Disadvantages   The Multilayer Perceptron can be used to learn non-linearly separable functions, and thus overcomes the problems of the Perceptron. The price to pay for this is, however, that learning usually is a lot slower. Whereas the Perceptron learns within a few learning steps, the Multilayer Perceptron typically requires several hundred learning steps to learn the desired input-output mapping. This is a problem for robotics applications, not so much for the computational cost, but for the fact that a robot would have to repeat the same sort of mistake hundreds of times, before it learns to avoid it[3]. For fundamental sensor-motor competences such as obstacle avoidance, this is usually not acceptable.

Further Reading on Multilayer Perceptrons

- [Rumelhart & McClelland 86, ch. 8].
- [Hertz *et al.* 91, pp.115-120].

Radial Basis Function Networks   Like the Multilayer Perceptron (MLP), the Radial Basis Function Network (RBF net) can learn non-linearly separable functions. It is a two-layer network, in which the hidden layer performs a non-linear mapping based on radial basis functions, whilst the output layer performs a linear weighted summation on the output of the hidden layer (as in the Pattern Associator). The fundamental mechanisms of RBF net and MLP are similar, but whilst the MLP partitions the input space using linear functions (hyperplanes), the RBF net uses nonlinear functions (hyperellipsoids). Figure 4.11 shows the general structure of a radial basis function network ([Lowe & Tipping 96]).

The hidden units have a Gaussian capture region which serves to identify similarities between the current input vector and a hidden unit's weight vector — each weight vector is a prototype of one specific input signal. The hidden layer performs a nonlinear mapping of the input space, which increases the probability that classes can be separated linearly.

The output layer then associates the classification of the hidden layer with the target output signal through linear mapping, as in the Perceptron and the MLP.

The output $o_{hid,j}$ of RBF unit j in the hidden layer is determined by equation 4.13:

$$o_{hid,j} = exp(-\frac{||\vec{\imath} - \vec{w}_j||}{\sigma}), \qquad (4.13)$$

with $\vec{w}_j$ being the weight vector of RBF unit j, $\vec{\imath}$ being the input vector, and σ being the parameter controlling the width of the bell curved capture region of the radial basis function (e.g. $\sigma = 0.05$).

---

[3] To use once perceived sensor patterns for repeated training is problematic, because of the high number of freak perceptions obtained with robot sensors.

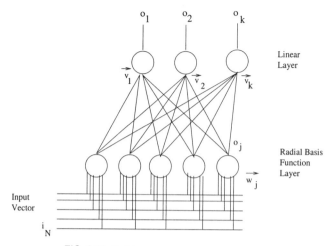

FIG. 4.11. RADIAL BASIS FUNCTION NETWORK

with $\vec{w}_j$ being the weight vector of RBF unit j, $\vec{\imath}$ being the input vector, and σ being the parameter controlling the width of the bell curved capture region of the radial basis function (e.g. $\sigma = 0.05$).

The output o_k of each unit of the output layer is determined by equation 4.14.

$$o_k = \vec{o}_{hid} \cdot \vec{v}_k, \tag{4.14}$$

where $\vec{o}_{hid}$ is the output of the hidden layer, and $\vec{v}_k$ is the weight vector of output unit k.

Training of the output layer is simple, and achieved by applying the Perceptron learning rule given in equations 4.6 and 4.7.

The RBF network works by mapping the input space onto a higher dimensional space through using a nonlinear function, for example the Gaussian function described above. The weights of the hidden layer, therefore, have to be chosen such that the entire input space is represented as evenly as possible. There are several methods for determining the weights of the units in the hidden layer. One simple method is to spread the cluster centres evenly over the input space ([Moody & Darken 89]). Alternatively, it is sometimes sufficient to position the cluster centres at randomly selected points of the input space. This will ensure that RBF cluster density is high where input space density is high, and low where the input density is low ([Broomhead & Lowe 88]). Finally, the weights of the hidden layer can be determined by a clustering mechanism such as the one used in the self-organising feature map (see next section).

Further Reading on Radial Basis Function Networks

- David Lowe, *Radial Basis Function Networks*, in [Arbib 95, pp. 779-782].
- [Bishop 95, ch. 5].

The Self-Organising Feature Map   All artificial neural networks discussed so far are trained by "supervised training": learning is achieved by using a target value, i.e. the desired output of the net. This target value is supplied externally, from a "supervisor" (which could be another piece of code, as in case study 1 on p. 69, or a human, as in case study 2 on p. 74).

However, there are applications where no training signal is available, for example all applications that have to do with clustering some input space. It is often useful in robotics to cluster a high dimensional input space and to map it automatically — in an unsupervised manner — onto a lower dimensional output space. This dimensionality reduction is a form of generalisation, reducing the complexity of the input space whilst, hopefully, retaining all the "relevant" features in the input space. Case study 3 (p. 80) gives an example of the application of unsupervised learning in mobile robotics.

The self-organising feature map (SOFM), or Kohonen network, is one mechanism that performs an unsupervised mapping of a high dimensional input space onto a (typically) two-dimensional output space ([Kohonen 88]).

The SOFM normally consists of a two-dimensional grid of units, as shown in figure 4.12.

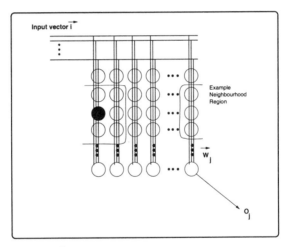

FIG. 4.12. SELF-ORGANISING FEATURE MAP

All units receive the same input vector $\vec{\imath}$. Initially, the weight vectors $\vec{w}_j$ are initialised randomly and normalised to unit length.

The output o_j of each unit j of the net is determined by equation 4.15.

$$o_j = \vec{w}_j \cdot \vec{\imath}. \tag{4.15}$$

Because of the random initialisation of the weight vectors, the outputs of all units will differ from one another, and one unit will respond most strongly to a particular input vector. This "winning unit" and its surrounding units will then be trained so that they respond even more strongly to that particular input vector, by applying the update rule of equation 4.16. After having been updated, weight vectors $\vec{w}_j$ are normalised again.

$$\vec{w}_j(t+1) = \vec{w}_j(t) + \eta(\vec{\imath} - \vec{w}_j(t)), \qquad (4.16)$$

where η is the learning rate (usually a value around $\eta = 0.3$). The neighbourhood around the winning unit, within which units get updated, is usually chosen to be large in the early stages of the training process, and to become smaller as training progresses. Figure 4.12 shows an example neighbourhood of one unit around the winning unit (drawn in black). The figure also shows that the network is usually chosen to be torus-shaped, to avoid border effects at the edges of the network.

As training progresses, certain areas of the SOFM become more and more responsive to certain input stimuli, thus clustering the input space onto a two-dimensional output space. This clustering happens in a topological manner, mapping similar inputs onto neighbouring regions of the net. Example responses of trained SOFMs are shown in figures 4.19, 4.23 and 5.19.

Application of SOFMs to Robotics Generally, SOFMs can be used to cluster an input space to obtain a more meaningful, abstracted representation of that input space.

A typical application is to cluster a robot's sensory input space. Similarities between perceptions can be detected using SOFMs, and the abstracted representation can be used to encode policies, i.e. the robot's response to a particular perception. Case study 6 (section 5.4.3) gives one example of how SOFMs can be used for robot route learning.

Further Reading on Self-Organising Feature Maps

- [Kohonen 88, ch. 5].
- Helge Ritter, *Self-Organizing Feature Maps: Kohonen Maps*, in [Arbib 95, pp. 846-851].

4.3 Further Reading on Learning Methods

On Machine Learning

- Tom Mitchell, *Machine Learning*, McGraw Hill, New York, 1997.
- Dana Ballard, *An Introduction to Natural Computation*, MIT Press, Cambridge MA, 1997.

On Connectionism

- John Hertz, Anders Krogh, Richard G. Palmer, *Introduction to the Theory of Neural Computation*, Addison-Wesley, Redwood City CA, 1991.
- R. Beale and T. Jackson, *Neural Computing: An Introduction*, Adam Hilger, Bristol, Philadelphia and New York, 1990.
- Christopher Bishop, *Neural Networks for Pattern Recognition*, Oxford University Press, Oxford, 1995.
- Simon Haykin, *Neural Networks : a Comprehensive Foundation*, Macmillan, New York, 1994.

4.4   Case Studies of Learning Robots

4.4.1   Case Study 1. *ALDER*: Self-Supervised Learning of Sensor-Motor Couplings

Having discussed the problem of robot learning in general, and the machine learning mechanisms that can be used to achieve competence acquisition in robots, we will now take a closer look at specific examples of mobile robots that learn to interpret their sensory perceptions to accomplish particular tasks.

The first case study presents a self-organising controller architecture which enables mobile robots to learn through trial and error, in a self-supervised learning process that requires no human intervention. The first experiments were conducted in 1989 ([Nehmzow *et al.* 89]), using the robots *ALDER* and *CAIRNGORM* (see figure 4.14), but the mechanism has since been used in many robots internationally to achieve autonomous acquisition of sensor motor competences (see, for instance, [Daskalakis 91] and [Ramakers 93]).

The fundamental idea of the controller is that a Pattern Associator (see section 4.2.3) associates sensory perception with motor action. Because this association is *acquired* through a learning process, rather than being pre-installed, the robot can change its behaviour and adapt to changing circumstances, if the appropriate training mechanism is provided. In *ALDER's* and *CAIRNGORM's* case performance feedback is received using so-called *instinct rules*. These instinct rules specify sensor states that must be maintained (or avoided) throughout the entire operation of the robot: behaviour is thus expressed in the form of sensor states, and the robot learns the appropriate behaviour in order to maintain (or avoid) the required states.

Figure 4.13 shows the general structure of the entire controller used in all experiments discussed in this section. The controller consists of fixed and plastic components, fixed components being the so-called instinct-rules, the robot morphology and various parameters within the controller; the plastic component being the Pattern Associator.

Instinct Rules   As the Pattern Associator is trained under supervised learning, a target signal — the desired response to a particular input — must be provided. As we want the robot to learn without human intervention, an independent method has to be devised to obtain these target signals.

We use fixed rules for this purpose which we call *instinct-rules*. They are similar, but not identical to *instincts* as defined by [Webster 81]:

> "[An instinct is a] complex and specific response on the part of an organism to environmental stimuli that is largely hereditary and unalterable though the pattern through which it is expressed may be modified by learning, that does not involve reason, and that has as its goal the removal of a somatic tension or excitation".

This describes behaviour and is therefore different to the instinct-rules used in the experiments described here, as instinct-rules are not behaviour, but constants

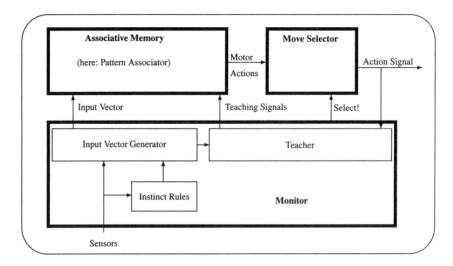

FIG. 4.13. COMPUTATIONAL STRUCTURE OF THE SELF-ORGANISING CONTROLLER

(sensor states) that guide the learning of behaviour. The goal of instinct and instinct-rules, however, is the same: the removal of a somatic tension (in the case of the robot such a "somatic tension" is an external sensor stimulus, or, in some experiments, the lack of it).

Each instinct-rule has a dedicated sensor in order that it can be established whether it is violated or not. This sensor can be a physical, external sensor (for example a whisker), or an internal sensor (for example a clock that is reset every time some external sensor stimulus is received).

To sum up, the instinct-rules are used to generate a reinforcement signal (the signal being the fulfilment of a previously violated instinct-rule), they do not indicate correct behaviour.

Input and Output Current and previous sensor signals constitute the input signals to the Pattern Associator. Typically, raw sensor signals are used, but sometimes it is useful to apply preprocessing to the sensor signals. Information about violated instinct-rules could similarly be used.

The output of the network denotes motor actions of the robot. Examples for such motor actions are swift left turn (i.e. right motor moving forward while left motor is moving backward), swift right turn, forward or backward movement. An alternative to using such "compound" motor actions is to use artificial motor neurons with analogue outputs to drive a differential drive system. Experiments of this kind are described in [Nehmzow 99c].

The idea behind this controller setup is that effective associations between sensor signals and motor actions arise over time through the robot's interaction with the environment, without human intervention.

Mechanism As said earlier, the Pattern Associator requires a teaching signal to develop meaningful associations between its input and its output. This teaching
signal is provided by the *monitor*, a "critic" that uses the instinct rules to assess the robot's performance and teach the network accordingly: as soon as any
of the instinct-rules become violated (i.e. as soon as a specified sensor status is
no longer maintained), an input signal is generated by the *input vector genera-
tor*, sent to the associative memory and the output of the network is computed
(fig. 4.13). The *move selector* determines which output node carries the highest output value and which motor action this output node stands for. That motor
action is then performed for a fixed period of time (the actual length of time depends on the speed of the robot). If the violated instinct-rule becomes satisfied
within this period of time, the association between original input signal and output signal within the Pattern Associator is taken to be correct and is confirmed
to the network (this is done by the monitor). If, on the other hand, the instinct-
rule remains violated, a signal is given from the monitor to the move selector
to activate the motor action that is associated with the second strongest output
node. This action is then performed for a slightly longer period of time than
the first one to compensate the action taken earlier; if this motor action leads to
satisfaction of the violated instinct-rule, the network will be taught to associate
the initial sensor state with this type of motor action; if not, the move selector
will activate the next strongest output node. This process continues until a successful move is found. Because the monitor is part of the robot controller, the
process of sensor-motor competence acquisition is completely independent from
an operator's supervision: the robot acquires its competences autonomously.

Figure 4.7 (left) shows the general structure of the Pattern Associator used.
The actual input to the network may vary from experiment to experiment, the
output nodes denote motor actions. The result of this process is that effective
associations between input stimuli and output signals (motor actions) develop.

Experiments This controller has been implemented on a number of different mobile robots by different research groups. The consistent finding is that it enables
mobile robots to acquire fundamental sensor-motor couplings very rapidly, using no more than 20 learning steps (and typically far less than that), taking a few
tens of seconds in real time. Due to the ability to autonomously re-map sensory
input to actuator output the robots have the ability to maintain task-achieving
competences even when changes in the world, the task, or the robot itself occur.

Learning to Move Forward The simplest experiment to begin with is to make a
robot learn to move forward. Assuming that the robot has some means of determining whether it is actually moving forwards or not[4], an instinct rule of the
form

"Keep the forward motion sensor 'on' at all times"

---

[4] This can be achieved, for instance, by detecting whether a swivelling caster wheel is aligned with
the main axis of the robot or not, using a suitably placed microswitch.

will lead to a mapping between sensory perception and motor actions that will result in the robot moving forward continuously.

Obstacle Avoidance The simple, acquired forward motion behaviour can be expanded to a forward motion and obstacle avoiding behaviour by adding one or more further instinct rules. For example, if we take the case of a simple mobile robot with just two whisker sensors mounted at the front (figure 4.5), the following two instinct rules would lead to that behaviour:

1. "Keep the forward motion sensor 'on' at all times!"
2. "Keep whiskers 'off' at all times!"

For robots with infrared or sonar sensors, the second instinct rule would have to be changed accordingly, for instance to "Keep all sonar readings above a certain threshold", or similar.

Experimental results with many different robots, using different sensor modalities show that the robots learn obstacle avoidance very quickly (less than a minute in most cases), and with very few learning steps (less than 10 in most cases).

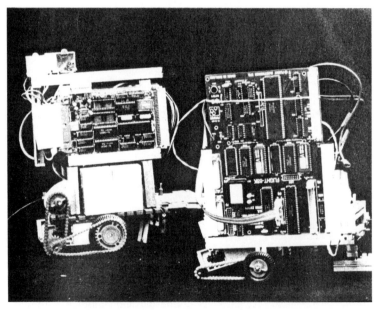

FIG. 4.14. *ALDER* (LEFT) AND *CAIRNGORM* (RIGHT)

Adapting to Changing Circumstances We stated earlier that the robot's ability to cope with unforeseen situations increases through its learning capability. Two experiments we conducted with *ALDER* and *CAIRNGORM* highlight this

([Nehmzow 92]). In the first experiment, the robots were placed in an environment containing convex obstacles (ordinary boxes), and quickly learned to turn away from a touched whisker. When encountering a dead end, however, the robots performed poorly to begin with (by turning back into the dead end, rather than towards the exit). Soon (within two minutes), though, they found the exit and had by then acquired a new behaviour: they were now turning in one and the same direction, regardless of whether the left or the right whisker was touched. This behaviour is best suited for leaving dead ends: the robots had adapted to their new environment.

In a second experiment, the robots' whiskers were physically swapped after they had acquired the obstacle avoidance competence. In between four and six learning steps they adapted the associations between sensor signals and motor actions within the artificial neural network, regained the ability to avoid obstacles and thus "repaired" the (in this case externally induced) fault.

We once found that one of our robots had been used for weeks, successfully learning many tasks, whilst inadvertently one of the eight infrared sensors had not been working due to a loose connection. Because of the redundancy in sensors (more than one sensor covering the area surrounding the robot), the robot had learned to avoid obstacles using the other sensors.

Contour Following By extending the set of instinct rules, the robots can acquire the ability to stay close to contours such as walls. In *ALDER's* and *CAIRNGORM's* case a third instinct-rule was added:

1. "Keep the forward motion sensor 'on' at all times!"
2. "Keep whiskers 'off' at all times!"
3. "Do touch something every four seconds!"

Using these three rules (or rules to the same extent), robots quickly learned to move forward, to steer away from obstacles, but to seek obstacles (i.e. walls) actively every four seconds. The resulting behaviour is that of wall following.

The following experiment demonstrates how quickly the robots can adapt to changing circumstances. When *ALDER* or *CAIRNGORM* were turned by 180° after having successfully learned to follow a wall on, say, their right hand side, they re-mapped sensory input to motor action within three to four learning steps such that they were able to follow a wall on their left hand side. If the robots' direction of motion is changed again, the re-learning process was even faster, because latent associations, acquired earlier, were still present within the network and only needed to be strengthened slightly to become active again.

Corridor Following By adding a fourth instinct rule, using short-term memory this time, the robots can learn to stay in the centre of a corridor by touching left and right walls in turn. The instinct rules for corridor following behaviour are:

1. "Keep the forward motion sensor 'on' at all times!"
2. "Keep whiskers 'off' at all times!"
3. "Do touch something every four seconds!"
4. "The whisker that was touched last time must not be touched this time!"

Phototaxis and Box-Pushing The possibilities of acquiring new competences are merely limited by a robot's sensors, and the fact that not all behaviours can be expressed in simple sensor states alone. The first case study will be concluded by looking at experiments with an IS Robotics R2 robot, which had infrared range sensors and light sensors.

Phototaxis was acquired within less than 10 learning steps, using an instinct-rule stipulating that the light sensors mounted at the front of the robot must return the highest value (i.e. face the brightest light).

Similarly, by using a instinct rule requiring the front facing infrared sensors to be "on" constantly (i.e. to return sensor values that indicate an object was situated in front of the robot), the robot acquired a box-pushing or object following competence in two learning steps, one for each of the two situations where the box is placed to the right or the left of the robot's centre respectively. The learning time to acquire a box-pushing competence is less than one minute.

4.4.2   Case Study 2. *FortyTwo*: Robot Training

The mechanism for autonomous competence acquisition, described in case study 1, can be adapted in such a way that the robot can be *trained* to perform certain sensor-motor tasks. This chapter explains how this can be done, and presents experiments conducted with *FortyTwo*.

Why Robot Training? For robotic tasks that are to be performed repeatedly and in structured environments, fixed installations (both hardware and software) for robot control are viable. Many industrial applications fall into this category, for example mass assembly tasks, or high-volume transportation tasks. In these cases, fixed hardware installations (robot assembly lines, conveyor belts, etc.) and the development of fixed, one-off control code are warranted. As robot hardware technology advances, sophisticated robots become available at constantly decreasing cost and even small workshops and service companies become interested in robotics applications ([Schmidt 95] and [Spektrum 95]), the development of control software becomes the governing factor in cost-benefit analysis. For low-volume tasks programming and re-programming the robot is not viable.

In this second case study we discuss experiments in which the robot is *trained* through supervised learning (training signals being provided by the operator) to perform a variety of different tasks. Simple sensor-motor competences such as obstacle avoidance, random exploration or wall following, as well as more complex ones such as clearing objects out of the way, area-covering motion in corridors ("cleaning") and learning simple routes are achieved by this method, without the need to alter the robot control code. During the training phase the robot is controlled by a human operator, and uses the received feedback signals to train an associative memory. After a few tens of learning steps, taking five to ten minutes in real time, the robot performs the required task autonomously. If task, robot morphology or environment change *re-training*, not *re-programming* is used to regain the necessary skills.

Related Work The method of providing external feedback to the learning process is as yet relatively rarely used in robotics. Shepanski and Macy use an operator-taught multilayer perceptron to achieve vehicle-following behaviour in a *simulated* motorway situation ([Shepanski & Macy 87]). The network learns to keep the simulated vehicle at an acceptable distance to the preceding vehicle after about 1000 learning steps. Colombetti and Dorigo present a classifier system with a genetic algorithm that enables a mobile robot to achieve phototaxis ([Colombetti & Dorigo 93]). *AUTONOMOUSE*, the robot used, began to show good light seeking behaviour after about 60 minutes of training time.

Unsupervised learning has also been used in robot control. Tasks such as obstacle avoidance and contour following ([Nehmzow 95a]), box-pushing ([Mahadevan & Connell 91] and [Nehmzow 95a]), coordination of leg movement in walking robots ([Maes & Brooks 90]) or phototaxis ([Kaelbling 92], [Colombetti & Dorigo 93] and [Nehmzow & McGonigle 94]) have successfully been implemented on mobile robots.

Teach-by-guiding ([Critchlow 85] and [Schmidt 95]) is still a common method of programming industrial robots. This method is different to work based on artificial neural networks, in that it does not show the generalisation properties of networks, but merely stores chains of locations to be visited in sequence.

Controller Architecture The central component in the controller used in the experiments is an associative memory, implemented as before through a Pattern Associator. The controller is shown in figure 4.15.

Inputs to the associative memory consist of preprocessed sensor signals. In the experiments presented here sensor signals from the robot's sonar and infrared sensors have been used, and preprocessing was limited to a simple thresholding operation, generating a '1' input for all sonar range signals of less than 150 cm distance (see figure 4.16). Experiments using visual input data are reported elsewhere ([Martin & Nehmzow 95]); in these experiments thresholding, edge detection and differentiation were used in the preprocessing stages.

The analogue output signals o_k of the associative memory are computed according to equation 4.17:

$$o_k = \vec{w}_k \cdot \vec{\imath}, \tag{4.17}$$

with $\vec{\imath}$ being the input vector containing the sensor signals, and $\vec{w}_k$ the weight vector of output node k (i.e. one of the two output nodes).

The two analogue output nodes of the associative memory drive the steering and translation motor of the robot, respectively (in the experiments presented here steering and turret rotation are locked, so that the front of the robot is always facing the direction of travel). This generates continuous, smooth steering and translational velocities, depending on the strength of the association between current sensory stimulus and motor response (see also [Nehmzow 99c]): the robot moves fast in situations which have been trained frequently and therefore have strong associations between sensing and action ("familiar" situations), and slowly in "unfamiliar" situations. If sensor signals are received which have

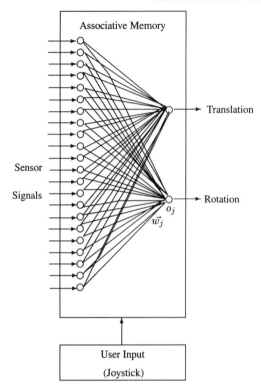

FIG. 4.15. THE CONTROLLER ARCHITECTURE

5 values	5 values	6 values	6 values
Left facing Sonars	Right facing Sonars	Left facing IRs	Right facing IRs

FIG. 4.16. THE INPUT VECTOR USED

never been encountered during the training phase, i.e. situations in which the network weights between sensory input and motor action output are zero, the robot does not move at all.

Training the Network Initially, there are no sensor-motor associations stored in the associative memory (i.e. all network weights are set to zero), and the robot is driven by the operator by means of the joystick. Information about the current environment (the input vector $\vec{i}$ to the controller) and the desired motor action in this situation (yielding the target output τ_k of equation 4.6 for each of the two output units of the network) is therefore available to the robot controller in the training phase.

Adjusting the weight vector $\vec{w}_k$ of output unit k is achieved by applying the Perceptron learning rule (equations 4.6 and 4.7).

The learning rate η was chosen at 0.3, and decreased by 1% every learning step. This eventually stabilises the associations stored in the associative memory of the controller. There are other ways conceivable of choosing the learning rate: an initially high, but rapidly falling rate will result in a robot learning only during the initial stages of the learning process, whilst a constant η will lead to continous learning behaviour. Thirdly, by means of a novelty detector a low η could be increased when drastic changes are detected.

Experiments The experiments described here were conducted in a laboratory of 5 m × 15 m, containing tables, chairs and boxes which were detectable by the robot's sensors.

Initially, there were no sensor-motor associations stored in the associative memory, and the robot was driven by the operator by means of the joystick. Using this information for training, meaningful sensor-motor couplings developed within the artificial neural network, and the robot improved rapidly in performing a specified task. After a few tens of learning steps the acquired information was usually sufficient to control the robot without any user intervention, the robot then performed the task autonomously, solely under network control.

Obstacle Avoidance Initially driving the robot with the joystick, *FortyTwo* was trained to avoid convex obstacles and cul-de-sacs. The robot learned this in less than 20 learning steps (one step being one application of equations 4.6 and 4.7), taking a few minutes in real time. The resulting obstacle avoidance motion was smooth, and incorporated translational and rotational movements at varying speeds, according to the strength of association between sensory perception and corresponding motor action (see also [Nehmzow 99c]).

Wall Following In the same manner as before, the robot was trained to stay within a distance of about 50 cm to the wall. As the only relevant part of the input vector for this task is the infrared one, the robot moved closer towards dark objects (little infrared reflection), and further away from light objects. Again, learning was achieved within 20 learning steps, and the acquired motion was smooth. The robot could be trained to follow left hand walls, right hand walls, or both.

Box-Pushing Both infrared sensor and sonar sensor range data is part of the input vector presented to the associative memory of the controller (see figure 4.16), and can therefore be used by the controller to associate action with perception. *FortyTwo's* infrared sensors are mounted low, about 30 cm above ground, whilst the sonar sensors are mounted high (ca. 60 cm above ground).

In a box-pushing experiment the robot was taught to move forward if a low object was detected straight ahead, and to turn left or right if an object was detected to the left or the right side of the robot respectively. During the training phase of about 30 learning steps, associations between the robot's infrared sensors (which are relevant to this task) developed, whilst sonar data delivered contradictory information in this experiment and strong associations between the "sonar part" of the input vector and the motor-driving outputs did not develop.

The robot acquired the ability to push a box quickly, in a few minutes of real time. After the initial training phase the robot was able to push and follow a box autonomously, staying behind the box even if the box moved sideways.

Clearing As the infrared sensors of the robot return identical signals for *any* object placed near the robot, it is impossible for the controller to differentiate between boxes, walls, or people. For example, the robot will attempt to push walls, as much as it will push boxes.

There is, however, a way of training *FortyTwo* to abandon boxes near tall obstacles: as the high mounted sonar sensors reach beyond a low box, the robot can be trained to pursue objects as long as they appear only in the "infrared part" of the input vector, but to abandon them as soon as tall obstacles appear in the "sonar part" of the input vector. Training for about 30 to 50 learning steps, taking between five and ten minutes in real time, the robot could be taught to acquire such a "clearing" ability. After the training phase, the robot pursued any object becoming visible to the infrared sensors only, and pushed it until tall obstacles were detected by the sonar sensors. *FortyTwo* then turned away from the object, looking for new boxes away from the tall obstacles. This resulted in a "clearing" behaviour: *FortyTwo* pushed boxes towards walls, left them there and returned to the center of the room to look for more boxes to move to the sides.

Surveillance Using the same method, and without any need to re-program the robot, *FortyTwo* could be trained to move in random directions whilst avoiding obstacles. During the training phase of approximately 30 learning steps, the robot was instructed to move forward when no objects were ahead, and to turn away from obstacles once they became visible to the robot's sensors. This developed associations between the sonar and infrared sensors and the motor-driving output units of the network. In this manner the robot acquired a general obstacle avoidance behaviour, also for input constellations that had not been encountered during the training phase (this is a result of the artificial neural network's capability to generalise).

The resultant obstacle avoidance behaviour was smooth and continuous; fast translational movement occured when familiar sensor states indicated free space. Smooth turning action was perceived when *distant* obstacles were detected, rapid turning action resulted from *nearby* obstacles being detected. The smooth motion of the robot was achieved through the direct association of the (analogue) outputs of the network with motor action, and the output itself being dependent on the strength of the input signal received (nearby objects will produce stronger input signals).

Such random exploration and obstacle avoidance behaviour forms the basis of a surveillance function of the robot. Using this behaviour, *FortyTwo* will, for example, follow corridors, avoiding moving and stationary obstacles as it moves.

Route Learning   As the robot effectively learns to associate sensory perception directly with a motor response, it can be taught to perform certain motor actions at particular locations, thus performing navigation. This is navigation along "perceptual landmarks", in which the perceptual properties of the environment are used to perform the desired motion at each physical location[5].

We have trained *FortyTwo* to follow a route as shown in figure 4.17. After about 15 minutes of training time the robot was able to follow the wall in the way indicated in figure 4.17, leave the laboratory through the door (which had about twice the width of the robot's diameter), turn and return through the door back into the laboratory and resume the path.

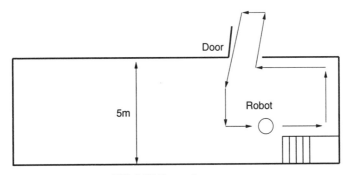

FIG. 4.17. ROUTE LEARNING

Cleaning   Cleaning tasks require the robot to cover as much floorspace as possible. For large, open spaces random exploration might be sufficient to accomplish the task over time. However, it is possible to train *FortyTwo* to cover floorspace in a more methodical manner.

Using the same training method as before, the robot was trained to move along a corridor in the Computer Science Department in the manner shown in figure 4.18.

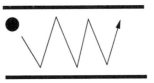

FIG. 4.18. CLEANING OPERATION

As before, learning is fast and the robot acquires the competence in a few tens of learning steps.

---

[5] The problem of "perceptual aliasing", which describes the fact that two different places may appear identical to the robot's sensors, is discussed in section 7.3.2.

Conclusions *Training*, rather than *programming* has a number of advantages. First of all, the Pattern Associator used here learns extremely fast; within a few learning steps meaningful associations between inputs and outputs develop.

Furthermore, it is able to generalise, i.e. to acquire input-output associations for input situations that have not been encountered explicitly. For large sensor spaces it is practically impossible that the robot encounters all possible sensor states during the training phase — the generalisation ability of artificial neural networks provides a solution to this problem.

Thirdly, as sensor stimuli are directly associated with (analogue) motor responses, the strength of an association determines the velocity of the action. This means that the robot moves fast in familiar territory, and slowly in unfamiliar territory; that the robot turns rapidly if nearby obstacles are detected, and gently in the presence of distant ones. This property is emergent, and not a design feature of the controller.

In addition to these points, "programming through teaching" provides a simple and intuitively clear man-machine interface. As the operator is able to instruct the machine *directly*, without the need of a middle man (the programmer), the risk of ambiguities is reduced.

And finally, through supervised training of artificial neural networks, an effective control strategy for a mobile robot can be established, even if explicit control rules are not known.

4.4.3 Case Study 3.
FortyTwo: Learning Internal Representations of the World Through Self-Organisation

For many robotics applications, for example those of object identification and object retrieval, it is necessary to use internal representations of these objects. These models — abstracted (i.e. simplified) representations of the original — are to capture the essential properties of the original, without carrying unnecessary detail.

The "essential properties" of the original are not always directly available to the designer of an object recognition system, nor is it always clear what constitutes unnecessary detail. In these cases the only feasible method is that of model *acquisition*, rather than model *installation*.

In this third case study, therefore, we present experiments with a self-organising structure that acquires models in an unsupervised way through robot-environment interaction. User predefinition is kept at a minimum.

In this particular instance, *FortyTwo's* task was to identify boxes within its visual field of view, and to move towards them. No generic model of these boxes was used, instead a model was acquired through a process of unsupervised learning in an artificial neural network.

Experimental Setup *FortyTwo's* task was to determine whether or not a box was present in its visual field of view, and, if present, to move towards the box. The camera was the only sensor used. The boxes carried no particular distinguishing features.

The trainable object recognition system shown in figure 4.19, based on a self-organising feature map, was used to achieve this.

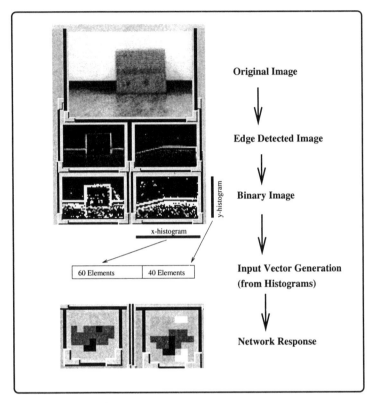

FIG. 4.19. THE BOX RECOGNITION SYSTEM

Vision Data Preprocessing System   As a first processing step, the raw grey level image of 320 by 200 pixels was reduced to 120 by 80 pixels by selecting an appropriate window that would show the target object at a distance of about 3 m.

The reduced grey level image was then subjected to a convolution with the edge-detecting template shown in figure 4.20, where each new pixel value is determined by equation 4.18.

$$e(t + 1) = |(c + f + i) - (a + d + g)| . \qquad (4.18)$$

The edge-detected image was then coarse coded by averaging the pixel values of a 2 x 2 square, yielding an image of 60 by 40 pixels.

-1	0	1
-1	0	1
-1	0	1

a	b	c
d	e	f
g	h	i

FIG. 4.20. EDGE DETECTING TEMPLATE

Following the coarse coding stage, we computed the average pixel value of the entire image, and used this value to generate a binary image (such as the one shown in figure 4.21) by thresholding.

FIG. 4.21. BINARY IMAGE

Finally, by computing the histogram along the vertical and horizontal axis of the binary image, we obtained a 60+40 element long input vector, which was used as input to our box detection algorithm. This is shown in figure 4.22.

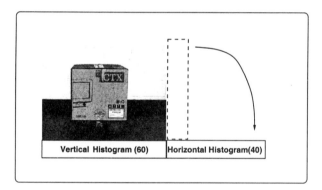

FIG. 4.22. INPUT TO THE BOX-DETECTING SYSTEM

The Box Detection Mechanism We then used this 100-element long input vector as an input to a self-organising feature map (SOFM) of 10 by 10 units (see section 4.2.3). The learning rate was set to 0.8 for the first 10 learning steps, after that to 0.2 for the entire remaining training period. The neighbourhood around the winning unit within which an update was performed remained static as ± 1 throughout the entire training period.

The idea behind this was, of course, to develop different network responses for images containing boxes than to images containing no boxes — based on self-organisation, and without any *a priori* model installation at all.

Experimental Results A test set of 60 images (30 with boxes, 30 without — see figure 4.23) was used to train the network, and evaluate the system's ability to differentiate between images containing boxes, and those not containing boxes.

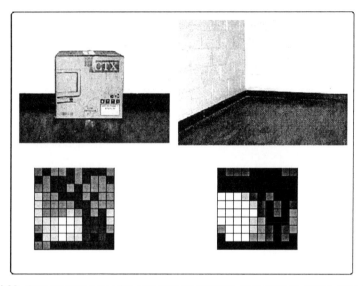

FIG. 4.23. TWO EXAMPLE IMAGES AND THE NETWORK'S RESPONSE TO THEM. THE GREY-LEVEL CODING INDICATES THE STRENGTH OF A UNIT'S ACTIVATION.

As can be seen in figure 4.23, the network's response in both cases is similar, but not identical. The difference in network response can be used to classify an image.

Fifty images of aligned boxes were used for the training phase of the network, of the remaining 10 test images all were correctly classified by the system.

In a second set of experiments, boxes were placed in *various* positions and angles. The training set consisted of 100 images, the test set contained 20 images. In the case of images showing boxes, 70% of all test images were classified correctly, 20% were wrong, and 10% were "not classified" (i.e. the excitation patterns of the SOFM neither resembled the "box" pattern, nor the "no box" pattern). Of the images not showing boxes, 60% were classified correctly, 20% were incorrectly classified and 20% were not classified.

To assess the ability of the system to classify images under more "realistic" situations, we conducted a third set of experiments, in which images were used that were similar to those in the previous experiment, i.e. they contained images of boxes in varying positions and angles. In addition to this, images of stairs, doors and other objects that had similarities with boxes were included ("difficult" images).

The training set consisted of 180 images, the test set comprised 40 images. Of the "box" images, 70% were classified correctly, 20% were incorrectly classified and 10% were not classified at all.

Of the "no box" images, 40% were classified correctly, 55% were incorrectly classified as "box" and 5% were not classified.

Associating Perception with Action Next, we were interested to use the system to guide the robot towards boxes, if any were identified within the image.

In SOFMs, this can be achieved by extending the input vector by adding an action component to it. The entire input vector (and therefore the weight vector of each unit of the SOFM) then contains a perception-action pair. In the training phase, the robot is driven manually towards a box in its field of view. Input vectors are generated by combining the preprocessed vision input and the user-supplied motor command.

In the recall phase, the robot is then able to move towards a box autonomously, by determining the winning unit of the SOFM (i.e. that unit that resembles the current visual perception most closely), and performing the motor action associated with that unit. Our observation was that *FortyTwo* was well able to move towards a single box in its field of view, regardless of orientation of the box, or initial orientation of the robot. As the robot approached the box, lateral movements of the robot decreased, and the approach became faster and more focused, until the box filled the entire field of view, and thus became invisible to the system. The robot approached boxes reliably under these conditions.

However, the robot could get confused by other box-like objects in the field of view (like the stairs in our robotics laboratory). In this case, the robot would approach the misleading object in question, to abandon it later when the error was detected. At this stage, however, the robot was often no longer able to detect the original box, because it had moved too far off the direct approach route.

Conclusions Developing internal representations is essential for many robotics tasks. Such models of the original objects simplify computation through their abstraction properties. In order to be useful, models need to capture the essential properties of the objects modelled whilst eliminating unnecessary detail.

As these characteristic properties are often not directly accessible to the designer, methods of (subsymbolic) model *acquisition*, rather than model *installation* are a possibility.

The box recognition system discussed here does not use any symbolic representations, and only very general information is supplied at the design stage (i.e. edge detection, thresholding and histogram analysis of images). Instead, models are acquired *autonomously* by clustering sensory perception, using a self-organising feature map.

The experiments showed that the acquired models could identify target objects with good reliability, provided the images contained no misleading (i.e. box-like) information.

Boxes are very regular objects. Whether a simple system such as the one described in this case study can construct representations of more complex objects (such as, for instance, people), is not clear. However, these experiments demonstrate that a robot *can* build internal representations of objects in its environment, without *a priori* knowledge, and without human support.

Case Study 3: Further Reading

- Ulrich Nehmzow, Vision Processing for Robot Learning, *Industrial Robot*, Vol. 26, No. 2, pp. 121-130, 1999.

4.5   Exercise 3: A Target-Following, Obstacle-Avoiding Robot

A mobile robot is equipped with two tactile sensors, one on its left side, and one on its right side. These sensors return "+1" when they touch something, otherwise "0". In addition to this, the robot has a centrally mounted beacon sensor, which can detect whether a beacon (which is placed somewhere in the environment) is to the right or to the left of the robot. The beacon sensor returns "-1" if the target is to the left, and "+1" if the target is to the right of the robot. Due to the asymmetries of the real world, the beacon sensor will never perceive the beacon as absolutely dead ahead, and therefore no third value for "ahead" exists.

The robot's motors will turn forward if a "+1" signal is applied, and backwards on a "-1" signal. The robot is shown in figure 4.24.

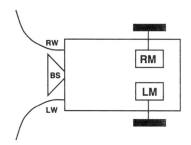

FIG. 4.24. A ROBOT WITH TWO TACTILE SENSORS AND ONE BEACON SENSOR

The task of the robot is to move towards the beacon, avoiding obstacles along the way.

- State the truth table required to achieve this function.
- Design an artificial neural network, using McCulloch and Pitts neurons, to implement the target seeking, obstacle avoiding robot.

The solution is given in appendix 2.2 on p. 220.

5 Navigation

Navigation

Summary. This chapter introduces the fundamental principles of navigation, giving examples of navigation in animals, humans, and robots. Five case studies of navigating mobile robots examine biologically inspired robot navigation, self-localisation, route learning and finding shortcuts in detail.

5.1 Principles of Navigation

5.1.1 Fundamental Building Blocks

For a mobile agent, the ability to navigate is one of the most important capabilities of all. Staying operational, i.e. avoiding dangerous situations such as collisions, and staying within safe operating conditions (temperature, radiation, exposure to weather, etc.) come first, but if any tasks are to be performed that relate to specific places in the agent's environment, navigation is a must.

In the animate world, some sort of navigation can be found in most living beings. Perhaps it is just the ability to reverse one's outward route, and thus to return home; perhaps it is a sophisticated ability to reason about spatial relationships; but animals that move can navigate.

In this chapter we will have a closer look at the skill of navigation, and try to identify the building blocks needed to build a robot navigation system. Examples of navigating mobile robots will also be given.

Navigation can be defined as the combination of the three fundamental competences:

1. Self-localisation;
2. Path planning;
3. Map-building and map-interpretation (map use).

Map in this context denotes any one-to-one mapping of the world onto an internal representation. This representation does not necessarily look like a map one can buy in the shop, in fact in robots it often takes the form of artificial neural network excitation patterns.

Localisation denotes the agent's competence to establish its own position within a frame of reference, *path planning* is effectively an extension of localisation, in that it requires the determination of the agent's current position and the position of a goal location, both within the same frame of reference. *Map-building* not only covers maps of the type we all know, i.e. metric maps of the environment, but any notation describing locations within the frame of reference. The map charts explored territory within this frame of reference. Finally, to use a map, the ability to *interpret* the map is needed.

5.1.2   The Navigational Frame of Reference

The frame of reference is the crucial component of any robot navigation system, as it effectively defines all three competences that constitute navigation. The frame of reference is a fixed point of reference that "anchors" the navigation competence.

In the simplest and most easily understood case, this frame of reference is a Cartesian co-ordinate system (see figure 5.1).

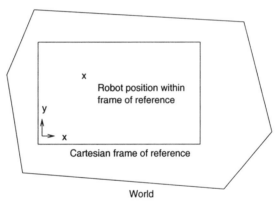

FIG. 5.1. NAVIGATION SYSTEM BASED ON CARTESIAN FRAME OF REFERENCE

For all internal processes in such a Cartesian navigation system, i.e. for localisation, path planning and charting territory, positions are recorded as co-ordinates within that frame of reference. Navigation is simple and perfect. Assuming the journey started from a known position, and assuming that speed and direction of travel are accurately known, the navigation system simply integrates the robot's motion over time, a process known as *dead reckoning*. Given a Cartesian frame of reference, a robot's position is always precisely definable, and so are all other locations.

However, there is one major problem: the frame itself is not anchored in the real world, i.e. the frame itself moves with respect to locations within the world. For a dead reckoning system to work, the robot has to measure its movement *precisely* — but this is impossible, owing to problems like wheel slippage, i.e. a movement that occurs *to* the frame of reference, but not *in* it. The robot can only measure how it moves via internal measurements, i.e. *proprioception*, and is therefore unable to detect changes to the entire frame of reference. Figure 7.16 on p. 193 shows an example of odometry drift error.

Navigation has to be achieved within the real world, however, not within the frame of reference, and therefore those drift problems, the drifting apart of frame of reference and position in the world, are a serious impediment. In practice, purely odometry-based navigation is unreliable over all but very short distances.

Much of the work to date concerning navigation of mobile robots uses internal geometrical representations of the robot's environment to perform navigational tasks. MOBOT III, for example, constructs such a geometrical representation autonomously from sensor data ([Knieriemen & v.Puttkamer 91]), other robots use maps supplied by the designer ([Kampmann & Schmidt 91]). Usually the maps are altered in the course of operation, depending on sensory perception.

This "classical" approach has the advantage that the resulting map is intelligible to the human operator, so a special interface between the robot's representation of its environment and the way a human sees it is not necessary. This allows for easy supervision of the robot operation by the designer. On the other hand, manual map installation is time consuming and requires large amounts of memory. Furthermore the resulting maps contain information not necessarily needed for the immediate task ahead. If, for example, the robot's task was to move ahead, avoiding one obstacle in front of it, information concerning objects *behind* the robot as well as in the *far distance* to the sides or ahead is irrelevant. To store such information puts an additional burden onto memory requirements.

5.1.3 Landmark-Based Navigation: Piloting

As navigation within the world is the goal, one way of overcoming the problems of proprioception-based systems is to anchor the navigation system within the world itself, rather than within an internal frame of reference. Detecting unique features in the world - landmarks - is one method of doing this. Navigation with respect to external landmarks is referred to as *piloting* - the required course to a goal location is not determined through path integration, as in dead reckoning, but through identifying landmarks or sequences of landmarks, and either following these landmarks in a specific order, or recalling the required compass direction from a recognised landmark, based on previous experience. Provided the robot is able to identify landmarks unambiguously, navigation is achieved with respect to the *world*, rather than with respect to an *internal* frame of reference (see figure 5.2), and therefore not subject to incorrigible drift errors. This is obviously desirable.

One way to do this is to use information concerning the neighbourhood relationships between certain landmarks the robot perceives. Such topological mappings occur, for example, in animals and humans in the mapping of sensors onto the cortex ([Knudsen 82] and [Sparks & Nelson 87], see also [Churchland 86]). As they only represent the topological relationship between locations, but not the distances, they require less time to build and less memory to store.

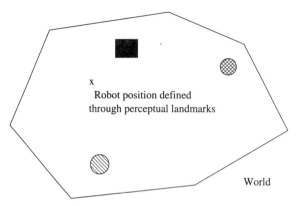

x
Robot position defined
through perceptual landmarks

World

FIG. 5.2. NAVIGATION, ANCHORED IN THE WORLD THROUGH PERCEPTION

What is Meant by "Landmark"? People usually refer to conspicuous, persistent perceptual features as "landmarks". Obvious examples are buildings and prominent
landscape features such as mountains or lakes. These are landmarks that require
scene understanding to be detected — only if you know what a church usually
looks like are you able to detect it in the environment.

There is a different possible definition of what constitutes a landmark, based
only on sensory perception, rather than the interpretation of that perception. Examples are the brightness of the sky (i.e. the position of the sun), the direction of
the wind, or sound emanating from a specific direction. All of these are location-
dependent perceptual features of the environment that can be detected by the
navigator, and can be used to maintain or determine a course without abstract
scene analysis.

As we are interested in minimising pre-definition (because of the problem of
perceptual discrepancy, introduced earlier and discussed on p. 110) we usually
use this second type of landmark, i.e. uninterpreted, location-dependent sensory
patterns such as sonar range patterns or images perceived at a particular location.
These are referred to as "perceptual landmarks" in this book.

"Perceptual Landmarks" for Robot Navigation If a whole robot navigation
system is to be based on landmark recognition, the question of what constitutes
a suitable landmark is obviously very relevant. In order to fulfil its purpose as a
guide to navigation, a landmark must be:

1. Visible from various positions;
2. Recognisable under different lighting conditions, viewing angles, etc.;
3. Either stationary throughout the period of navigation, or its motion must be
   known to the navigation mechanism.

Points 1 and 2 require that some generalisation regarding the internal representation of the landmark within the navigation mechanism is achieved. Storing
raw sensory perceptions of a landmark, for instance, will not be very useful,

because the robot will almost certainly perceive the same landmark slightly differently on a subsequent visit, meaning it won't recognise the landmark unless that generalisation has somehow been achieved. Often, artificial neural networks can be used to generalise representations of landmarks. Examples for this can be found in section 5.4.2.

Point 1 refers to a specific problem in landmark recognition: if the robot has learned to recognise a landmark from one position, can it recognise the same landmark from a different position, even though it has never seen the landmark from there? This would be a great achievement, as it would allow very efficient storage of landmarks, and the construction of very robust navigation systems.

In a robot like *FortyTwo*, i.e. a robot that has sensors that are equally spaced over 360 degrees, rotating for instance the 16 sonar range readings to a uniquely identifiable position (e.g. the centre of gravity of those readings) would convert any string of 16 readings into the canonical string. The principle is shown in figure 5.3.

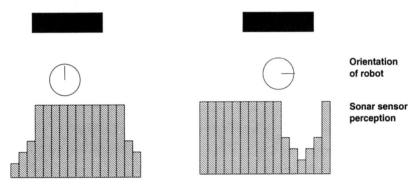

FIG. 5.3. USING SOME CHARACTERISTIC PROPERTY OF ALL SONAR RANGE READINGS - SUCH AS CENTRE OF GRAVITY - PERCEPTIONS FROM DIFFERENT VIEWING ANGLES CAN BE CONVERTED INTO IDENTICAL (CANONICAL) READINGS BY APPLYING A "MENTAL SHIFT"

However, because of the special characteristics of sonar sensors, in particular specular reflections (which are determined by incident angle), this method will not always work. Figure 5.4 shows a situation where the physical position of the robot is crucially important for the perception obtained, and mere "mental shifts" such as rotating the inputs will not generate one canonical view in both situations shown.

5.1.4 Foundations of Navigation: Summary

To be able to navigate entails the ability to determine one's own position, and to be able to plan a path towards some goal location. The latter usually requires the use of a representation of the environment (a "map"), and the ability to interpret that representation.

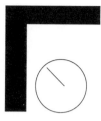 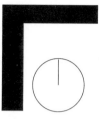

FIG. 5.4. BECAUSE OF SPECULAR SONAR REFLECTIONS, 'MENTAL SHIFTS' CANNOT ALWAYS BE USED TO GENERATE CANONICAL VIEWS OF LANDMARKS

That an animal must stay alive, or that a robot must stay operational in order to navigate at all, is obvious. Staying operational is therefore a fundamental, enabling competence — but it alone is not navigation.

All navigation has to be anchored in some frame of reference, that is, navigation is always relative to this fixed frame of reference. Dead reckoning strategies estimate the agent's direction of travel and speed, and integrate the agent's movement over time, starting from a known location. Dead reckoning navigation systems are relatively easy to implement, easy to interpret, and easy to use. They suffer, however, from the problem of incorrigible drift error, which is a serious problem for all but short range navigation tasks.

The alternative to dead reckoning is landmark-based navigation, which is based on *exteroception*, i.e. the agent's perception of the environment. Drift error is no problem here, but if the environment contains few perceptually unique clues, or confusing information (e.g. perceptual aliasing – see p. 195), the performance of such systems deteriorates.

5.2 Fundamental Navigation Strategies of Animals and Humans

To discuss the navigation strategies of animals and robots exhaustively is beyond the scope of an introductory textbook on mobile robotics. Nevertheless, I shall look at the most common navigation mechanisms used by animals and humans, and give examples of experiments that demonstrate these mechanisms. This will hopefully reveal the marvellous and astonishing beauty of living navigators, as well as provide some pointers to how we might achieve robust and reliable robot navigation.

To date, no machine performs navigation anywhere nearly as competently as animals. Whilst for example ants, bees and birds, to name but three examples, are able to navigate reliably and robustly over long distances, in unmodified, changeable, noisy and inconsistent environments, robots typically depend on very structured environments that change little throughout the period of operation. Robots have great difficulties when navigating over long distances, in environments that contain conflicting (inconsistent) information - they work best in environments containing artificial cues such as markers or beacons, along fixed routes that are identified by such markers. The greater the required degree of flexibility, the harder it is for a mobile robot to navigate reliably. The hope is that perhaps some mechanisms used by the competent biological navigators can be adapted for use in autonomous mobile robots.

We begin by looking at some fundamental navigation strategies found in animals, and continue with five detailed case studies of navigating robots that use strategies copied from living beings.

5.2.1 Piloting

Piloting, i.e. navigation by landmarks that are identified by their perceptual features, is very common in animals. Animals orientate themselves not only by local landmarks, that is landmarks that are relatively close to the animals and change their azimuth position as the animal moves, but also by global landmarks such as distant objects (e.g. mountains), the stars and the sun, which do not change their position with respect to the animal as the animal moves.

Local Landmarks One common strategy when piloting by local landmarks is to store a retinal image at a specific location that is needed in future navigation (for example the nest, or a feeding site), and to move in such a way that on a subsequent journey the current image and the stored image are brought to agreement through appropriate movements.

Desert ants (*Cataglyphis bicolor*), for instance, use visual stimuli to identify a home location ([Wehner & Räber 79]). The experiment shown in figure 5.5 demonstrates that in order to move to a particular location ants can match the current retinal image and a stored image. Figure 5.5 (top left) shows the initial situation: two identical markers of width x at equal distances to the left and the right of the nest serve as landmarks. The small dots indicate homing positions of individual ants. If these markers are moved apart to twice the original distance (which makes it impossible for the ant to find a position in which both the angle α and the angle β are the same as in the original situation) the ants return to either of the two markers (figure 5.5, top right). If the size of the markers is also doubled (which means that both angles α and β are identical to the original situation again), the ants return to the original home location (figure 5.5, bottom).

Similarly, piloting is observed in honey bees (*Apis mellifera*). Gould and Gould ([Gould & Gould 88, p. 148]) report von Frisch's findings concerning the use of landmarks in the navigation of bees: bees who have been trained on a dog-leg route with the turn near a prominent tree will continue to fly to the food by way of the tree, whereas bees trained on a similar dogleg route in the open country will fly along the shortest route. Prominent landmarks such as forest edges will be used predominantly for navigation by honey bees, the sun is merely used as a reference point, a compass sense, in the bees' dance, indicating the direction to the food source ([Gould & Gould 88, pp. 148ff.] and [Waterman 89, p. 177]).

In the vicinity of the hive, bees perform image matching, just like the desert ants. Cartwright and Collett ([Cartwright & Collett 83]) report experiments with bees that show a striking similarity to the experiments with ants by Wehner and

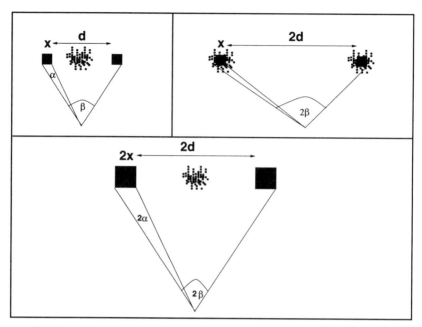

FIG. 5.5. LANDMARK USE IN *Cataglyphis bicolor* (AFTER [WEHNER & RÄBER 79])

Räber ([Wehner & Räber 79]). Like ants, bees use the angular extent of local landmarks for navigation: displacement of artificial landmarks leads to a corresponding displacement in return position. Cartwright and Collett conclude from these observations ([Cartwright & Collett 83]):

> "[Bees] do not find their way using anything analogous to a floor plan or map of the spatial layout of landmarks and food source. The knowledge at their disposal is much more limited, consisting of no more than a remembered image of what was present on their retina when they were at their destination. ... Bees find their way, the experiments seem to say, by continuously comparing their retinal image with their snapshot and adjusting their flight path so as to lessen the discrepancy between the two."

Waterman ([Waterman 89, p. 176]) confirms this by reporting that honey bees stop foraging if artificial landmarks are introduced (or removed) into their territory and make orientation flights before they continue to forage; similarly they make reconnaissance flights in unknown territory before they begin to forage.

Global Landmarks Although desert ants are theoretically able to navigate by local landmarks, this method is not always applicable due to the habitat they live in. Often the desert environment in which they forage is completely devoid of landmarks, and the ants have to resort to other navigation methods in order to get back home.

And they are able to achieve this, too. Desert ants are able to return to their nest directly after completion of a foraging trip of typically 20 m. This can be established experimentally by displacing an ant sideways after the outward journey of a foraging trip is completed, and logging its return trip. Typically, the ant starts searching for the nest after it has overshot the "imaginary" nest location by 10% of total distance travelled, using an ever widening search pattern centred on the location where the ant suspects the nest to be ([Wehner & Srinivasan 81] and [Gallistel 90, p. 61]).

From the logged return trips it is very clear that desert ants do not retrace their outward journey (by, for instance, following a pheromone trail). Instead, their navigation is purely based on dead reckoning ([Wehner & Srinivasan 81]), using the polarisation pattern (the pattern of polarised light on the blue sky — the so-called E-vector — that is determined by the sun's position) of the sky as a global landmark ([Wehner & Räber 79]). Such patterns can be regarded stationary over the relatively short foraging time of desert ants and therefore provide reliable directional cues. As an ant does not perform pitching and rolling movements during foraging and homing, the sky pattern changes only in relation to rotations about the vertical axis - the relevant information for performing path integration, and homing by dead reckoning.

Like ants, bees also use the position of the sun and the polarisation pattern of the sky for navigation ([Gould & Gould 88, p. 126] and [Waterman 89]). One experiment demonstrating this is shown in figure 5.6. The results show that bees' paths in relation to the hive are determined by the position of the sun. If the hive is moved by several kilometres over night (figure 5.6, top), the bees will leave the hive in the morning in the same direction as they did the previous day. If the hive is moved while the bees are away feeding (figure 5.6, middle), they will return to the old location, discover their error and fly to the new location of the hive. If, thirdly, the hive is moved over whole continents, i.e. the apparent movement of the sun is a different one to what it was at the original location, bees will fly off in the same angle to the sun they used to fly at the original location, but get confused in the course of the day (figure 5.6, bottom).

Birds also use global landmarks for navigation. In fact, celestial bodies are the backbone of the bird's navigation system. One example of many is the indigo bunting. Planetarium experiments with indigo buntings (*Passerina cyanea*) about to migrate show that birds use the stars for navigation. In the planetarium the birds orientated themselves in the same direction they would have done in the open country. If the artificial sky was shifted, their flight orientation changed accordingly ([Waterman 89, p. 109]).

The most important cue for the birds is the apparent rotation of the entire sky around the celestial pole. Planetarium experiments demonstrate that birds are able to orientate correctly, as long as the artificial sky rotates around a fixed celestial pole, even if the artificial star constellations are different from constellations observed on a true night sky. Observing the star movement over time, they

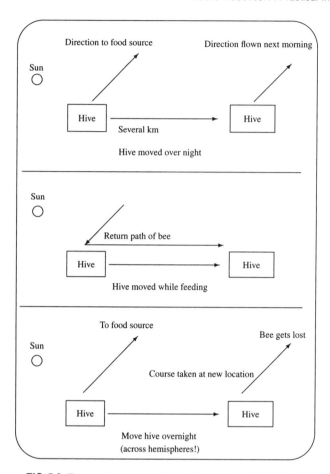

FIG. 5.6. THE USE OF REFERENCE LANDMARKS IN *Apis mellifera*

are able to determine the position of the celestial pole, like humans are when looking at a long-time exposure photograph of the night sky.

5.2.2 Path Integration (Dead Reckoning)

In environments where landmark cues are not available animals are able to navigate by path integration, i.e. dead reckoning. An example is the desert ant mentioned already.

Dead reckoning can be observed in many animals as an additional navigation strategy. In experiments with geese, for instance, Ursula von St. Paul showed that geese are able to determine the direct path home through path integration ([St. Paul 82]). When geese were either led to an unknown release site, or wheeled there in an open cage, they set off directly towards the home pen when released. They did not retrace the detoured route, demonstrating their ability to determine the direct course home. When, however, the geese were wheeled to the unknown release site in a covered cage, they were generally disorientated and refused to leave the site. This observation indicates that geese can use *optic flow* (the apparent movement of the image on the retina) for path integration.

As discussed on p. 88, dead reckoning is prone to accumulated drift errors. It is interesting to note that the magnitude of this error is dependent on the movement pattern of the navigator (turns induce more error than translations), and that the error can therefore be reduced by a suitable motion strategy. Humans, for instance, have developed interesting navigational strategies to minimise this accumulation of error. Before the time of inertial navigation systems and global positioning systems, maritime navigation was performed using the position of celestial bodies, and ephemeris tables. Computational error and measurement error were reduced by "sailing the parallels", that is by sailing due east or west and north or south respectively, rather than diagonally in the desired direction. The trade winds and ocean currents, which are predominantly parallel to the latitudes, were a further reason for this strategy.

Using a similar method, Polynesian navigators steer their canoes parallel or across the waves — even slight deviations from the straight course can thus be detected by the resulting rolling motion of the canoe.

5.2.3 Routes

Following canonical paths is another common navigational strategy of animals. Wood ants (*Formica rufa*), for example, use the same paths between their food sources and their nest so intensely that the forest floor shows these paths clearly: in the course of many years the covering vegetation has been removed and black trails indicate the usual way of the ants ([Cosens 93]).

A further example of the use of canonical paths in animal navigation are Canvasback ducks. In the Mississippi valley they have very narrow flight paths which they follow each year during migration ([Waterman 89, p. 176]).

Routes are such powerful navigational aids that humans have shaped entire environments around fixed routes (e.g. roads and rivers).

5.2.4 Survey Knowledge: The Navigation of Birds

Apart from exploiting cues such as local landmarks, canonical routes, or using dead reckoning based for instance on a sun compass, there are examples of navigators that are able to return home from a completely unknown location: birds. If carrier pigeons are released from an unknown site, they nevertheless are usually able to return to their home loft ([Emlen 75]). How do they do it?

Through experimental design (transport to the release site in a closed container) one can rule out that the pigeons perform path integration on the way out. Likewise, piloting is impossible, because they have never seen the release site before, and are too far away from known landmarks to be able to perceive them once airborne.

The most fundamental element in a current hypothesis of long range bird navigation ([Wiltschko & Wiltschko 98]) is the existence of a compass sense, which is demonstrated very clearly through experimentation with birds. In fact, birds possess a number of different compass senses: first, there exists a magnetic compass that measures the inclination of the magnetic field (i.e. it determines "towards the equator" and "away from the equator", rather than "north" and "south" ([Wiltschko & Wiltschko 95]). Second, there exists a sun compass. Because the movement of the sun is dependent on the geographical location, this compass is learned when the birds are young (but can be modified later if necessary). The sun compass is not genetically fixed. Once learned, the sun compass is the compass sense used predominantly by the pigeons (the use of the sun compass is very widespread amongst birds in general, not just carrier pigeons).

There is experimental evidence that birds mainly rely on site-specific information to determine their homeward direction, rather than on information collected *en-route* ([Walcott & Schmidt-Koenig]), which leads to the concept of the *navigational map*.

This navigational map (or "grid map") is assumed to be a directionally oriented representation of navigational factors. Specifically, these navigational factors are naturally occurring gradients (e.g. fluctuations in the earth's magnetic field strength) that are detectable by the birds, and whose angle of intersection is not too acute. There is no experimental evidence that gradients are indeed used, but the assumed use of gradients explains the experimental observations well (in particular the observation that birds are able to return home directly from sites which they have never visited before). Hypotheses about what these gradients might be include infra-sound, emanating from mountain ranges or the sea, and field strength of the earth's magnetic field.

Using this concept of a navigational map large scale navigation could be achieved like this:

> "When flying around, young pigeons register the direction in which they are flying with the help of their compass mechanisms; at the same time, they register changes in their gradient values encountered *en route*. These two pieces of information are linked together and incorporated in the "map" by associating changes in gradients with the current direction of flight. This gradually leads to a mental representation of the navigational factors which reflects the distribution of gradients within the home region in a realistic way" ([Wiltschko & Wiltschko 98]).

The navigational map is used over long and middle scale navigation, but experiments show that even for navigation at extremely familiar sites pigeons continue to use their compass sense for navigation. Clock-shift experiments (i.e. externally introduced changes to the sun compass) reveal that pigeons do not use landmarks (alone) near familiar sites, but still rely on their sun compass.

Once the birds get close to home, it is impossible to use the navigational map any more, because the local gradient values can no longer be distinguished from the home values. At this point, it is postulated that birds use a "mosaic map" for navigation which is a directionally oriented representation of the positions of prominent local landmarks.

In summary, birds use a navigational mechanism that is highly adaptable to their specific situation (sun compass, navigational map and mosaic map are learned and can be modified through learning in adult birds), and that covers the entire range of distances, from several hundred kilometres (sun compass and navigational map) to the immediate vicinity of the loft (mosaic map and sun compass).

5.2.5 Human Navigation

People do not possess as sophisticated a navigation sense as for example birds (we do not have a compass sense, for instance), and yet people are able to navigate reliably, over long distances, under difficult circumstances. What are the mechanisms used?

Man's main ability with respect to navigation is to notice even very small changes and features in the environment, to pay careful attention to all available landmarks (which may well be features such as wave patterns, occurrence of certain animals, or specific cloud formations).

The fundamental principle in human navigation is the use of landmark information. Recognised landmarks are then memorised in *cognitive maps*, which are a distorted representation of space, having a high resolution near home, and decreasing resolution with increasing distance from home. [Lynch 60] investigated people's representation of their home city, by interviewing citizens of four American cities of very different layout. He found that their cognitive maps contained:

- Prominent landmarks, such as their homes, places of work, churches, theatres or conspicuous signs;
- Important routes, such as motorways;
- Crossings of such routes, and
- "Edges", i.e. borders between two quarters, such as lakes or parks.

Administrative boroughs did not feature very prominently on people's cognitive maps.

Polynesian Navigation Without using compasses or geometrical maps the inhabitants of the Polynesian islands are able to navigate successfully over several thousand kilometres of open sea: the journey between Tahiti and Hawaii — 6000 km long — was travelled by the *Hokulea*, using traditional navigation methods ([Kyselka 87], [Lewis 72], [Gladwin 70] and [Waterman 89, ch. 3]). Such navigation was successful because all available sources of information (local landmarks and reference landmarks as well as special properties of the environment) were exploited by the navigators.

To determine an initial course, the navigators use the stars, moon and sun as reference landmarks. For example, the position of a particular star, when rising or setting (i.e. when apparently moving vertically near the horizon) gives the direction towards a particular island (see figure 5.7). They also align local landmarks of the island they are departing from to determine their initial course ([Waterman 89, ch. 3]).

On the way, wind and wave patterns (which are usually unique for certain parts of the ocean, because they are influenced by the position of islands) are used as local landmarks; in fact the weather patterns in many parts of the world are so reliable that they are used for navigation not only by humans, but also by animals. Sparrows and warblers, for example, fly 2000 to 3000 km from Canada and New England to South America's north coast. Computer modelling suggests that, provided the departure is closely timed (which indeed seems to be the case according to observations), the birds will be directed to their destinations by the repeating wind patterns ([Waterman 89, p. 27]).

Although a navigator in a canoe has a view of only 15 km, islands can be detected from a much greater distance. Because land is warm in comparison to the sea, air masses rise over land, cooling down in the process and forming stationary clouds above the island (see figure 5.7). Clouds over islands can be differentiated from clouds over open water by their colour: atolls reflect a green light underneath these white clouds.

Certain land birds fly out over the sea for a certain distance and can reliably be used as an indication of nearby land. Noddies and White Terns always head for land at dusk, so does the Sooty Tern. The Booby is the navigators' favourite bird, because of its striking behaviour: at dusk, the Booby heads to a passing canoe and circles it, as if intending to land. Even the most inattentive navigator cannot fail to notice this. When the sun is about to set, the Booby heads straight for home. All that remains to be done by the navigator is to follow the leader!

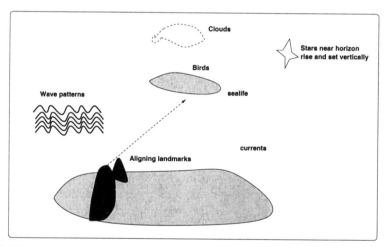

FIG. 5.7. NAVIGATION IN POLYNESIA AND THE CAROLINE ISLANDS USES SEVERAL METHODS SIMULTANEOUSLY FOR RELIABLE NAVIGATION

In addition to these cues, navigators exploit other properties of the environment they are navigating in. The Hawaiian islands, for example, stretch out in a chain 750 km long (but only 150 km wide). This means that aiming at the broad side of the islands the navigator has to get the bearing only roughly right; as soon as one island is detected, local landmarks can be used to sail to the actual destination of the journey. It is observed that in general Polynesian navigators tend to be conservative, i.e. they take a safer route, even if this involves a detour ([Gladwin 70]).

Navigation in the Caroline Islands   Both Polynesian navigators and Caroline Islanders are dependent on reliable navigation over long sea journeys, and use fundamentally the same principles. However, the methods they use are specifically adapted to their environment, and a navigator from the Caroline Islands would not be able to navigate in Polynesia, nor vice versa ([Gladwin 70]).

The method employed by Caroline navigators is based on dead reckoning. Initially, a course is determined by means of sky marks and landmarks. Being near the equator, stars rise and set almost vertically, and their rising and setting points at the horizon therefore provide useful directional indicators. Each destination has its own navigational star associated with it, and the knowledge about the "right" stars is handed down from generation to generation. To determine the "right" stars in the first place is not difficult. While it is hard to find the right direction (and hence the right star) coming from a big island and heading for a small one, the opposite is fairly easy. And, looking back, the navigator can determine the right star for heading towards the small island!

Once en route, the task of maintaining course is achieved by observing wave patterns. In the Carolines, there are three major types of wave patterns, coming from three major compass directions. The navigator can therefore use the waves to determine whether the canoe's course is still correct, or not. As in Polynesia, navigators prefer to sail directly parallel or across the waves, which induces a sideways or pitching motion of the canoe. Even slight deviations from the course can then be detected by the resulting rolling motion of the boat.

Once near the destination, clouds and other obvious route marks are again used to pinpoint the destination island precisely.

5.2.6   Conclusions for Robotics

One fundamental feature of animal and human navigation is the use of multiple information sources. The navigator does not rely on one mechanism alone, but combines information from multiple sources to make his decision where to go.

Examples for the use of multiple information sources are the use of magnetic and sun compasses in birds, the use of waves, sea life and weather patterns in human navigation, or the navigation by sun and landmarks in insects.

In mobile robots, a number of individual navigational competences and mechanisms have been developed. As in biological navigators, their combination and parallel use make robot navigation systems more reliable and more robust.

5.2.7 Further Reading on Navigation
of Animals and Humans

On Animal Navigation

- Talbot H. Waterman, *Animal Navigation*, Scientific American Library, New York, 1989.
- C.R. Gallistel, *The Organisation of Learning*, MIT Press, Cambridge MA, 1990.
- *The Journal of Experimental Biology*, January 1996.

On Human Navigation

- Thomas Gladwin, *East is a Big Bird*, Harvard University Press, Cambridge MA, 1970.
- D. Lewis, *We, the Navigators*, University of Hawaii Press, Honolulu, 1972.

5.3 Robot Navigation

5.3.1 Guided Vehicles

The easiest way of making a mobile robot go to a particular location is to *guide* it. This is usually done by burying an inductive loop or magnets in the floor, painting lines on the floor, or by placing beacons, markers, barcodes etc. in the environment. Such Automated Guided Vehicles (AGVs, see figure 2.1) are used in industrial scenarios for transportation tasks. They can carry several thousand pounds of payload, and their positioning accuracy can be as good as 50 mm.

AGVs are robots built for one specific purpose, controlled by a pre-supplied control program, or a human controller. Modifying them for alternative routes is difficult, and may even require modifications to the environment.

AGVs are expensive to install or to modify after installation, because they require specially prepared environments. It would be desirable, therefore, to build robot navigation systems that would allow a mobile robot to navigate in unmodified ("natural") environments.

As said before, the fundamental competences of navigation are localisation, path planning, map-building and map-interpretation. If we want to build an *autonomous* navigating robot that operates in unmodified environments, we would have to "anchor" all of these competences in a some frame of reference, rather than following a pre-specified path.

In robotics, typically such a frame of reference is either a Cartesian (or related) co-ordinate system, or a landmark-based system. The former uses dead reckoning strategies based on odometry, the latter sensor signal processing strategies to identify and classify landmarks. There are also hybrid models (in fact, most systems today have elements of both dead reckoning and landmark recognition). David Lee ([Lee 95]) provides a useful taxonomy of world models, distinguishing recognisable locations, topological maps, metric topological maps and full metric maps.

5.3.2 Navigation Systems Based Predominantly on Cartesian Reference Frames and Dead Reckoning

Because of the odometry drift problems it is rare to find mobile robot navigation systems based solely on dead reckoning. It is more common to find navigation systems that are fundamentally based on dead reckoning, but that use sensory information in addition.

One good example of a robot navigation system purely based on a Cartesian reference frame and dead reckoning is the use of *certainty grids* (or evidence grids, [Elfes 87]). Here, the robot's environment is divided into cells of finite size, which are initially labelled "unknown". As the robot explores its environment, estimating its current position by dead reckoning, more and more cells are converted into "free" or "occupied" cells, dependent on range sensor data, until the entire environment is mapped in this fashion.

Occupancy grid systems start with an empty map, which is completed as the robot explores its environment. They therefore face the problem that any error in the robot's position estimate will affect both the map-building and the map-interpretation.

One can get round some of these difficulties by supplying the robot with a ready-made map. [Kampmann & Schmidt 91] present one example of such a system. Their robot *MACROBE* is supplied with a 2D geometric map before it starts to operate. *MACROBE* then determines free space and occupied space by tessellating the environment into traversable regions, and plans paths using this tessellation. To be able to do this, the robot needs to know precisely where it is. *MACROBE* does this by a combination of dead reckoning and matching the map against precise range data obtained from a 3D laser range camera.

A similar system, again based on a Cartesian co-ordinate system, is *Elden*. The *Elden* system ([Yamauchi & Beer 96] uses "adaptive place networks" to construct spatial representations. In these adaptive place networks, units correspond to a region in Cartesian space, while links represent the topological relationships (more precisely, the compass directions) between these "place units", based on odometry. As this system is crucially dependent on accurate odometry, the robot returns to a fixed calibration position every 10 minutes to calibrate the odometry.

The *OxNav* navigation system ([Stevens *et al.* 95]) is also based on a Cartesian map, which, in this case, contains discernible sonar features, and is supplied before operation by the user. The robot uses stereo sonar sensors to track features, and then fuses odometry data, feature data and the prior map information to estimate its current position, using an extended Kalman filter.

There are many related examples (for instance, Maeyama, Ohya & Yuta [Maeyama *et al.* 95] present a similar system for outdoor use), all based on the use of a Cartesian map and dead reckoning, often augmented by landmark information.

5.3.3 Navigation Systems Based Predominantly on Landmark Information

The alternative to a navigation system that is fundamentally based on a global Cartesian reference frame within which the robot integrates its own motion through odometry would be to use a system in which the robot navigates using landmarks. "Landmark" here stands for a location-dependent sensory perception, as explained on p. 90. A number of components are needed to make such systems work.

First of all, sensory perception is subject to noise and variation. To use raw sensory data is therefore not a good idea. Instead, some kind of generalisation, which retains the salient features of a landmark, but discards the noisy components, is needed.

Clustering Techniques One way to achieve this is to use clustering mechanisms that cluster data in a topological fashion: similar looking data are grouped together. When clustering noisy sensory data this means that even if two perceptions are not identical, but merely similar, they will nevertheless be clustered together. Examples of self-organising clustering mechanisms are:

- Kohonen's self-organising feature map ([Kohonen 88], see p. 67). Applications of this can be found in case studies 5 and 6.
- Restricted Coulomb Energy networks (RCE). An example for the use of an RCE net can be found in [Kurz 96].
- Growing neural gas networks ([Fritzke 95]). An application example is the mobile robot *ALICE* ([Zimmer 95]) which uses dead reckoning for navigation, and corrects drift errors by using clustered sonar perceptions. An extension of this approach, using video images for navigation, is the work by von Wichert ([Wichert 97]).

Perceptual Aliasing In certain applications one can make the assumption that the robot will only visit a fixed number of locations, and obtain a *unique* perception for each location. In this case, sensory information can be used directly. Franz, Schölkopf, Mallot and Bülthoff ([Franz *et al.* 98]), for example, use a *graph* to represent their robot's environment. In their case no metric information at all is used, instead, nodes represent 360 degree camera snapshots, while edges represent adjacency relationships between snapshots. The robot is able to traverse edges by means of a homing procedure, without using metric information.

Unfortunately, however, the assumption of unique perceptual signatures does not hold in many cases. Typically, a mobile robot has to navigate over large distances in environments that have a more or less uniform appearance. Offices are an example. In such environments, there are usually many locations that look alike (perceptual aliasing). Perceptual aliasing obviously is a fundamental problem for navigation systems that rely on localisation by perception. There are several ways of dealing with it.

One possible method to distinguish similar looking locations is to use more and more sensory information from an increasing number of sensor modalities. Bühlmeier *et al.* ([Bühlmeier *et al.* 96]) have successfully used this method.

Case study 5 (p. 110) provides another example. Obviously, there are natural limits to this method. First, the number of sensors cannot be increased *ad infinitum*. Second, increasing acuity means increasing the influence of small fluctuations, leading to less reliable systems and increasing memory requirements. For a featureless environment such as a long corridor, however, one would like to do the opposite, i.e. reduce acuity and the amount of memory dedicated to representing that location. Finally, for complex environments we cannot assume the absence of perceptual aliasing, and therefore need to use mechanisms that assume perceptual aliasing exists, and deal with it.

Another approach for dealing with perceptual aliasing is to incorporate history of local sensor sequences into the recognition of locations. In case study 5 we combine past and present sensor and motor experience of the robot in the input to a self-organising feature map. Similarly, Tani and Fukumura ([Tani & Fukumura 94]) add previous sensor patterns to the input field of an artificial neural network controller.

A disadvantage of this approach is that the identical set of previously stored locations must be revisited for matching of history information to be possible. In complex environments, this can only be achieved by restricting the navigational behaviour of the robot, often to following fixed paths — a severe restriction. Case study 5 on p. 110 will show that a *range* of temporal horizons or "time windows" of history is required to localise in an environment containing perceptual aliasing, i.e., one fixed length of history is insufficient. In general, overcoming perceptual aliasing by looking at temporal patterns of perceptions is limited by the amount of history stored, and does not generalise to cover arbitrarily large areas of perceptual ambiguity in the robot's environment. Also, these methods are not robust to sensor noise; one freak perception will affect the next n inputs to the system, where n is the number of previous perceptions taken into account for localisation.

Yet another approach is to use the combination of perception and dead reckoning to disambiguate similar looking locations. Here, the position estimate provided by dead reckoning is corrected by matching observed features of the environment against an internal world model (see, for instance, [Atiya & Hager 93], [Edlinger & Weiss 95], [Horn & Schmidt 95], [Kuipers & Byun 88], [Kurz 96], [Yamauchi & Langley 96] and [Zimmer 95]). For example, Kuipers and Byun ([Kuipers & Byun 88]) move the robot itself towards locally distinctive places as a means of correcting the drift error due to odometry. These methods are very effective, provided the robot knows roughly where it is at the start. For the "lost robot" problem they are not suited.

The maps used in these localisation methods are often graph-based, using topologically connected "place" nodes. Metric information, corresponding to the relative translational and rotational displacement of the robot between places, may be added ([Kurz 96], [Yamauchi & Langley 96] and [Zimmer 95]). Position updates may be continuous ([Kurz 96]) or episodic ([Yamauchi & Langley 96]). Some methods are capable of dealing with dynamic environments ([Yamauchi & Langley 96] and [Zimmer 95]), and even of distinguishing transient changes such as moving people from lasting changes in the environment ([Yamauchi & Langley 96]).

Relationship to Hippocampal Models of Localisation Topological maps, developed through mechanisms of self-organisation, are related to hippocampal models of localisation in animals (see [Recce & Harris 96] for an introduction). In the robot case the map used consists of a discrete set of distinct locations; these are analogous to place cells of the hippocampus. Robot localisation is essentially a competitive learning scheme in which the location in the map with the highest "activation" provides the position estimate. Case study 7 is an example.

5.3.4   Discussion

We said (in section 5.2.6) that the strength of living navigators was their ability to combine multiple information sources, and doing exactly this is a promising way forward in robot navigation.

Each navigation principle alone, be it dead reckoning or landmark-based navigation, has peculiar strengths and weaknesses, and only through the combination of systems can we overcome the drawbacks of each system while retaining their strengths.

Dead reckoning systems suffer from drift errors and, what is worse, these errors cannot be corrected without external perceptions.

Being based on exteroception, landmark-based navigation systems do not suffer from incorrigible drift errors. However, they are affected severely by perceptual aliasing. Perceptual aliasing is not always unwanted: it is, after all, a generalised (i.e. memory-efficient) representation of the robot's world. Problems only arise if two identical-looking locations require different actions by the robot.

Hybrid systems try to retain the positive aspects of both approaches, while getting rid of the problems. Different environments, however, require different signal processing etc., so the risk here is that hybrid approaches are too carefully geared towards particular environments. Learning, especially self-organisation would help here.

In fact, self-organisation would also help to overcome another major problem: man and machine perceive the environment differently, and man is therefore not ideally placed to identify the landmarks by which the robot is to navigate. A better approach is to let the robot select landmarks itself.

Further Reading on Robot Navigation

- J. Borenstein, H.R. Everett and L. Feng, *Navigating Mobile Robots*, A K Peters, Wellesley MA, 1996.
- G. Schmidt (ed.), *Information Processing in Autonomous Mobile Robots*, Springer Verlag, Berlin, Heidelberg, New York, 1991.

5.4 Case Studies of Navigating Robots

We said above that it is desirable to build robot navigation systems that are not dependent on modifications of the environment. Such systems are more flexible and cheaper to install than automated guided vehicles.

Because of the accumulating drift errors in odometry-based navigation systems, it is furthermore desirable to build robot navigation systems that are based on exteroception rather than proprioception.

We will now look in detail at some robot navigation systems based on these principles that have been developed and tested on real robots. These case studies provide detailed information, and are intended to help the student to understand the issues at hand when trying to make a mobile robot navigate in unmodified environments, using external cues.

5.4.1 Case Study 4.
GRASMOOR: Ant-like Robot Navigation

The principles of compass-based dead reckoning as observed in ants (see p. 94) can easily be explored with a simple robot, equipped with nothing more than four light sensors (see figure 5.8 for the design principles of such a robot).

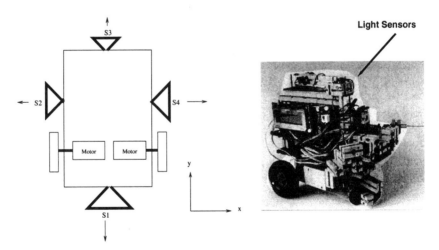

FIG. 5.8. A SIMPLE MOBILE ROBOT WITH DIFFERENTIAL DRIVE SYSTEM AND FOUR LIGHT SENSORS (S1 TO S4). EACH LIGHT SENSOR FACES A DIFFERENT DIRECTION, AND IS SENSITIVE WITHIN AN ANGLE OF ABOUT 160 DEGREES.

In situations where a defined light gradient exists, for example in rooms with windows at only one wall, or outdoors in sunshine, or in environments with artificially created light gradients (i.e. light source at one far end of the room), a simple but effective compass-based navigation system can be designed using the light sensors of the robot.

In a Cartesian co-ordinate system we can determine the robot's current heading using the differences between opposite sensors (hence the name *Differential Light Compass* for this type of compass) as follows:

$$dx \propto S4 - S2,$$
$$dy \propto S3 - S1,$$

where dx and dy are the x and y component of the robot's movement per time unit, and S1 to S4 are the readings of the four light sensors. This would indicate the robot's current heading correctly in all environments where the overall intensity of light is constant, so that dx and dy are determined only by the robot's orientation, not the brightness of the environment.

However, to eliminate the influence of changes in overall light intensity, we can normalise the readings for dx and dy as follows:

$$dx = \frac{S4 - S2}{\sqrt{(S4-S2)^2 + (S3-S1)^2}},$$
$$dy = \frac{S3 - S1}{\sqrt{(S4-S2)^2 + (S3-S1)^2}}.$$

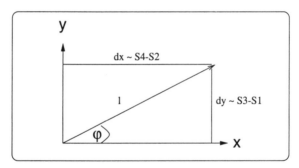

FIG. 5.9. TRIGONOMETRY OF THE DIFFERENTIAL LIGHT COMPASS

For implementation on the robot, it is sometimes convenient to use trigonometric functions (which can be tabulated in lookup tables, for quick processing):

$$\tan \varphi = \frac{S3-S1}{S4-S2},$$
$$dx = l \cos \varphi,$$
$$dy = l \sin \varphi,$$

where l is the distance travelled (which, at constant speed, is proportional to time travelled), and φ is the angle measured by the differential light compass.

Assuming that the robot travels at constant speed, the current position of the robot is continuously being updated according to equations 5.1 and 5.2.

$$x(t+1) = x(t) + dx \ , \tag{5.1}$$

$$y(t+1) = y(t) + dy \ . \tag{5.2}$$

If the robot does not travel at a constant speed, the actual distance travelled has to be measured by some other means, for example by using odometry.

During the outward journey, the robot's current position is continuously being updated using equations 5.1 and 5.2. To return home (or to go to any other location), the required heading can be determined as shown in figure 5.10, but the simplest and most robust strategy for homing is to let the robot head in the "right" direction, by ensuring that the signs of x and dx and y and dy respectively are different (assuming that the home position is at the origin of the co-ordinate system). Such a return behaviour is shown in figure 5.11.

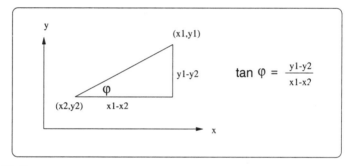

FIG. 5.10. HOMING BY DETERMINING THE PRECISE DIRECTION FOR THE HOME LOCATION (x_2, y_2) FROM POSITION (x_1, y_1)

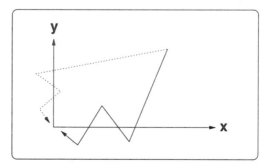

FIG. 5.11. HOMING TO $(0, 0)$ BY ITERATIVELY REDUCING THE ERROR IN X AND Y DIRECTION, USING A LOCAL STRATEGY ONLY

5.4.2   Case Study 5. *ALDER*: Two Experiments on the Application of Self-Organisation to Map-Building

We said earlier that there are good reasons to use landmark-based navigation systems: landmark detection based on exteroception will produce a more robust navigation procedure that does not suffer from odometry drift error. The robot will *observe* where it is, rather than *estimate* through dead reckoning. This, of course, is only true if landmarks can be identified uniquely. Considerable confusion is created if several places in the real world share the same perceptual signature, or if one and the same place exhibits a different perceptual signature on subsequent visits. Both these problems do occur in the real world, and ways of dealing with them are discussed later in this chapter. For the time being, we will assume that unique places in the robot's world have unique perceptual signatures.

A landmark-based navigation system obviously needs a way of identifying landmarks. The first idea that comes to mind is perhaps that certain features of the environment could be defined by the human operator as landmarks, and a detection algorithm is built that detects these landmarks and uses them for navigation. This will work well in environments that have been modified for robot operation, for example by placing perceptually distinctive and easily identifiable objects (e.g. beacons or markers) in it. Environments within which robots can operate would thus be similarly created to environments in which humans can operate: after all, we have placed easily detectable sign posts everywhere in our world to aid our navigation.

The Problem of "Perceptual Discrepancy" However, what about landmark-based navigation in *unmodified* environments? To define landmarks *a priori* is not a good idea here, because we may choose to define landmarks that we *believe* to be easily detectable by the robot, but which turn out to be hard to perceive. Likewise, we may overlook very easily detectable landmarks, simply because they are not easily detectable by humans (an example of the latter are door posts, which protrude slightly from a smooth wall. While they do not normally catch the human's attention, they are easily detectable by robot sonar sensors, because the sonar burst gets reflected very well by them. Door posts act like beacons!)

This is the "problem of perceptual discrepancy" introduced in section 4.1.1. This problem provides a strong motivation for limiting pre-definition as much as possible, and to use learning and self-organising mechanisms wherever possible.

It would be better, therefore, to equip the robot with the ability to identify "good" landmarks autonomously, to put them on a map, and to use them for navigation. That is, the robot is first left to explore an unknown environment for some time, identifying perceptually unique features in the environment and differentiating different perceptual signatures from one another. Once this perceptual map is built, it can then be used for various navigation tasks. In this section we will show how such a map can be used for localisation. Case study 6 then shows how such a map can be used for learning routes.

So, in summary, a mechanism is needed that allows the robot to cluster its perceptions autonomously, to pinpoint perceptually unique features and to identify them when seeing them again.

Definition of "Map" We take a map to be any one-to-one mapping (bijection) of a state-space onto map-space. Examples of such maps are the plan of the London Underground, the Manchester telephone directory, and a family tree. The connections between stations, phone owners and numbers, and family members are represented in all these cases. A map is therefore not just a representation of a birds-eye-view of the world the robot inhabits.

In the mapping scheme described in this case study the state-space that is represented using a self-organising network has nothing to do with actual physical locations in the real world, at least not directly. What *is* represented by these maps is the *perceptual* space of the robot. If no perceptual aliasing is present, there will be a unique one-to-one relationship between perceptual space and physical space that can be exploited in robot navigation systems.

Whenever the term "map" is used, therefore, it is used in the wider sense of this definition.

Experiment 1: Localisation Using Perception Using a ring-shaped, one-dimensional self-organising feature map (SOFM) of 50 units, experiments have been conducted with *ALDER* (see figure 4.14), to achieve autonomous map-building through self-organisation, and to use the map for self-localisation.

The behaviour of this network was previously described on p. 67. The neighbourhood within which weight vectors were updated was $\pm$ 2 cells (constant over time). A typical response of the network is shown in figure 5.12 (in this figure the ring is cut and shown as a line).

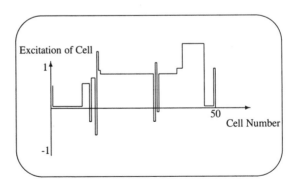

FIG. 5.12. A TYPICAL RESPONSE OF THE RING AFTER HAVING SETTLED IN

Performing a wall following behaviour, the robot negotiated its way around the perimeter of its enclosure and the network responses became correlated with being at corners.

The Input Vector A self-organising network clusters the input information presented to it in a (statistically) meaningful way. If the input to the net contains no meaningful information (meaningful in relation to the task of constructing a state-space representation of the robot in its world, that is) the network will not develop any meaningful structure. The very first input vector we used simply contained information about whether the robot had received a signal on its left or on its right hand side, plus information about two previous sensor readings (again only whether the obstacle was seen on the left or on the right), plus crude odometry information (simply the number of wheel rotations). Such information was too weak to construct a meaningful state-space representation (at least without requiring a great many input vectors), and consequently the network response in the settled state of the net had little correlation with particular locations in the real world.

This was obviously due to a lack of sufficient structure in the input vector presented to the net. We therefore enriched the input vector by preprocessing the sensory information obtained. Instead of taking data straight from the sensors and feeding it into the net, sensor readings were used to detect convex and concave corners[1]. This information was then used as input to the net. The input vector eventually used to obtain the results presented below contained information about the present corner and previous corners encountered as well as the distance travelled between the present and the previous corner (see figure 5.13, top).

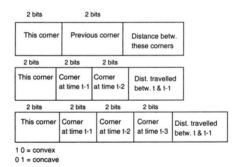

FIG. 5.13. THE INPUT VECTORS USED IN THE THREE STAGES OF EXPERIMENT 1

Brief Summary of the Experimental Procedure

1. Initialise the ring-shaped self-organising network by filling the weight vectors of all cells with randomly chosen values;
2. Normalise all the weight vectors;
3. Present an input stimulus to the network;

---

[1] This is very easily achieved: if the time the robot needs to turn towards the wall exceeds a certain threshold time, then it is assumed that a convex corner is detected. Similarly, if the time it takes the robot to get away from a detected obstacle exceeds a certain threshold time, it is assumed that a concave corner is detected.

4. Determine the response to this stimulus for each cell of the ring according to equation 4.15 (p. 67);
5. Determine the unit that is responding most strongly;
6. Update the weight vectors of the five units within a neighbourhood of ± 2 cells of the maximally responding cell, according to equations 4.6 and 4.7;
7. Normalise those five weight vectors again;
8. Continue with step 3.

Experimental Results The experiment was conducted as follows. The robot was placed within an experimental arena such as the one shown in figure 5.14, and allowed to explore it, following the wall always in the same direction for several rounds. The arena was composed of walls that were detectable by the robot's whiskers, and contained convex and concave corners.

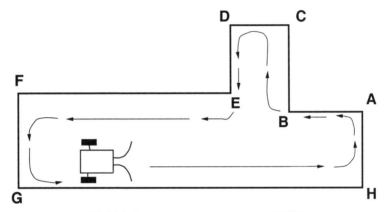

FIG. 5.14. A TYPICAL ENVIRONMENT FOR *ALDER*

Whenever a convex or concave corner was detected an input vector as described in figure 5.13 was created and presented to the ring. The gain η for updating weight vectors (see equations 4.6 and 4.7) was initially very high (5.0) and decreased by 5 per cent after every presentation of an input vector. The longer the robot went around in the enclosure, the more settled the ring became and the more precise the response to a particular input stimulus. After about three rounds a particular corner was marked by pressing the "attention" button on the robot. The response of the ring for that particular ("marked") corner was then stored, all subsequent responses were compared with the target response by calculating the Euclidean difference between them; the smaller this value, the closer the match. Obviously, if the robot is able to construct a meaningful internal state-space representation this difference should be small when the robot is at the marked corner, and it should be noticeably larger at any other corner.

Figure 5.15 shows the results for recognising corners H (left) and F (right). The bar diagrams at the various locations of the enclosure indicate the Euclidean distance between the excitation of the net at the particular location and that at the target location. The horizontal axis in the bar diagrams denotes time.

For corner H, the results are perfect: only at corner H is there a small Euclidean distance between target excitation pattern and observed excitation pattern, meaning that corner H is uniquely identified, and not confused with any other corner. At this stage the robot is able to return to position H, regardless of the starting position along the perimeter of the experimental enclosure.

For corner F, the situation is different. Because the input vectors generated at locations F and C look similar, the network response at those two corners is equally similar, meaning that the robot is unable to tell whether it is at corner F or corner C (however, the robot is still able to differentiate between corner F/C and all the other corners).

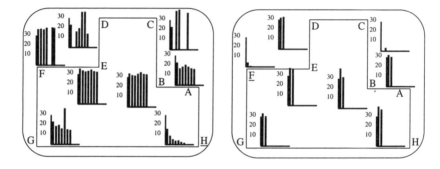

FIG. 5.15. RECOGNISING CORNERS H (LEFT) AND F (RIGHT). THE SIZE OF BARS AT INDIVIDUAL LOCATIONS INDICATES THE EUCLIDEAN DIFFERENCE BETWEEN THE NETWORK RESPONSE AT THAT LOCATION AND AT LOCATION H AND F RESPECTIVELY. EACH BAR DENOTES ONE VISIT TO THE RESPECTIVE LOCATION.

The same applies to corners B and E: they are both convex, both have previous corners that are concave, and again the distances between them are similar. Again, our expectations that these two corners might have an identical representation on the resulting map are experimentally verified (see figure 5.16): as in the case of corners F and C, the robot cannot differentiate between corners B and E.

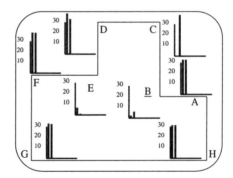

FIG. 5.16. RECOGNISING CORNER B, LOOKING AT ONE PREVIOUS CORNER

Dealing with Perceptual Aliasing by Extending the Input Vector One answer to
the problem of perceptual aliasing is to increase the information contained in the
input vector. In the experiments here, we have done this by extending the input
vector shown in figure 5.13 (top), and testing the effect on the robot's ability to
recognise corner B, and to differentiate it from all other corners in its enclosure.
We have extended the input vector by first adding one more component (now
containing information about the types of the *two* previous corners, fig. 5.13,
middle), and then one more component again (*three* previous corners, fig. 5.13,
bottom). Figure 5.17 shows the results.

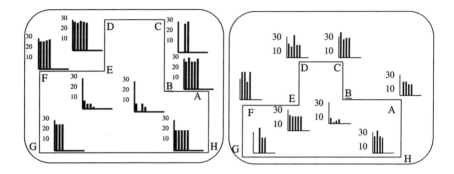

FIG. 5.17. RECOGNISING CORNER B, LOOKING AT TWO PREVIOUS CORNERS (LEFT) AND
THREE PREVIOUS CORNERS (RIGHT)

The information about the previous two corners is still not sufficient to differentiate corners B and E (I leave it as an exercise to the reader to justify this
statement), and consequently even with an extended input vector the robot is
unable to distinguish these two locations (figure 5.17, left). However, when the
information about three previous corners is used (fig. 5.13, bottom), that distinction is possible (figure 5.17, right).

Summary of Experiment 1 In summary, this is what happened: having had sufficient time to explore the environment, the robot was able to recognise particular
corners that had been marked by the experimenter. In cases where the input
vector presented to the self-organising net contained insufficient information,
ALDER confused corners that looked alike, simply because their input vectors
were identical. This was to be expected.

The robot's ability to recognise the marked corner reliably increased with experience, and the difference between excitation of the net at the marked corner at
time t and excitation at the marked corner at time $t + 1$, decreased continuously.
It eventually became zero.

There are, interestingly, similarities between *ALDER's* use of self-organising
feature maps for landmark recognition, and bee navigation (see p. 94). Like
bees, *ALDER* does not generate a floor plan (a conventional map), instead it

uses "snapshots" (distinctive excitation patterns of the self-organising network as a response to the sensory input) to recognise locations.

Like in the case of bees, the mechanism described here is very robust and fairly immune to noise. "Undetected" corners, varying distance measurements and even moving the robot to a different location (without the control algorithm realising this) do not impair *ALDER's* ability to recognise locations. Cartwright and Collett's comment on the bee's navigation system was: "The bee's guidance system is immune to a considerable amount of noise" ([Cartwright & Collett 83]).

Experiment 2: Using Different Input Stimuli for Localisation   In the first experiment we used processed sensor information (denoting corner types) to achieve location recognition. The second experiment demonstrates that self-localisation can also be achieved without using direct sensory information. Instead, the history of the *motor action commands* of the robot controller are used as input to the self-organising neural network.

Sensing and acting are often treated as separate functions in robotics, but are really two aspects of *the same* function. They cannot successfully be analysed in isolation.

The actions of a robot, just like those of a person, determine to a large extent the sensory signals it will receive, which will in turn influence its actions. Breaking this tight interaction into two separate functions leads to an incorrect decomposition of the robot control problem.

The input vector used for the following experiments demonstrates this point: it contains no direct information about sensory input. Instead, the information it contains is derived from the motor action commands of the robot controller, but these, as we have said, are themselves influenced by the sensory signals received by the robot as a result of its actions. Information derived from the motor action commands of the robot controller form a smaller set of signal types, they are much less subject to noise, but they still adequately characterise the interactions between the robot and its environment as it seeks to achieve its task — wall following, in our case.

For the location recognition experiments the robot was again placed in an enclosure as shown in figure 5.14; it then followed the wall using a pre-programmed wall following and obstacle-avoidance behaviour. The robot was governed by its pre-programmed wall following behaviour which, of course, did use sensory information. The process of constructing the SOFM is, however, independent of the wall following behaviour: it simply "looks" at the motor action commands issued by the controller as the robot follows the walls.

Every time a new motor action command was issued, that is, every time the wall following or the obstacle-avoidance behaviour forced the robot to change direction, a motor action vector was generated. The 9-bit motor action vector shown in figure 5.18 formed the input to the SOFM.

Thus, from figure 5.18 we can see that no information concerning sensor signals is directly presented to the SOFM. The only information available to the network concerns motor action commands.

Motor Action		Duration
Forward	01 01	00000 less than 0.9s
Left	01 10	00001 0.9 - 1.3s
Right	10 01	00011 1.3 - 1.7s
		00111 1.7 - 2.1s
		01111 2.1 - 2.6s
		11111 over 2.6s

FIG. 5.18. THE MOTOR ACTION VECTOR

Experiments with a 10 x 10 SOFM The robot was left to explore its enclosure by following walls, generating input vectors as shown in figure 5.18 each time a new motor action command was issued by the robot controller for any reason. Figure 5.19 shows response of a 10×10 cell SOFM to different input stimuli.

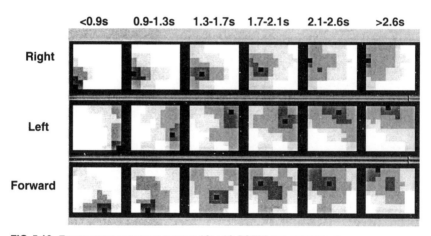

FIG. 5.19. EXCITATION PATTERNS OF THE 10×10 SOFM FOR DIFFERENT TYPES OF MOTOR ACTION VECTOR INPUTS. THE DARKER THE COLOUR, THE GREATER THE EXCITATION OF THE CELL. ROWS FROM TOP TO BOTTOM GIVE THE MAP RESPONSE TO "RIGHT", "LEFT" AND "FORWARD" MOTOR ACTION RESPECTIVELY, COLUMNS FROM LEFT TO RIGHT DENOTE THE LENGTH OF THE MOTOR ACTION IN THE SIX STAGES INDICATED IN FIGURE 5.18, IN INCREASING ORDER.

Comparison with Biological Mappings Two observations can be made from these pictures of the response of the SOFM to different types of input vector:

- The size of the excited area is roughly proportional to the frequency of occurrence of the input signal that caused the excitation.
- Related inputs excite neighbouring areas. In this example, we can see that "forward" movements stimulate the central region of the network, "left"

movements stimulate the right hand region, and "right" movements the left hand region of the net. Within these basic regions there are variations, depending on the duration of the movement.

Mappings with these same properties — development through self organisation, preservation of neighbourhood relationships, and a representation of signal frequency in the size of the excitation area — are common in living beings.

[Churchland 86] gives a good overview of somatotopic mappings, so called because they map the body's touch, pressure, vibration, temperature and pain sensors onto the cortex. These somatotopic mappings retain the neighbourhood relationships of the sensors (i.e. signals from neighbouring sensors excite neighbouring areas of the cortex), and furthermore occupy larger areas of the cortex for regions where the sensor density is high. Experiments show that where the nature of the stimuli is altered, the resulting mapping onto the cortex also changes. ([Clark *et al.* 88]) have shown in experiments that if two fingers of a hand are surgically joined, the cortex area they excite changes accordingly.

Topological mappings are also found in the visual cortex. [Allman 77] gives an overview of these. In the macaque monkey, to name one example, the striate cortex — part of the visual system of primates — is organised in a topological manner ([Hubel 79]).

Location Recognition, Using Motor Actions In the previous experiment, it was the *sequence* of previous features (corners) that had been detected immediately prior to the current feature (corner) that was used to determine recognition. Clearly, a similar approach is needed here. As it turned out, looking at the motor actions performed in one fixed time interval was not sufficient for reliable localisation: some locations are uniquely identified by a short sequence of actions, others by long ones.

We therefore used a system of *seven* independent, two-dimensional SOFMs, working in parallel. Each SOFM consisted 12×12 cells. The input vectors to each of these networks were different, but all were built from motor action vectors as shown in figure 5.18. By combining 2, 4, 6, 8, 12, 16, and 24 of these basic motor action vectors we formed seven SOFM input vectors which correspond to increasingly longer histories of the robots motor action changes.

The lengths of histories are chosen to cover adequately the expected spectrum of action periodicity. If we think of the sequence of actions generated as the robot circles its enclosure as a periodic series, with period roughly equal to the average number of action-vectors generated in a single circuit, then the use of SOFMs tuned to different "frequency bands" allows us to sample the temporal structure of the series across its spectrum and associate these samples with the physical locations whose signatures they are.

The set of excitation patterns of the seven SOFMs produced as the robot arrives at a particular location in its enclosure, therefore, can be used to distinguish this location from all other locations.

Experimental Procedure The robot was set to wall follow its way around the enclosure. Every time a new motor action command was issued as a result of the

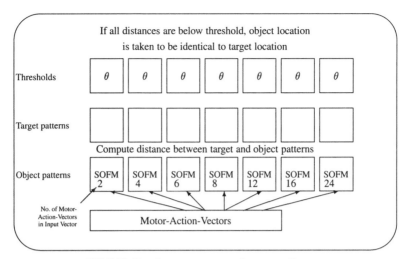

FIG. 5.20. THE SYSTEM USED FOR LOCATION RECOGNITION

built in wall following or obstacle avoidance behaviour of the robot, a motor action vector was generated. This vector, together with the respective number of previous motor action vectors, was presented to each of the seven SOFMs. After a sufficient time (about five times round the enclosure) these feature maps had organised themselves into stable structures corresponding to the topological interrelationships and proportional densities of the input vectors.

After this learning period the excitation patterns of all seven networks at a particular location (the *target patterns*) were stored. All subsequent sets of seven excitation patterns generated by new input vectors (*object patterns*) were then compared to the set of seven target patterns. This was done by computing the Euclidean distance (or, alternatively, the city-block distance) between pairs of target and object patterns. If the distance values between each of the seven pairs of object and target patterns was less than a threshold defined for each pair, the robot identified the location as the target location.

Results Data recorded from the robot was used to compute these results, however the actual computation was done off-line on a workstation.

The robot recognised corner H four times out of five rounds, and corners E and F in five out of the five times. At no time was a non-target corner erroneously "identified" as a target corner.

Case Study 5: Summary and Conclusions In both experiments the robot's task was to recognise particular locations in a simple enclosure. In the first experiment we showed that this task can be accomplished using self-organising feature maps. The input vector used there contained explicit information about landmarks encountered: that the robot was at a corner, what sort of corner (convex or concave), and information about previous corners encountered.

In the second experiment we tried to reduce the explicit information content in the input vector. We also tried to generate input vectors to the network(s) that contain no direct information about sensor signals.

The input vector contained information only about the motor commands of the robot controller, and their duration. Vectors put together from varying numbers of these motor action vectors (2, 4, 6, 8, 12, 16 and 24) were presented to seven separate self-organising feature maps, each two-dimensional of 12×12 cells. In order to identify a particular corner, all seven excitation patterns had to be close enough to a stored set of target patterns.

The location recognition system performed well in this experiment, recognising corner H in four out of five times, corners E and F in five out of five times, with no erroneous identifications in either case.

Using self-organising feature maps to recognise locations adds a high degree of freedom to the robot controller. The robot is able to build its own representations of the environment, independently of the designer.

There are three main conclusions we can draw from these experiments. First, it is possible to achieve robot self-localisation through self organisation, without providing *a priori* knowledge such as maps, and without modifying the environment by installing artificial landmarks.

Second, sensing and acting are closely coupled. The "sensor" in the second experiment is actually the behaviour of the robot. Choosing an input vector that contains no direct information about sensory signals makes the system independent of the actual sensors used. Whether tactile, ultrasonic, infrared or other sensors are used: the location recognition system stays the same.

Third, with this approach the features to be identified by the SOFMs are spread out over time, meaning that not only spatial features, but also temporal features are used for location recognition. This technique will be used again later in this book, in case study 7.

Case Study 5: Further Reading

- The fifth case study is based on [Nehmzow & Smithers 91] and [Nehmzow *et al.* 91], where detailed information about the experimental procedures and further references are given.

5.4.3   Case Study 6. *FortyTwo*: Route Learning in Unmodified Environments

The previous case study has shown how map-building through self-organisation can be used for self-localisation. While map-building is a fundamental component to any robot navigation system, the question is whether such maps can be used for other navigational tasks. For example, is it possible to use such maps to associate perception with action, i.e. to generate goal-directed motion?

In this sixth case study, we discuss a route learning system that allows a mobile robot to first map its environment through a process of self-organisation, and then use this map to follow a particular route autonomously. The navigation system has been tested extensively on the mobile robot *FortyTwo*, is reliable and copes with noise and variation inherent in the environment.

At the heart of the map-building and navigation system is again a Self-Organising Feature Map (SOFM, see p. 67).

The association between location and action which is necessary for route learning can be achieved by extending the input and weight vectors to include the required actions (fig 5.21). During the operator-supervised training phase, the operator's driving actions become part of the input vector and thus, through self-organisation, become part of the weight vector of the trained units.

During route recall, the action part of the input vector is set to zero, and the required action can be retrieved from the weight vector of the winning unit. Used in this way, the SOFM becomes an associator between sensory information and action (see [Heikkonen 94]).

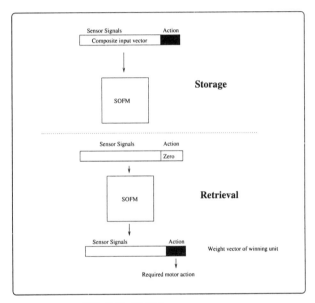

FIG. 5.21. SOFM AS ASSOCIATOR

Figure 5.21 shows the general principle of the SOFM as associator, as well as the sequence of events for action *retrieval*. First the robot receives its sensory information. The input vector is formed by inserting zeros into the action part of the vector, and this is then fed into the network and a winner found.

The winner is the cell whose weights most closely match the sensor data; due to the topological mapping achieved by the SOFM this winner is likely to be within the same region that was excited at this physical location during training. The final step is then to retrieve the action from the winner's weight vector.

There are therefore two phases of operation:

1. Training phase — action and sensory information are combined, and the winner's weights and those of its neighbours updated;

2. Recall phase — sensory information alone fed to network (zeros for action), and action retrieved from weights of the winner (no weight update takes place in the recall phase).

Experimental Procedure The sensor section of the input vector contained 22 components, 11 integer range values between 0 and 255 inches obtained from the sonar sensors indicated in figure 5.23, and 11 binary values obtained from the infrared sensors shown in figure 5.23. This input vector is shown in figure 5.22.

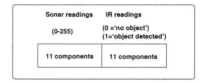

FIG. 5.22. SENSOR SECTION OF THE INPUT VECTOR

FIG. 5.23. SENSORS USED

During training, the motion signal from the operator's joystick is recorded in the 2-component action section of the input vector as follows:

1 0 — forward (by constant velocity)
0 1 — left (by constant angular velocity)
0 -1 — right (by constant angular velocity)
1 1 — forward and left
1 -1 — forward and right

The action section combined with the sensor section therefore gives an input vector with a total of 24 components.

In order to achieve a balanced interpretation of each section of the weight vector (sonar, IR and action), these components are then normalised independently.

The size of the network used in these experiments was 15×15 cells with a learning rate of 0.2 and a neighbourhood size of 1. The network was torus-shaped to avoid edge effects[2], and the weights of the cells were initially random.

---

[2] In a torus-shaped network there are no edges, because the network "wraps round" both in up/down and left/right directions.

Experimental Results *FortyTwo* was trained to learn and navigate four different routes. In each experiment the robot navigated the route successfully for five consecutive runs. For each route the experiment was repeated four times, with a freshly initialised network on each occasion (i.e. 20 successful completions of the entire route for each of the four routes trained). For each of these trials the number of training visits required at each turning location was recorded. This is the number of times that the robot needed to be trained at that location before autonomous operation was achieved at that position within the route.

The total training time is also given for each trial. This is the time taken until the end of the robot's first totally independent circuit of the route without error (with four subsequent circuits also being completed successfully).

Route 1 Figure 5.24 shows the first route on which *FortyTwo* was trained in the laboratory.

The route is simple and the average training time was approximately 18 minutes. A network response for this route is shown in figure 5.25 (taken from trial 1). This figure shows the change in the position of the maximally excited network unit as the robot moves through the environment. The results for this route are given in figure 5.26.

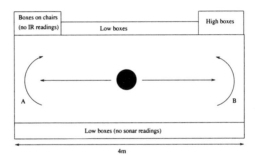

FIG. 5.24. ROUTE 1

Route 2 Again this was a simple laboratory route (see figure 5.27), the average training time was approximately 23 minutes. A sample network response for this route (taken from trial 1) is shown in figure 5.27. Here the robot started and finished in region A, the cells activated at each particular location are marked accordingly. The results for this route are given in figure 5.28.

Route 3 This was the first route that was attempted outside the robotics laboratory (figure 5.29). Again it is a relatively simple route, but one much longer than anything previously attempted in the laboratory, and with a greater number of turns to be learned. To learn this route perfectly took on average 36 minutes.

As can be seen from the results shown in figure 5.30, the most difficult locations for the system to differentiate were C and E. The cause of this was that these two locations were perceptually quite similar. Looking at figure 5.29 one

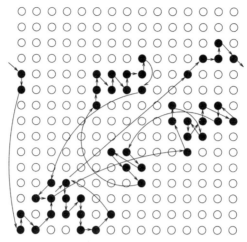

FIG. 5.25. A NETWORK RESPONSE FOR ROUTE 1. ONE CAN SEE HOW THE STRAIGHT MOVE IN PHYSICAL SPACE (FIGURE 5.24) MAPS ONTO PERCEPTUAL SPACE.

Trial 1

Location	Training visits required
A	4
B	5
Approx. total training time	14 min

Trial 2

Location	Training visits required
A	3
B	5
Approx. total training time	19 min

Trial 3

Location	Training visits required
A	3
B	4
Approx. total training time	15 min

Trial 4

Location	Training visits required
A	3
B	5
Approx. total training time	21 min

FIG. 5.26. ROUTE 1 RESULTS

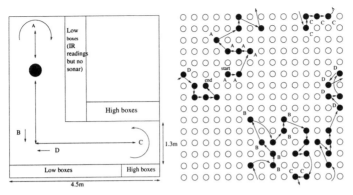

FIG. 5.27. ROUTE 2, AND ITS REPRESENTATION BY THE NETWORK

Trial 1

Location	Training visits required
A	3
B	4
C	4
D	5
Approx. total training time	25 min

Trial 2

Location	Training visits required
A	4
B	4
C	3
D	4
Approx. total training time	22 min

Trial 3

Location	Training visits required
A	3
B	4
C	3
D	4
Approx. total training time	24 min

Trial 4

Location	Training visits required
A	3
B	4
C	5
D	4
Approx. total training time	20 min

FIG. 5.28. ROUTE 2 RESULTS

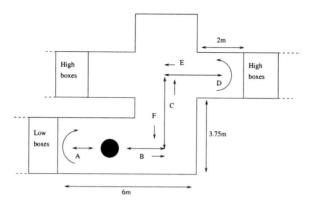

FIG. 5.29. ROUTE 3

Trial 1

Location	Training visits required
A	3
B	3
C	5
D	4
E	5
F	3
Approx. total training time	28 min

Trial 2

Location	Training visits required
A	3
B	3
C	6
D	3
E	5
F	4
Approx. total training time	41 min

Trial 3

Location	Training visits required
A	4
B	3
C	6
D	3
E	4
F	3
Approx. total training time	34 min

Trial 4

Location	Training visits required
A	3
B	3
C	4
D	3
E	6
F	3
Approx. total training time	38 min

FIG. 5.30. ROUTE 3 RESULTS

can see that the robot is presented with similar situations at these two points on the route, in each case there is a corridor to the front and a corridor to either side of the robot. Although these corridors are of different length, they are similar enough to cause confusion in the early stages of network development.

Route 4 This route (figure 5.31) followed a different format to the previous routes being more obviously circular in nature. To learn this route *FortyTwo* took 49 minutes on average.

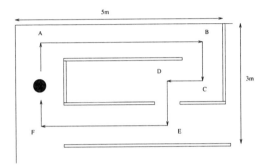

FIG. 5.31. ROUTE 4

As can be seen from the results in figure 5.32 the most difficult location to learn was D. This was because, as can be seen in figure 5.31, the gap through which the left turn was to be made at D was very narrow, and consequently more precision was necessary in the robot's actions at this point to enable it to pass through the gap. This extra precision required additional training.

Fault Tolerance A test of the robustness of the system was carried out using route 4. Once the network for trial 1 had been fully trained, two arbitrarily chosen sonar sensors were "disabled" by replacing their readings with zeros in the input vector (see figure 5.33).

With the sensors disabled in this way the robot was still able to complete the whole route successfully. The reason for this is that in this case the remaining sensors supply perceptual stimuli to the network that are sufficiently close to the original ones so that the learned actions can be retrieved correctly (just as in the case of an undetected sensor fault, described on p. 73). Obviously, the more sensors fail the higher the probability for erroneous recall due to perceptual aliasing — the navigation mechanism is dependent on distinctive sensor readings, although it can cope with a certain amount of degradation in acuity.

Generalisation To test the generalisation ability of the system the robot was trained to perform a right turn at an intersection, and then presented with slight variations of that intersection. Figure 5.34a shows the intersection at which the robot was trained, figures 5.34b and 5.34c show the two variations with which the robot was presented on completion of training. Training for the intersection took

Trial 1

Location	Training visits required
A	3
B	1
C	2
D	7
E	3
F	2
Approx. total training time	53 min

Trial 2

Location	Training visits required
A	4
B	2
C	4
D	6
E	3
F	2
Approx. total training time	40 min

Trial 3

Location	Training visits required
A	3
B	2
C	3
D	6
E	4
F	3
Approx. total training time	42 min

Trial 4

Location	Training visits required
A	4
B	2
C	3
D	6
E	4
F	2
Approx. total training time	61 min

FIG. 5.32. ROUTE 4 RESULTS

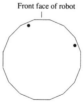

FIG. 5.33. DISABLED SONARS IN FAULT TOLERANCE EXPERIMENT

approximately four minutes, with the robot requiring to be guided around the turn three times before fully autonomous operation was successful.

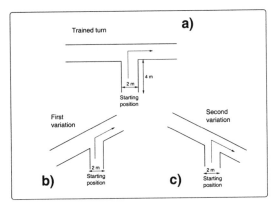

FIG. 5.34. GENERALISATION: THE ROBOT WAS TRAINED TO TURN RIGHT AT INTERSECTION A), BUT WAS ABLE TO TURN CORRECTLY AT INTERSECTIONS B) AND C) WITHOUT ANY FURTHER TRAINING

When presented with the two variations of the turn, the exit trajectory was correct in both cases without any re-training. However, the robots motion was not as smooth as for the trained turn. In actual route learning experiments we observed a similar robustness when landmarks (stacks of boxes) were shifted by up to 50 cm: the robot was able to complete the routes successfully, albeit in a more wavering manner.

Case Study 6: Discussion These experiments show how a map-building mechanism based on self organisation can be used to teach a robot routes — completely independently from previously installed maps, or artificial landmarks. The experiments presented here were chosen to demonstrate the mechanism, and the four short routes discussed here do not mean that this mechanism couldn't be used over longer distances. In fact, *FortyTwo* now regularly roams the corridors of the University of Manchester on routes of over 150 m length!

One would obviously like to know how good *exactly* such a route learning system is, rather than trusting statements like "it worked very well". Case study 11 (p. 191) presents such a quantitative performance analysis of this route learning system.

Case Study 6: Further Reading

- Carl Owen and Ulrich Nehmzow, Route Learning in Mobile Robots through Self-Organisation, *Proc. Eurobot 96*, pp. 126-133, IEEE Computer Society, 1996.
- Carl Owen and Ulrich Nehmzow, Map Interpretation in Dynamic Environments, *Proc. 8th International Workshop on Advanced Motion Control*, IEEE Press , ISBN 0-7803-4484-7, 1998.

5.4.4   Case study 7. *FortyTwo*: Localisation Through Hypothesis Formation

"That map may be all right enough, ... if you know whereabouts in it we are now." (Jerome K. Jerome, *Three Men in a Boat*).

The seventh case study addresses the problem of localisation in autonomous mobile robots in environments that show a high degree of perceptual aliasing. In particular, this section is concerned with the more general problem of re-localisation (in other words, the robot is initially completely lost).

During an exploration phase, the robot builds a map of its environment, using a self-organising neural network to cluster its perceptual space. The robot is then moved to a randomly chosen position within that environment, where it will attempt to localise. By actively exploring, and accumulating evidence through the use of relative odometry between local landmarks, the robot is able to determine its location with respect to perceptual landmarks very quickly.

As we are interested in the use of autonomous mobile robots in *unmodified* environments, we again avoid the use of pre-installed maps or external devices such as markers or beacons for position evaluation. To be fully autonomous, the robot must therefore rely on its own perceptions for dealing with the interrelated sub-problems of exploration, map-building and re-localisation. To achieve this, proprioception and/or exteroception can be used. For the reasons given earlier (section 3.1.9), in case study 7 we have chosen a landmark-based method, accumulating evidence over time.

Experimental Procedure   The robot begins by building a map of its environment, using an Adaptive Resonance Theory self-organising neural network (ART2) to cluster its perceptual space. The robot is then moved to a random position in its environment, its sensors being disabled during that move. An active exploration phase follows, during which the robot accumulates evidence based on relative odometry between perceptually distinctive locations. Hence, previous sensory experience is used to choose between competing hypotheses of the robot's possible location. The resulting position estimates are corrected by reference to the previously acquired world model.

Both the map-building and localisation competences operate independently of the exploration strategy used. In this case study, performance is demonstrated using two different exploration behaviours (contour following and wandering), both having been acquired autonomously by the robot using instinct rules (see case study 1). The system as a whole is composed of a hierarchy of behaviours (see figure 5.35), each being resilient to a significant degree of error in the preceding levels. Thus, the localisation system is highly robust, and has localised successfully in hundreds of laboratory trials, both on a real robot and using a simulator.

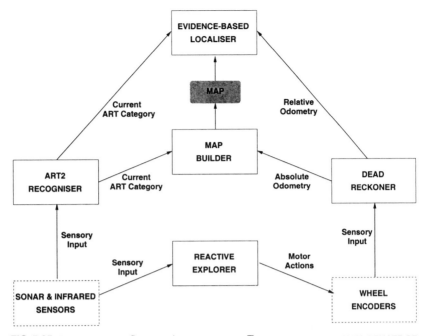

FIG. 5.35. LOCALISATION SYSTEM ARCHITECTURE. THE SOLID-EDGED BOXES DENOTE BE-HAVIOURAL MODULES, AND ARROWS THE DEPENDENCIES BETWEEN DIFFERENT PARTS OF THE SYSTEM. THE SHADED BOX DENOTES THE REPRESENTATION USED FOR THE MAP, AND THE DASHED BOXES SHOW HARDWARE COMPONENTS.

Case Study 7: Dealing with Perceptual Aliasing In this case study, evidence based on past sensory experience is used to mediate between competing position estimates, which are corrected by matching current perceptions to an autonomously acquired world model. The map used is similar to the graph-based models described in [Yamauchi & Langley 96] and [Kurz 96].

Perceptual Clustering The first stage of the problem is for the robot to recognise distinct places in its perceptual space. This is complicated by the problems of using sensors in the real world. For example, the robot will often obtain different sensor readings when revisiting a previously encountered location. Individual sensory perceptions may therefore be inconsistent, imprecise and unreliable. Hence, the robot should be capable of generalising in order to extract the salient features in a given situation, without being distracted by the finer detail of individual sensor patterns.

To keep the use of pre-defined information low, a self-organising classification system is used. The neural network architecture ART2 ([Carpenter & Grossberg 87]) is responsible for clustering input patterns into distinct classes or categories, such that similar patterns are grouped into the same class and dissimilar patterns are grouped into separate classes. The stored class definitions may be said to correspond to prototypes or templates for matching with current perceptions of the world.

Reasons for Using Self-Organisation   The motivation for choosing self-organisation is that clustering the robot's perceptions autonomously using a self-organising classifier helps to avoid the problem of matching individual environmental features against an internal world model. There is no attempt to recognise specific objects in the robot's environment, rather the raw sensor readings are grouped according to their similarity. This means that the robot's perceptual groupings (ART classifications) may bear no direct translation to obvious human categorisations of environmental features (e.g., "corner", "wall", "box", etc.). Suitable perceptual landmarks emerge rather than being defined arbitrarily by a human designer.

ART is not the only methodology that could be used for the localisation task. In case studies 5 and 6 we have used self-organising feature maps (see also[Kurz 96], [Nehmzow *et al.* 91] and [Owen 95]). Other possibilities are Restricted Coulomb Energy networks ([Kurz 96]), Growing Cell Structures ([Fritzke 94] and [Zimmer 95]), Vector Quantisation networks ([Kohonen 95]), etc. The specific advantages and disadvantages of using ART are discussed below.

In the wider context of the map-building and localisation competences, which are presented later in the section, the ART network is effectively used as a "black box" for classifying sensor patterns. Readers who are not interested in the details of the ART architecture might wish to skip over some of the following material.

Characteristics of ART   Some of the important characteristics of ART are listed below, explaining the motivation for choosing this particular classification strategy.

- *Unsupervised Learning.* Self-organisation means that suitable prototypes emerge rather than being hand-crafted by the designer.
- *Real-Time Learning.* No off-line processing is required.
- *Lifelong Learning.* Learning is continuous during normal operation, so there are no separate training and testing phases.
- *Solution to the "Stability-Plasticity Dilemma".* The network can learn new information without forgetting old information, simply by adding more prototype nodes to the network. In other competitive learning schemes (e.g. SOFM) the size of the network and therefore the amount of storable information must be fixed in advance.
- *Variable Sensitivity to Perceptual Detail.* A pre-specified variance parameter known as the "vigilance" determines the size of the clusters. A high value results in fine categories, a low value in coarse categories.
- *Closed Classification Boundaries.* An input pattern cannot be classified in a particular category if the similarity falls below the vigilance threshold. Thus, ART can detect whether an input pattern has been "seen" before or not. Other competitive networks, e.g. Vector Quantisation, SOFM, etc., will

always match with the closest node, even if the input pattern bears little resemblance to any of the stored patterns. This has the advantage that there is a clear criterion for distinguishing familiar from unfamiliar input patterns, while losing the ability of competitive networks to "second guess" an appropriate classification based on noisy input data.

- *Self-Scaling Property.* This prevents any pattern that is a subset of another from being classified in the same category. Thus, patterns which share common features but are in different classes can still be distinguished. Grossberg ([Grossberg 88]) calls this "the discovery of critical features in a context sensitive manner".

However, ART does have some disadvantages too. The general complexity and reliance on details of architecture have been criticised, and there are a large number of parameters or "magic numbers" which must be determined experimentally by the designer. The solution to the "stability-plasticity dilemma" of adding more nodes means that ART may continue to come up with new prototypes even if the robot stays within a previously explored part of the environment. Another problem is *over-training*, where new categorisations occur in physical locations which have previously been associated with a different ART category.

The ART Information Processing Model The basic ART architecture consists of two fully connected layers of units, a feature layer (F1) which receives the sensory input, and a category layer (F2) where the units correspond to the perceptual clusters or prototypes (see figure 5.36). There are two sets of weights between the layers, corresponding to feedforward and feedback connections. A "winner-takes-all" criterion is used during the feedforward phase, and a similarity criterion is used to accept or reject the resulting categorisation in the feedback phase.

When a pattern is presented to the network, the input is compared to each of the existing prototypes (through the feedforward weights) to determine a winning node. If the similarity between the input pattern and the winning node (through the feedback weights) exceeds the vigilance threshold, then adaptive learning is activated and the stored pattern is modified to be more similar to the input pattern (the learning method depends on the particular ART network used). Otherwise a "reset" occurs, where the current winner is disabled, and the network searches for another node to match the input pattern. If none of the stored prototypes is similar enough to the given input, then a new prototype will be created corresponding to the input pattern.

In earlier clustering experiments, the ART1 network ([Grossberg 88]) was tried, but was found to be unreliable because of its requirement of binary inputs. The individual sensor readings had to be coarse coded into "bins" (i.e. '0' or '1') according to a threshold level. It was found that sensor noise around the threshold and variations in the exploration behaviour of the robot produced too many inconsistent input patterns, resulting in misclassifications and spurious prototypes being created. The ART2 network was therefore implemented, which is capable of handling continuous-valued inputs.

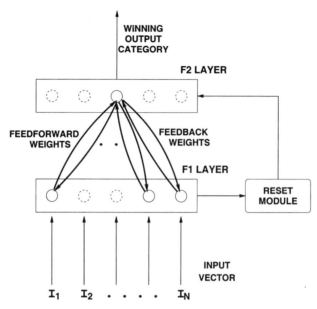

FIG. 5.36. BASIC ART ARCHITECTURE. THE UNITS IN THE FEATURE LAYER (F1) ARE COMPLETELY CONNECTED TO EACH OF THE UNITS IN THE CATEGORY LAYER (F2), THROUGH TWO SEPARATE SETS OF WEIGHTS. FOR CLARITY, ONLY A FEW OF THE FEEDFORWARD AND FEEDBACK CONNECTIONS ARE SHOWN.

ART2 Implementation in Case Study 7 The ART2 architecture is a generalisation of ART1, being capable of learning and recognising continuous-valued input patterns. The basic connectivity is the same as in ART1, except that the units in the feature layer (F1) are each constructed from a subnetwork of six nodes (see figure 5.37). Each subnetwork acts as a buffer between the input signal and the feedback from the category layer (F2), being used to normalise and combine the two signals for comparison by the reset module. In addition to the basic architecture, an extra preprocessing layer (F0), consisting of a subnetwork of four nodes per unit, was added to further reduce noise and enhance the contrast of the input patterns, as suggested by Carpenter and Grossberg ([Carpenter & Grossberg 87]).

In ART2, the F1 units are implemented as six individual nodes, among which much of the control processing is distributed. A preprocessing layer F0 was added to enhance the contrast further and to reduce noise in the input patterns. The mechanism used for updating the weight vectors was based on the implementation of ART2 by Paolo Gaudiano at the CMU Artificial Intelligence Repository (http://www.cs.cmu.edu/Groups/AI/html/repository.html).

F0 Layer Equations The equations describing the dynamics of the F0 and F1 levels are given as follows, in order of bottom-up flow through the network. I is the input vector presented to the network, a, b, c, d, e and θ are constants (see page 137), and $f(x)$ is a noise filtering function (see page 137).

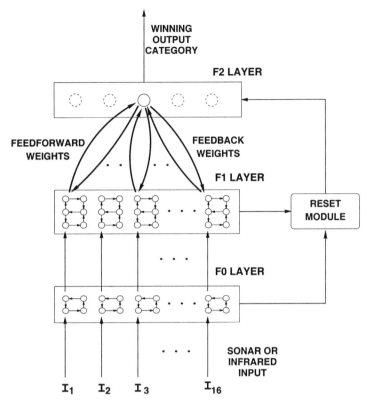

FIG. 5.37. ART2 ARCHITECTURE USED FOR LOCALISATION. EACH F1 UNIT CONSISTS OF A SUB-NETWORK OF SIX NODES, AND EACH F0 UNIT CONSISTS OF A SUB-NETWORK OF FOUR NODES. THE F1 AND F2 LAYERS ARE COMPLETELY CONNECTED; FOR CLARITY ONLY A FEW OF THE CONNECTIONS ARE SHOWN.

$$w'_i = I_i + au'_i \,,$$

$$x'_i = \frac{w'_i}{e + \|w'\|} \,,$$

$$v'_i = f(x_i) \,,$$

$$u'_i = \frac{v'_i}{e + \|v'\|} \,.$$

F1 Layer Equations Similarly, the equations describing the dynamics of the F1 layer are given as follows, again in order of bottom-up flow through the network.

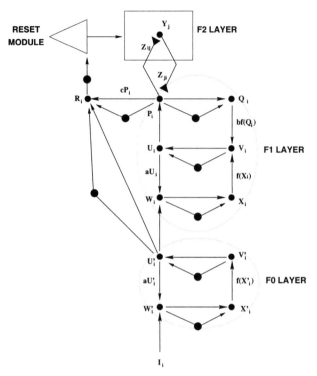

FIG. 5.38. ART2 ARCHITECTURE. THIS SHOWS THE F2 LAYER (NODE Y), F1 LAYER (NODES P, Q, U, V, W AND X), F0 LAYER (NODES U', V', W' AND X'), RESET MODULE, FEEDFOR-WARD WEIGHTS (ZIJ) AND FEEDBACK WEIGHTS (ZJI), FOR A SINGLE ELEMENT, I, IN THE IN-PUT VECTOR, I. THE ARROWS SHOW PROCESSING STEPS BETWEEN THE NODES, AND THOSE WITH A SHADED CIRCLE DENOTE A NORMALISATION OPERATION ON THE ASSOCIATED VEC-TOR. ADAPTED FROM [CARPENTER & GROSSBERG 87].

$$w_i = u_i' + au_i \,,$$

$$x_i = \frac{w_i}{e + \|w\|} \,,$$

$$v_i = f(x_i) + bf(q_i) \,,$$

$$u_i = \frac{v_i}{e + \|v\|} \,.$$

$$p_i = \begin{cases} u_i & \text{if F2 is inactive} \\ u_i + dz_{Ji} & \text{if the } J^{th} \text{ F2 node is active} \end{cases}$$

$$q_i = \frac{p_i}{e + \|p\|} \,.$$

Noise Filter The following equation was used to cut out background "noise" below a given threshold θ at nodes v_i' and v_i;

$$f(x) = \begin{cases} 0 \text{ if } 0 \leq x < \theta \\ x \text{ if } x > \theta \end{cases}$$

Weight Vectors The bottom-up (z_{ij}) and top-down (z_{ji}) weights between layers F1 and F2 are initialised as follows, where M is the number of units in the F1 layer.

$$z_{ij} = \frac{1}{(1-d) \times \sqrt{M}} \text{ for all units } i \text{ in F1}, j \text{ in F2} \,,$$

$$z_{ji} = 0 \text{ for all units } j \text{ in F2}, i \text{ in F1} \,.$$

The following differential equations were used to adjust the weights for the winning F2 unit J, and these were solved using the Runge-Kutta method (see [Calter & Berridge 95] for a description of this method).

$$\frac{dz_{iJ}}{dt} = d(1-d) \left[\frac{u_i}{1-d} - z_{iJ} \right] \,,$$

$$\frac{dz_{Ji}}{dt} = d(1-d) \left[\frac{u_i}{1-d} - z_{Ji} \right] \,.$$

Reset Module The activation of the reset module r is determined using the following equation:

$$r_i = \frac{u_i' + cp_i}{e + \|u'\| + \|cp\|} \,.$$

The F2 layer is reset when the following criteria is met after the feedback phase, given the vigilance parameter ρ:

$$\frac{\rho}{e + \|r\|} > 1 \,.$$

Parameter Values The following parameter values were used throughout all of the experiments and simulations documented in this section:

$$a = 5.0, b = 5.0, c = 0.225, d = 0.8, e = 0.0001, \theta = 0.3 \,.$$

Different values were used for the vigilance threshold ρ depending on the particular experiment or simulation being carried out (see also next appendix). On both the real robot experiments and the simulations using infrared input, $\rho = 0.9$ was used. In the simulations using sonar, $\rho = 0.75$ was used. In general, the value of the vigilance parameter was found to have a critical effect within the range of approximately $0.7 \leq \rho < 1.0$, where high values result in a fine categorisation and low values in a coarse categorisation.

Param.	Description	Value in Real Robot Experiments	Value in Wall Foll. Simulations	Value in 2-D Simulation
ρ	Vigilance threshold used in ART2 net	0.9	0.9	0.75
D	Distance threshold used in map-building	0.25 m	0.25 m	0.25 m
$GAIN$	Gain factor used in localisation	8.0	3.0	3.0
$DECAY$	Decay factor used in localisation	0.7	0.7	0.7
MIN	Min. confidence level allowed in localisation	0.5	0.5	0.5
T	Match distance used in localisation	0.50 m	0.50 m	0.50 m

Table 5.1. PARAMETERS USED IN THE LOCALISATION SYSTEM

Table 5.1 shows the values of the variable parameters or "magic numbers" used in the various components of the localisation system during the different experiments and simulations.

In ART2, adaptive learning is carried out by moving the stored weight vectors in the direction of the input vector (the magnitude of vectors is ignored due to vector normalisation). The "fast" mode of learning was implemented, where the network is allowed to stabilise completely after each training pattern is presented. This means that the weight vectors are moved to the fullest extent possible, allowing locations to be remembered by the robot after a single visit. The Runge-Kutta method was used to solve the differential equations for the weight adjustment.

The input vector to the ART2 network was taken from either the 16 infrared or 16 sonar sensors mounted on the turret of *FortyTwo*, depending on the experiment or simulation being carried out. The sensor patterns were always presented in the same orientation, regardless of the direction travelled by the robot. This was done by keeping the robot's turret stationary whilst travelling.

The implementation was used successfully to classify the robot's perceptual space consistently between discovering and revisiting the same locations. Figure 5.39 shows the results of a simulation where ART2 was run in parallel with a wall following behaviour. The robot's physical space is divided into regions according to the ART classification category (these areas are termed "perceptual regions" in the rest of the section). An example of perceptual aliasing is shown by the shaded areas; these regions all share the same ART category.

Problems using ART Networks In ART networks, a novel perception always results in the creation of a new prototype. Thus, noisy or "rogue" input patterns can result in spurious ART categories being created as well as misclassification errors. In the real world using real sensors, no classification method will probably ever give completely error-free performance. However, the ART2 implementation rarely suffered from either of these problems, and performance was sufficiently good for the localisation algorithm to succeed every time in the experiments conducted.

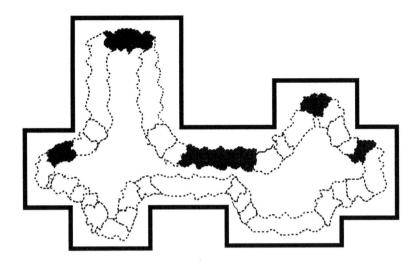

FIG. 5.39. ART2 CLASSIFICATIONS DURING WALL FOLLOWING SIMULATION. AS THE ROBOT FOLLOWED THE WALLS OF A ROOM, THE PHYSICAL SPACE COVERED WAS DIVIDED INTO RE-GIONS ACCORDING TO THE ART CATEGORY RECORDED. AN EXAMPLE OF PERCEPTUAL ALIAS-ING IS SHOWN BY THE SHADED REGIONS; THESE ALL SHARE THE SAME ART CLASSIFICATION.

In addition, over-training was found to be a problem during prolonged use of the ART2 network under normal operation, e.g. after five or six laps of a room by the wall follower, where new classifications started to occur which were inconsistent with the results in previous laps. This was because the prototype vectors continue to be adjusted during lifelong learning, as the stored patterns are continuously moved closer to the input patterns presented. It was found that new prototypes were occasionally created to fill the "holes" which appeared between the existing, previously overlapping clusters moved by adaptive learning.

This problem was avoided in the localisation system presented here by switch-ing training off after map-building had been carried out. The patterns remained fixed during localisation. For example, during wall following, training was fin-ished once a complete circuit of the robot's enclosure had been detected by dead reckoning.

Map-Building After perceptual clustering has been carried out, the next stage is to build a map of the locations visited during exploration. The map created contains stored "locations", where a location is an ART category associated with an (x, y) co-ordinate obtained by dead reckoning. New locations are entered into the map either when a new ART category is perceived, or the robot has moved by more than a distance of $D = 25\,cm$.

The map represents a clustering of the Cartesian space within the regions defined by the ART classifier, consisting of a discrete set of stored points. The stored locations could therefore be said to correspond to "place prototypes".

The representation accommodates perceptual aliasing because there may be a one-to-many relationship between perceptual signatures (ART categories) and stored locations in the map.

In Lee's taxonomy ([Lee 95]), the world model might be described as "Recognisable Locations", except that metric information is also represented. If the map were to be incorporated into a complete navigation system, it would probably be necessary to store topological links as well for path planning, etc.

Method The x and y co-ordinates of the robot are averaged continuously as the robot moves across a perceptual region corresponding to a particular ART category, as shown in figure 5.40. Whenever the robot moves into a different perceptual region, a new location point is created. This point will keep moving towards the approximate centre of the cluster due to the averaging process, until a new cluster is formed. This is similar to the map-building system described by Kurz ([Kurz 96]).

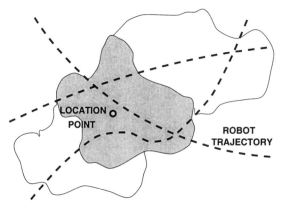

FIG. 5.40. CREATION OF LOCATION POINTS. AS THE ROBOT MOVES THROUGH A REGION CORRESPONDING TO A PARTICULAR ART CLASSIFICATION (SHADED), THE X AND Y CO-ORDINATES ARE AVERAGED CONTINUOUSLY TO GIVE THE POSITION OF THE CORRESPONDING LOCATION POINT. ADAPTED FROM [KURZ 96].

In addition, when the displacement of the robot from the current (nearest) point location exceeds the threshold of $D = 25\ cm$, a new point location is also created. This leads to multiple point locations within large perceptual regions (see figure 5.41). Also, this handles the problem of perceptual aliasing, because different places which share the same perceptual signature will be represented by different points in the map, provided they are more than distance D apart. Otherwise, for example, averaging the x and y co-ordinates of all the shaded regions in figure 5.39 would result in a point somewhere in the middle of the room. This would be an incorrect mapping, as this point would correspond to none of the individual places from which it had been derived.

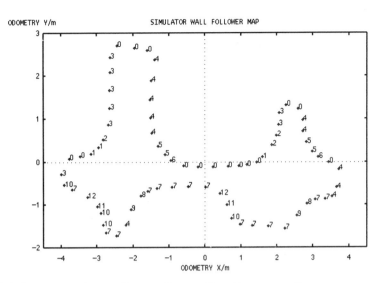

FIG. 5.41. LOCATION POINTS CREATED DURING WALL FOLLOWING. THE LOCATION POINTS PLOTTED HERE CORRESPOND TO THE PERCEPTUAL REGIONS SHOWN IN FIGURE 5.39. THE NUMBERS SHOWN CORRESPOND TO THE ART2 CLASSIFICATIONS, E.G. THE POINTS NUMBERED '0' LIE WITHIN THE SHADED AREAS SHOWN IN FIGURE 5.39.

Coping with Odometry Drift A major weakness of this part of the work is the reliance on global odometry for supplying the metric component of the map. (This problem does not affect the localisation algorithm as that only uses short distance odometry between local landmarks.) While the averaging process will smooth out local variations in odometry, the map as a whole will be subject to global drift errors. This was not a problem in the experiments conducted here as only relatively short routes were travelled, e.g. with the wall follower, only one lap of a room was used to build the map. However, in large, complex environments this could result in matching with the wrong "nearest" point during the map-building phase.

This problem could be eliminated by combining the map-building and localisation phases, or in other words, implementing lifelong learning. Thus, the map would be used to correct the current position estimate, which is used to build the map itself! Referring back to figure 5.35, this would effectively mean creating a link back from the localiser to the dead reckoner, applying appropriate corrections to the absolute odometry values based on the results of the localisation algorithm. This is discussed further in the conclusions below.

Localisation The basic principle of the localisation method is similar to that of ART and other competitive learning schemes; the location point in the map with the highest "activation" or confidence level is selected as the winner. Thus, the location points are analogous to the "place cells" found in hippocampal models of localisation (see, for instance, [Recce & Harris 96]). The confidence levels

are adjusted by accumulating evidence based on relative odometry between locations. The algorithm works by comparing old and new information at each
iteration, or in other words, by considering the *changes* in the moving robot's
perceptions over time.

Localisation Algorithm Possible locations are stored as a list of hypotheses in working memory, each with an associated confidence level. Whenever the robot perceives a new location, either by recognising a change in the current ART category or a change in odometry bigger than the maximum distance between the
stored location points, another set of possible locations is created. (The maximum distance between the stored locations will be $2D$ because the averaging
process used in the map-building means that the robot should be within the distance threshold D of the nearest point on either side.) A matching procedure is
then used to combine both sources of evidence to produce an updated list of hypotheses. The algorithm is given as follows, and explained in more detail below.

0. *Initialisation.* Formulate set of hypotheses, $H = \{h_0, ..., h_N\}$, consisting of
   location points which match the current ART category. Initialise confidence
   levels: $\forall h_i \in H$, assign conf(h_i) = 1.
1. Wait until the ART category changes or robot has moved distance $2D$, where
   D is the distance threshold used during map-building.
2. For each hypothesis h_i add change in odometry ($\triangle x, \triangle y$) to the co-ordinates
   of h_i, (x_{h_i}, y_{h_i}).
3. Generate second set of candidate hypotheses, $H' = \{h'_0, ..., h'_N\}$.
4. For each h_i, find the nearest h'_j, recording distance apart, d_{h_i}.
5. Accumulate evidence, given distance threshold T, minimum confidence level
   MIN, gain factor $GAIN > 1$ and decay factor $0 < DECAY < 1$:
   $\forall h_i \in H$
       if $d_{h_i} < T$ then
           replace (x_{h_i}, y_{h_i}) with $(x_{h'_j}, y_{h'_j})$ from the matching h'_j
           let conf(h_i) = conf(h_i) $\times GAIN$
       else
           let conf(h_i) = conf(h_i) $\times DECAY$
           if conf(h_i) < MIN then delete h_i.
6. Delete any duplicates in H, preserving the one with the highest confidence
   level.
7. Add all remaining h'_j from H' which are not already contained in H to H,
   assigning conf(h'_j) = 1.
8. Return to step 1.

In step 2, the existing set of location estimates are updated by adding on the
change in position recorded by relative odometry. A new set of candidate hypotheses is then enumerated by selecting all possible location points from the
map which matches the current ART category. A search procedure follows where
each of the existing hypotheses is matched to its nearest neighbour in the new
candidate set.

Step 5 then uses a threshold criterion to determine whether each of the matched hypotheses should be increased or decreased in confidence. This means that if the matched position estimates are sufficiently close to each other, then this is judged to be evidence in favour of this particular hypothesis. The confidence level is therefore raised by a gain term, and the position estimate from the old hypothesis is replaced by the new value. Thus, good position estimates are continually corrected on the basis of perception.

Conversely, if the match distance exceeds the threshold, then the associated confidence level is scaled down by a decay term, and the position estimate is left uncorrected, i.e. it is not replaced by its nearest neighbour in the candidate set. Hypotheses which fall below a certain confidence level are rejected and pruned from the list of possible locations, eliminating the bad hypotheses quickly and minimising the search space. Duplicates created by the matching process are deleted here too.

Any unmatched location points remaining in the candidate set are also added to the current list of hypotheses, and are assigned an initial confidence value. This will be the case for all of the candidate hypotheses on the first iteration, as the hypothesis set will initially be empty. (Initialisation has been included as step 0 here for clarity, although this is actually unnecessary.) All possible locations with the current perceptual signature are always considered, so that the algorithm can cope with unexpected, arbitrary changes of position.

Eventually, one of the hypotheses emerges as a clear winner. For example, in the experiments conducted on a real robot, this took an average of 7 iterations through the algorithm, in a mean time of 27 seconds with the robot travelling at $0.10ms^{-1}$. If the robot becomes lost again, confidence in this particular hypothesis gradually decays as a new winner emerges.

Performance The current version of the algorithm localises to the nearest stored location point. Thus, the accuracy of the position estimate depends on the resolution of the map, which in turn depends on the distance threshold D used in the map-building process. After localisation has been achieved, the error between the actual and estimated position should therefore vary between 0 and D.

Results Experimental results obtained with this self-localisation system and a quantitative performance analysis are presented in case study 11 on p. 197.

Case Study 7: Discussion This localisation system can localise even in environments where no single place has a unique perceptual signature. No prior estimate of position is required, so the robot can recover even after becoming completely lost. The localisation algorithm implements a competitive learning scheme, which is related to hippocampal models taken from biology. During an exploration phase, evidence is accumulated to support competing place estimates. Perceptual changes (from sonar, infrared and relative odometry) are correlated with an internal world model to provide positive or negative reinforcement of the emerging hypotheses.

The algorithm has some other interesting emergent properties. One is that the robot continues to collect useful evidence even when moving between location points which share the same perceptual signature. More generally, it can be seen that a winner emerges once a perceptually unique path has been traced through the map. This applies regardless of the length of the path, or in other words, the amount of past sensory experience required to disambiguate similar looking locations. In principle, the algorithm therefore generalises to cover arbitrary levels of perceptual aliasing in the environment, provided that the following conditions are upheld:

1. That the environment has a finite size (i.e. that the environment has boundaries which are perceptually distinctive from its interior);
2. That the robot has a compass sense, or can recover its orientation unambiguously from landmarks in the environment, and;
3. That the exploration strategy of the robot will eventually find a perceptually unique path through the environment. (Conditions 1 and 2 guarantee that such a path will exist.)

The reasoning behind this is that if the environment has a finite size, then by heading in any direction, the robot will eventually find a boundary. Following the boundary of the enclosure would eventually allow the robot to find its location, provided that it could distinguish repeating patterns of perceptions around the enclosure. In the worst case of a circular or radially symmetric room, the robot would need a compass to find its location. Otherwise, the relative position of landmarks should allow the robot to recover its original orientation.

Of course, this assumes a perfect world; in practice, the above assumptions may be undermined to some extent by the inherent uncertainties of using a real robot in the real world. However, the results (given in case study 12 on p. 197) show that the localisation algorithm presented here is very robust, experiencing only a graceful degradation in performance with respect to the errors introduced. With regard to the third condition, the results also demonstrated the superiority of following canonical paths over random exploration.

Case Study 7: Further Reading

- An in-depth discussion of this work, together with proposal for its extensions with respect to lifelong learning, pro-active exploration, recognition of familiar landmarks from novel perspectives and scaling up can be found in [Duckett & Nehmzow 96] and [Duckett & Nehmzow 99].

5.4.5 Case Study 8: Radial Basis Function Networks for Determining Shortcuts

In 1948, Tolman ([Tolman 48]) introduced the term "cognitive map" to describe an animal's representation of its environment, encoding routes, landmarks and the relationships between these navigational factors. In particular, Tolman argued that the ability to determine novel routes (shortcuts) demonstrates the existence of a cognitive map.

Similarly, O'Keefe and Nadel ([O'Keefe & Nadel 78]) argued that the ability to make shortcuts was the feature that differentiated animals with cognitive maps from those without.

Andrew Bennett ([Bennett 96]) discusses the question of whether the ability to determine shortcuts indicates the presence of a cognitive map or not, and argues that shortcuts could also be discovered through path integration, i.e. trigonometry.

In this eighth case study we will look at a robot navigation system that is able to do just that: to determine shortcuts by using trigonometry. The interesting aspect is that the robot's trigonometry is not based on path integration, however, but on landmark recognition.

The following experiment describes a scenario in which a Nomad 200 robot associates perceptions with "virtual co-ordinates" — quasi-Cartesian co-ordinates that are recalled from memory as a landmark is identified — and then uses those co-ordinates to determine the shortest routes between locations, even if those routes had never been traversed before.

Experimental Setup For the experiments, the robot was equipped with an omnidirectional CCD camera (see figure 5.46) that produced 360-degree images such as the one shown in figure 5.45. The robot was driven manually through the environment shown in figure 5.42, along the trajectory shown in figure 5.43.

FIG. 5.42. THE NOMAD 200 MOBILE ROBOT (RIGHT), AND THE ENVIRONMENT USED FOR THE NAVIGATION EXPERIMENTS (THE OMNIDIRECTIONAL CAMERA USED IN THE EXPERIMENTS IS NOT VISIBLE IN THE IMAGE ON THE RIGHT)

During the traversal of this route over 700 images of the robot's omnidirectional CCD camera and their corresponding positions in Cartesian space (as obtained from the robot's odometry system) were logged. Thirty of those percep-

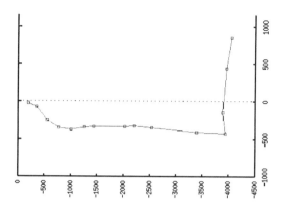

FIG. 5.43. TRAJECTORY TAKEN BY THE ROBOT IN CARTESIAN SPACE. DIMENSIONS ON x AND y AXES ARE IN UNITS OF 2.5 MM.

tions were then used off-line for the experiments described here. The positions where these images were taken are shown in figure 5.44.

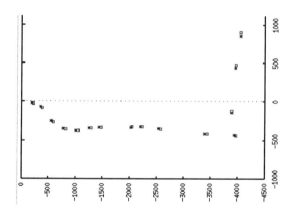

FIG. 5.44. TRAINING AND TEST DATA OBTAINED ALONG THE TRAJECTORY SHOWN IN FIG-URE 5.43. THE 15 TRAINING PERCEPTIONS (ASTERISKS) WERE USED TO TRAIN THE NETWORK, THE 15 TEST PERCEPTIONS (BOXES) WERE USED TO DETERMINE THE CORRESPONDENCE BE-TWEEN VIRTUAL AND CARTESIAN CO-ORDINATES. DIMENSIONS ARE IN UNITS OF 2.5 MM.

Mechanism The fundamental idea here is to associate perception (the camera image) with location (the virtual co-ordinate). However, before the raw camera image can be used for that purpose, some preprocessing has to be done.

The omnidirectional camera used an upward looking camera and a conical mirror to produce a 360-degree image (this setup is shown in figure 5.46).

Obviously, if the robot rotates, the image rotates similarly, which is a problem if one specific location is to be associated with exactly one perception, and one virtual co-ordinate.

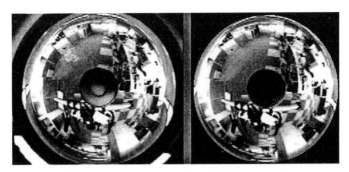

FIG. 5.45. IMAGE PREPROCESSING I. THE IMAGE ON THE LEFT SHOWS RAW DATA OBTAINED FROM THE ROBOT'S OMNIDIRECTIONAL CCD CAMERA, THE IMAGE ON THE RIGHT SHOWS THE PROCESSED IMAGE, WITH IRRELEVANT DATA BEING REPLACED BY ZEROS (SHOWN BLACK IN THE IMAGE).

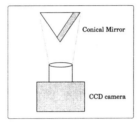

FIG. 5.46. AN OMNIDIRECTIONAL CCD CAMERA, USING AN UPWARD LOOKING CAMERA AND A CONICAL MIRROR

In order to remove the orientation dependency of the images, we segmented the image into 90 concentric rings (see figure 5.47), and used the power H of the image along each concentric ring, according to equation 5.3.

$$H = \sum_j^N h_j^2 \tag{5.3}$$

with h_j being the grey level value of pixel j of the selected radius, and N the total number of selected pixels along the radius ($N = 314$ in our experiments, irrespective of radius).

This yielded a 90-element long (normalised) input vector per image. Three such power spectra are shown in figure 5.48. One can see that they differ, meaning that the camera perceptions at these three locations differed as well.

Finally, the 90-element input vectors were associated with their logged Cartesian co-ordinates, using a Radial Basis Function network as described on p. 65. The net used 15 input units — one for each landmark to be learned — and two output units for the x and y value of the virtual co-ordinate.

Experimental Results Fifteen images of the data, which were evenly distributed along the robot's trajectory were then used to train the net, by simply making

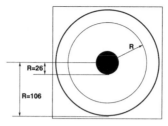

FIG. 5.47. IMAGE PREPROCESSING II. TO REMOVE ORIENTATION DEPENDENCY, THE POWER CONTAINED IN THE IMAGE IS COMPUTED ALONG 90 CONCENTRIC RINGS BETWEEN R=26 AND R=106. ALONG EACH RING GREY LEVEL VALUES ARE TAKEN IN INCREMENTS OF 1.14°, 314 VALUES PER RING.

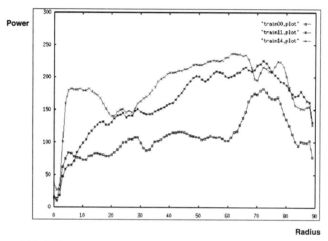

FIG. 5.48. POWER SPECTRA FOR THREE DIFFERENT LANDMARKS

the weights of each of the 15 input units identical to one of the 15 landmarks respectively. Each unit therefore became a detector of a particular landmark.

To test the localisation ability of the net, 15 different locations, which were near, but not identical to the trained locations (see figure 5.44) were presented to the net for localisation. Figure 5.49 shows the actual trajectory taken by the robot (using test data), and the trajectory as it was perceived by the network. The two trajectories coincide closely, indicating that the robot had a good idea of where it was.

Finding Shortcuts These virtual co-ordinates can now be used for global spatial reasoning, for example to determine shortcuts. To determine how accurate the robot would turn towards a location it had never visited along a novel route, we determined the difference between the correct heading and the computed heading, using virtual landmarks, if the robot was to travel between the four positions shown in table 5.2. This heading error in degrees is shown in table 5.3.

The error is very small, meaning that all hypothesised shortcuts were very close to the actual shortest route between two locations. Although the robot had

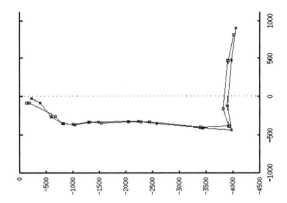

FIG. 5.49. ACTUAL TEST TRAJECTORY TAKEN (ASTERISKS) AND THE TRAJECTORY PERCEIVED IN VIRTUAL CO-ORDINATES (BOXES)

Location	(x,y)
A	-362,-816
B	-362,-2572
C	-122,-3882
D	895,-4050
E	-27,-212

Table 5.2. THE CARTESIAN POSITIONS OF THE FOUR LANDMARKS USED TO DETERMINE THE ROBOT'S ABILITY TO FIND SHORTCUTS (SEE TABLE 5.3). COORDINATES ARE AS SHOWN IN FIGURE 5.49.

	To A	To B	To C	To D
From E	7	2	3	-1
From A		1	0	-1
From B			-3	-4
From C				-2

Table 5.3. DETECTING NOVEL PATHS BETWEEN THE LOCATIONS GIVEN IN TABLE 5.2. THE NUMBERS IN THE TABLE INDICATE THE ERROR IN DEGREES THAT THE ROBOT MAKES, COMPUTING THE REQUIRED HEADINGS USING VIRTUAL CO-ORDINATES RATHER THAN THE POSITION'S TRUE CO-ORDINATES.

never actually traversed these routes, it was able to determine them, based on other knowledge it had gained through exploration.

Case Study 8: Discussion

Localisation Far Away from Known Landmarks The network will *always* generate
virtual co-ordinates from perception, whether the robot is at a known position
or far away from any known place. This is a serious disadvantage, because the
computed virtual co-ordinates may be meaningless. One effective way to address
this problem is to take the actual level of excitation of the strongest responding
RBF unit into account (equation 4.13): if there is no close match (i.e. if the robot
is lost), this output is low and can be used to detect that localisation is weak.

It is interesting to see what happens when the robot is presented with landmarks that are far away from known landmarks (albeit still within visual range
of those known landmarks). We used the seven landmarks given in table 5.4 to
determine the robot's ability to localise and compute route headings outside the
immediate vicinity of known landmarks. Landmarks F to H have been visited
before by the robot, landmarks I to L are away from known locations.

Location	(x,y)
F	-32,181
G	-432,-3932
H	852,-4044
I	-422,-3192
J	-324,-3929
K	194,-3906
L	-351,-1733

Table 5.4. THE TRUE CO-ORDINATES OF THE LANDMARKS USED TO DETERMINE THE ROBOT'S
ABILITY TO FIND SHORTCUTS AWAY FROM KNOWN LOCATIONS. COORDINATES ARE AS SHOWN
IN FIGURE 5.49.

The "far" positions I, J, K and L and their associated virtual co-ordinates
are shown in figure 5.50. The distances of these four positions to the nearest
landmark known to the robot are 50 cm, 61 cm, 72 cm and 27 cm respectively.

Although the discrepancy between true and virtual co-ordinates is larger here
than in the case where test landmarks were close to training landmarks (figure 5.49), the correspondence is nevertheless remarkably good. In all four cases
the virtual co-ordinates are in the "right ballpark", navigating using these virtual
co-ordinates may work in cases where the robot heads off in the indicated direction, and then encounters further familiar landmarks which allow more precise
localisation.

As before, we determined the robot's heading error for novel routes, using the
virtual co-ordinates of the positions shown in table 5.4. These heading errors in
degrees are shown in table 5.5.

These errors show that often path planning is possible with high accuracy,
but that there are also routes where the robot would deviate from the correct
direction by up to 50 degrees. It depends on the situation. However, provided
the robot repeats the path planning process regularly as it moves, there is a good

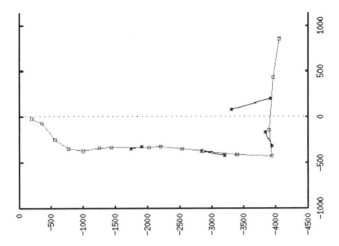

FIG. 5.50. LOCALISATION FAR FROM KNOWN LANDMARKS. BOXES INDICATE THE LOCATIONS OF KNOWN LANDMARKS, AND LINKED ASTERISKS THE TRUE AND VIRTUAL CO-ORDINATES OF LOCATIONS I, J, K AND L (TABLE 5.4).

	To F	To G	To H
From I	-1	-2	-12
From J	5	23	-7
From K	-1	50	-34
From L	0	-1	1

Table 5.5. HEADING ERROR IN DEGREES COMPUTED FOR VARIOUS NOVEL ROUTES BETWEEN THE "FAR" LANDMARKS I, J, K, AND L AND THE KNOWN LANDMARKS F, G AND H.

chance that it can use the landmarks encountered *en route* to get the correct heading with continuously increasing precision.

Shortcuts and the Cognitive Map: Further Reading

- *The Journal of Experimental Biology*, January 1996.
- J. O'Keefe and L. Nadel, *The Hippocampus as a Cognitive Map*, Oxford University Press, Oxford, 1978.
- J. Gould, The Locale Map of Honey Bees: Do Insects Have Cognitive Maps?, *Science*, Vol. 232, 1986.
- Ulrich Nehmzow, Toshihiro Matsui and Hideki Asoh, "Virtual Coordinates": Perception-based Localisation and Spatial Reasoning in Mobile Robots, *Proc. Intelligent Autonomous Systems 5 (IAS 5)*, Sapporo 1998. Reprinted in *Robotics Today*, Vol. 12, No. 3, The Society of Manufacturing Engineers, Dearborn MI, 1999.

Simulation: Modelling Robot-Environment Interaction

Summary. This chapter discusses the relationship between the inter-action of a real robot with its environment, and a numerical model (a simulation) of that interaction. A case study presents a method to achieve high fidelity simulation of one specific robot, interacting with one specific environment.

6.1 Motivation

To conduct experiments with mobile robots can be very time consuming, expensive, and difficult. Because of the complexity of robot-environment interaction, experiments have to be repeated many times to obtain statistically significant results. Robots, being mechanical and electronic machines, do not perform identically in every experiment. Their behaviour sometimes changes dramatically, as some parameter changes. *ALDER*, for instance, had the annoying property of turning slightly to the left when instructed to move straight. However, as battery charge decreased, the robot began to curve to the right! Such hardware-related issues make simulation an attractive alternative.

If it was possible to capture the essential components that govern robot-environment interaction in a mathematical model, predictions regarding the outcome of experiments could be made using a computer, instead of a robot. This is faster, cheaper, and has the additional benefit that simulations can be repeated with precisely defined parameters. This enables the user to identify the influence of single parameters upon performance, something that cannot be done with real robots (because there are never two truly identical situations in the real world).

This is the aim of computer simulations:

> "[To construct a] model which is amenable to manipulations which would be impossible, too expensive or impractical to perform on the entity it portrays. The operation of the model can be studied and, from it, properties concerning the behaviour of the actual system or its subsystem can be inferred." ([Shubik 60, p. 909]).

There are many advantages to simulation, apart from speed, simplicity and low cost. Provided a faithful model can be found, simulation is a means of making predictions of systems that are too complex to analyse (e.g. national economies), or for which there is no data (yet) to perform a rigorous analysis (e.g. space exploration before the first man ever entered space). Simulation allows the controlled modification of parameters, and this modification in turn can lead to a better understanding of the model. Simulations can be used for teaching and training, stimulating interest (e.g. games). "What if" scenarios can be analysed using models, and simulation can give insights into how to best break up a complex system into subcomponents.

6.2 Fundamentals of Computer Simulation

The fundamental idea of simulation is that a *model* is defined of a *system*. Such a system could be a national economy, a factory, or, for that matter, a mobile robot delivering mail in the Computer Science Department at Manchester University. *Input variables* and *output variables* of the system — which could for example be raw materials going into a factory, and products leaving it — are represented through the *exogenous variables*, i.e. the variables that are outside the model, whilst elements of the model are represented by *endogenous variables*, variables that are internal to the model.

The model itself is constructed such that it describes only those aspects that are relevant for the question asked by the user. In mobile robotics, this is a very difficult decision to make, because so little is known about the governing rules of robot-environment interaction. There is always a great risk that the model either misses out some vital aspect, or includes an aspect that is irrelevant.

6.2.1 Models

The first distinction to be made is that between *random* or *stochastic models* and *deterministic models*. A random model approximates the system by using processes based on (pseudo) random numbers. An example would be the model of traffic flow along a motorway, in which the number of cars and their speeds are chosen randomly. A deterministic model, on the other hand, uses deterministic (mathematically defined) relationships between input and output variables. An example would be a model of a bouncing rubber ball, which uses the laws of energy conservation and motion to predict the ball's behaviour.

Then there is the distinction between *analytic solutions* and *numerical solutions* of a model. The former is a mathematically tractable instantiation of the model, using differential and integral calculus, whilst the latter uses numerical approximation methods, such as numerical integration or Newton's algorithm for finding roots of a function, etc.

Finally, a distinction is made between *Monte Carlo methods*, which use random number generators and take no account of a time dimension, and *simulations*, which incorporate a consideration of time. A Monte Carlo simulation, therefore, is a model that takes time into account, and uses random numbers.

Almost all models used in simulations are *discrete*, rather than *continuous*. This is because they are run on a digital computer, which operates in discrete states. In practice this means that the status of a system (for example a robot) performing some task in the real world, that is in continuous time, is sampled at regular intervals, and then modelled. As long as the sampling frequency is twice that of the highest frequency occurring in the physical system, this is not a problem. The difficulty is, however, to know what that highest frequency is!

6.2.2 Validation, Verification, Confirmation and Other Problems

Having constructed a model of a system, for example that of a mobile robot in the corridors of Manchester University, the question is: what can be said about the accuracy of the model's predictions? If the model predicts a collision with a wall, for instance, is this collision definitely going to happen, or is this just a "good guess"?

Oreskes, Shrader-Frechette and Belitz ([Oreskes *et al.* 94]) discuss this problem with respect to modelling soil and surface properties and security assessments for building nuclear power stations in particular locations. If the model proclaims a site to be "safe", how safe is it really? They differentiate between three classifications of a model: verified, validated, and confirmed.

Verification, they state, is the demonstration of truth of a proposition, which can be achieved only for closed systems (systems that are completely known). Given two statement of the form "*p* entails *q*", and "*q*", we infer that "*p*" is true, i.e. verified. Unfortunately, models of physical systems are never closed, because closed systems require input parameters that are incompletely known (simulation literature (e.g. [Kleijnen & Groenendaal 92]) often refers to verification merely as the proof that no programming errors have been made when the model was built. These different usages of the word can be confusing).

Validation is described as "establishment of legitimacy" by [Oreskes *et al.* 94], describing a model that does not contain any detectable flaws and is internally consistent. The term can therefore be usefully applied to generic computer code, but not necessarily to actual models. Whether a model is valid or not depends on the quality and quantity of input parameters. Contrary to co-workers in the field, Oreskes *et al.* maintain that verification and validation are not synonymous.

Finally, a model as a theory or general law can be *confirmed* by observations, if these observations agree with predictions made by that theory. But however many confirming observations there are, neither veracity nor validity of the model can be inferred from them. "If a model fails to reproduce observed data, then we know that the model is faulty in some way, but the reverse is never the case" ([Oreskes *et al.* 94]).

Regarding the modelling of robot-environment interaction, this, unfortunately, means that the best we can hope for is a confirmed model, that is a model whose (preferably large number of) predictions are met by (large numbers of) observations. We cannot establish that the predictions of the model are actually the truth.

Although there are good reasons for simulation — see above — there are also good reasons not to simulate. In some circumstances, to obtain an accurate model can be far more work than to run a robot. And to run the robot will give you "true" answers, whilst running a simulation won't.

There is also the risk of simulating something that isn't a problem in the real world. For example, the situation that two robots meet at crossroads, at exactly the same moment and on collision course, is usually a simulation problem, not one in the real world. In the real world, almost always one of the robots is going to be at the junction first, and will claim the right of way. Deadlock situations such as this one really only occur in simulation.

Here is a second example, showing that simulations can make life harder. A real robot, moving about in the real world, will occasionally shift objects slightly as it circumnavigates them: the environment changes through robot-environment interaction, corners become "smoother", etc. In simulation, this doesn't happen, meaning that a simulated robot will be stuck at a corner, whilst a real one might push the obstacle out of the way.

The greatest risk is that "simulations are doomed to succeed" (Takeo Kanade). Very often, the designer of a simulation system is also the one who uses it to design robot application programs with it. Should he have made some erroneous assumption in designing the model, then there is a good chance he will make the same assumption when using the model. The error will not be exposed, due to lack of independent confirmation.

6.2.3 Example: The Nomad Simulator

FortyTwo has a numerical model, which models some of the parameters that govern the robot's sensory perceptions, and actions ([Nomad 93]). Table 6.1 shows parameters that determine the perception obtained from the simulated sonar and infrared sensors of the model.

The parameters shown in this table indicate which physical properties of the sensors are modelled, and their current values. For example, it is assumed in the model that the sonar burst is a circle segment of 25°. The true beam pattern of a sonar sensor is shown in figure 3.2 — it is not a circle segment, but rather more complicated with main and side lobes.

FortyTwo's model makes a few more simplifying assumptions, for instance, that the incident angle beyond which specular reflections occur is constant. This is synonymous with the assumption that all objects in the simulated environment have the same surface texture (an assumption that doesn't hold in reality). *FortyTwo's* simulation environment is shown in figure 6.1.

Simplifying assumptions can lead to dramatic errors. Figure 6.2 shows the sonar readings of one sensor of *FortyTwo*, as it followed a wall, as well as the predicted readings by the model. When the robot passes a door with a smooth surface (this happens at sample 20), specular reflections create a wrong range

```
[sonar]
firing_rate      = 1     ; 0.004 sec
firing_order     = 1 2 3 4 5 6 7 8 9 10 11 12 13 14 15 16
dist_min         = 60    ; minimum detectable distance is 6.0 in
dist_max         = 2550  ; maximum detectable distance is 255.0 in
halfcone         = 125   ; sonar cone opening is 25 deg
critical         = 600   ; specular reflections start at 60.0 deg
                         ; incident angle
overlap          = 0.2   ; 20% (a segment is visible if
                         ; greater than 0.2x25 deg
error            = 0.2   ; returned range readings are between
                         ; 80% and 120% of true value


[infrared]
calibration      = 0 20 40 60 80 100 120 140 160
                   180 200 220 240 260 280 300 320
                         ; dist. values in inches
                         ; corresponding to the 15 range bins
firing_order     = 1 1 1 1 1 1 1 1 1 1 1 1 1 1 1 1
dependency       = 0     ; 0% (no evening out of readings over time)
halfcone         = 100   ; 10.0 deg simulated beam width
incident         = 0.05  ; error factor for oblique incident angles
error            = 0.1   ; returned range readings are between
                         ; 90% and 110% of true distance
```

Table 6.1. SIMULATION PARAMETERS FOR THE SONAR AND INFRARED MODELS OF *FortyTwo*

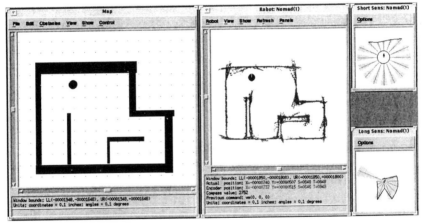

FIG. 6.1. SIMULATION ENVIRONMENT OF *FortyTwo*. THE SIMULATED ENVIRONMENT IS SHOWN ON THE LEFT, THE ROBOT'S PERCEPTION OF IT (SIMULATED SONAR AND INFRARED READINGS) IN THE MIDDLE. THE SMALL WINDOWS ON THE RIGHT SHOW THE CURRENT INFRARED SENSOR SIGNALS (TOP) AND SONAR SENSOR SIGNALS (BOTTOM). USED WITH PERMISSION OF NOMADIC TECHNOLOGIES INC.

reading, which the model is unable to predict, because it assumes uniform surface structure of all objects in the simulated environment.

The strength of the numerical models discussed so far is that they provide a generalised, abstracted description of robot-environment interaction. Such descriptions are compact, and relatively straightforward to analyse.

The weakness of such models, on the other hand, is that they do not describe robot-environment interaction very faithfully. They make simplifying assump-

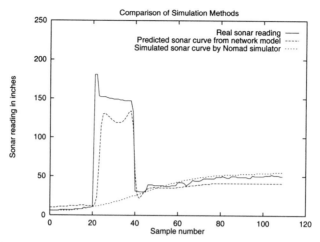

FIG. 6.2. SIMULATION OF SONAR RANGE READINGS DURING WALL FOLLOWING. THE SUDDEN INCREASE AT SAMPLE NUMBER 20 ("REAL SONAR READING") IS DUE TO SPECULAR REFLECTION OFF A WOODEN DOOR. *FortyTwo's* MODEL ("NOMAD SIMULATOR") FAILS TO PREDICT THIS, BECAUSE THE MODEL ASSUMES UNIFORM SURFACE STRUCTURE THROUGHOUT THE ENTIRE ENVIRONMENT.

tions, such as uniform surface structure and surface colour of objects throughout the environment, which leads to sometimes drastic errors (as shown in the example above). Standard numerical models are useful as a "first guess", but cannot make accurate predictions about the behaviour of one specific robot, performing one specific task in one specific environment. The following section will describe how a more faithful simulation can be achieved in that situation.

6.3   Alternatives to Numerical Models

Robot, task and environment have to be considered together. The same robot, performing the same task in a different environment, will behave differently. The same applies to a different robot, performing the same task in the same environment, etc. The conclusion from this fact is that if we want to simulate as faithfully as possible, we have to simulate the interaction of one specific robot with one specific environment.

6.3.1   Example: Wall Following in the Real World

Let's do exactly that now, look at one specific robot performing one specific task in one specific environment: *FortyTwo*, following walls in the robotics laboratory at Manchester. Figure 6.3 shows the actual trajectories taken by *FortyTwo* and its simulation.

There are two possible sources of error in a robot model, that could lead to the observed discrepancies between the behaviour of the real robot, and that of its simulation: the model of the robot's sensors, and the model of the robot's

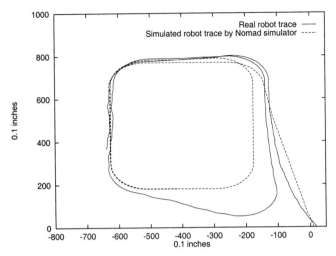

FIG. 6.3. TRAJECTORIES FOLLOWED BY *FortyTwo* AND ITS SIMULATION, BEING CONTROLLED BY THE THE SAME WALL FOLLOWING PROGRAM. THE WALL AT THE BOTTOM HAS A SMOOTHER SURFACE THAN THE OTHER THREE WALLS, RESULTING IN A DISCREPANCY BETWEEN THE TRAJECTORY TAKEN BY THE SIMULATED ROBOT AND THAT BY THE REAL ROBOT.

actuators. One way to find out which is the dominant source of error would be to supply the simulator with real sensor readings , and to run the real robot with simulated sensor readings (if the discrepancies persist, then it is the actuator model that introduces the error). Figure 6.4 shows that in both these cases the trajectories of simulated and real robot coincide.

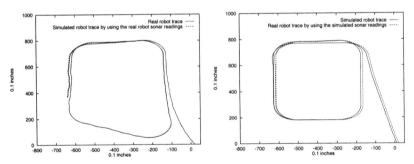

FIG. 6.4. THE TRAJECTORY OF THE SIMULATED ROBOT RESEMBLES THAT OF THE REAL ROBOT IF THE SIMULATED ROBOT'S CONTROLLER IS SUPPLIED WITH SONAR READINGS OBTAINED FROM THE REAL ROBOT (LEFT). LIKEWISE, THE TRAJECTORIES OF THE REAL AND THE SIMULATED ROBOT RESEMBLE ONE ANOTHER IF THE REAL ROBOT'S CONTROLLER IS SUPPLIED WITH SIMULATED SONAR RANGE FINDER DATA (RIGHT).

The conclusion to be drawn from this observation is that it is the model of the *sensors* that introduces the greater error. Consequently, we will focus on faithful *sensor* modelling in the first instance, and stick with a generalised, simple model of the robot's actuators for the time being.

The fundamental idea behind faithful sensor modelling is depicted in figure 6.5: as a sensor (for example a sonar sensor) gives different readings in different locations, the model aims to associate location with sensor reading, based on exploration of the environment and acquisition of the model during that exploration.

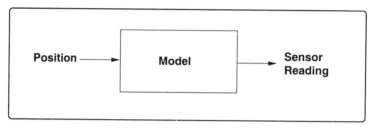

FIG. 6.5. FUNDAMENTAL PRINCIPLE OF MODELLING A SPECIFIC ROBOT'S INTERACTION WITH A SPECIFIC ENVIRONMENT: THE ROBOT EXPLORES THE ENVIRONMENT, AND LEARNS A MODEL THAT ASSOCIATES LOCATION WITH SENSORY PERCEPTION.

It is obviously impossible for the robot to visit every location in the world. If this was possible, and if an unlimited amount of memory was available, one could simply store the sensory perception of every location in a lookup table. However, as this can't be done, the model needs to incorporate an element of generalisation to predict sensory readings for locations that have never been visited before.

Case study 9 will discuss one example of how this can be done.

6.4 Case Study on Simulation of Robot-Environment Interaction

6.4.1 Case Study 9. *FortyTwo*: Autonomous Model Learning

The ninth case study presents a mechanism that can learn location-perception mappings through exploration, and that is able to predict sensor readings for locations that have never been visited. A multi-layer Perceptron is used to achieve this.

The structure of the two-layer network is shown in figure 6.6. It is a multilayer Perceptron that associates the robot's current position in (x, y) co-ordinates with the range reading of the one sonar sensor being modelled. Sixteen networks were used, one for each sonar sensor of *FortyTwo*.

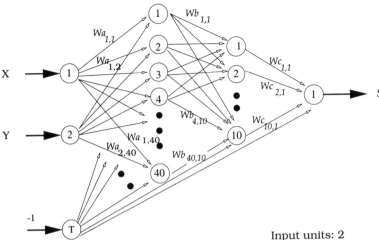

T: Threshold unit

W: Weight

X: Robot's x position in Cartesian system

Y: Robot's y position in Cartesian system

S: Robot's sonar reading

Input units: 2
Output units: 1
First hidden-layer units: 40
Second hidden-layer units: 10
Threshold units: 51
Threshold value: -1
Total weights: 490

FIG. 6.6. THE MULTILAYER PERCEPTRON USED TO SIMULATE A SONAR SENSOR OF *FortyTwo*

6.4.2 Experimental Procedure

To obtain training data, *FortyTwo* was moved through the target environment in a methodical and regular manner, obtaining sonar sensor readings in regular intervals. The (x, y) location as obtained from the robot's odometry and the reading of the sensor were logged for later off-line training of the net. To minimise the error introduced by odometry drift, the robot's wheel encoders were frequently calibrated, and the path of the robot was chosen to be straight, rather than curved, which introduces less odometry error. Figure 6.7 shows two such experimental setups, indicating the paths the robot took for acquiring training data.

The robot was then led along a different, more "interesting" path to collect test data. As can be seen from figure 6.7, training and test paths coincide in only very few points. If the acquired model has any *general* explanatory power about *FortyTwo's* interaction with those two environments at all, it will be revealed when the network's predictions about sensory perception along the test path are compared with the actual sensory perception of the robot.

6.4.3 Results

Predicting Sensory Perception Figure 6.2 shows those predictions versus the actual sensor readings for the test path given in figure 6.7 (top). As can be seen,

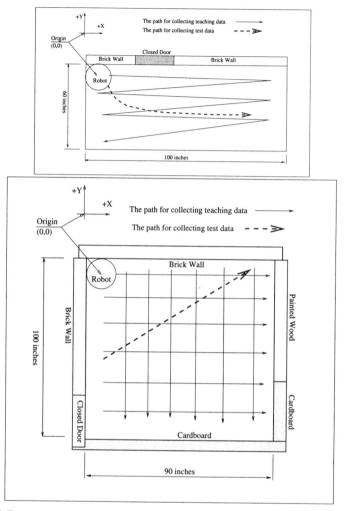

FIG. 6.7. EXPERIMENTAL SETUP FOR DATA ACQUISITION IN TWO DIFFERENT ENVIRONMENTS

the network is able to predict the sudden increase in range reading at sample number 20, which is due to a specular reflection off the smooth wooden door. The result of the simplified numerical model ("Nomad simulator") is shown for comparison.

Likewise, figure 6.8 shows the prediction of sensory perception of the learned model along the test path given in figure 6.7 (bottom).

Again, the acquired model is able to predict the sudden rise in range reading near location (400, -400).

Predicting Robot Behaviour So far, there is an indication that the network model is able to predict *FortyTwo's* sonar sensor readings in the target environment.

Sonar reading in inches

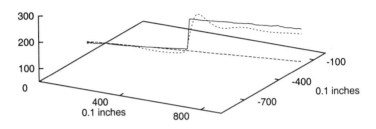

FIG. 6.8. NETWORK RESPONSE TO TEST DATA. THE NOMAD SIMULATOR IS UNABLE TO PREDICT THE SUDDEN INCREASE IN RANGE READING DUE TO SPECULAR REFLECTION, WHILE THE NETWORK SIMULATOR PREDICTS THIS CORRECTLY.

Clearly this is useful, but really we are interested to predict the robot's *behaviour* in that environment, executing a particular control program.

For example, one could take a hardwired control program, i.e. a program that uses a fixed control structure without learning, to achieve a wall following behaviour, and execute that program on the real robot, on its network simulation, and on the simple numerical simulator.

The result is astonishing! Because of the specular reflection off the door in the environment shown in figure 6.7 (top), *FortyTwo* actually crashes into the door, assuming there is more space ahead than there actually is. This is shown in figure 6.9.

Because the simple numerical model assumes a uniform surface structure throughout the environment, it fails to predict that collision ("Nomad simulator" in figure 6.9), whereas the network simulator sees it all coming. Figure 6.9 is one illustration of the fact that we are not necessarily talking about minor differences between the behaviour of a robot and its simulation: these are major discrepancies, leading to qualitatively completely different behaviour!

Let's run another simple hardwired control program, this time in the environment shown in figure 6.7 (bottom). The program now is a "find-freest-space" program, which first takes all 16 sonar readings of the robot, then moves one inch in the direction of the largest reading, then repeats the process until either a distance of 100 inches has been covered, or the robot's infrared sensors detect an obstacle. This is a "critical" program, because even slight deviations will take

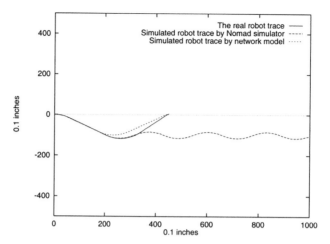

FIG. 6.9. ASSUMING A HOMOGENEOUS WALL SURFACE, THE NOMAD SIMULATOR FAILS TO PREDICT THE COLLISION THAT THE REAL ROBOT ENCOUNTERS, DUE TO SPECULAR REFLECTIONS. THE NETWORK SIMULATOR PREDICTS THE COLLISION CORRECTLY.

the robot into a different area of the environment, resulting in a totally different trajectory. The results are shown in figure 6.10.

In a uniform environment, one would expect that a find-freest-space program would lead the robot towards the geometrical centre of the environment, and make the robot oscillate around that centre. This is precisely what the simple numerical simulator predicts.

However, in real life the robot actually moved towards the edge of the environment, which was predicted quite accurately by the network simulator.

Predicting the Behaviour of a Learning Controller

So far, the control programs we used to predict the robot's behaviour were relatively simple hardwired programs. These programs take sensor readings as inputs, and perform one specific, user-defined action in response.

Two components dominate the robot's behaviour in these experiments: the robot's sensory perception, and the control strategy used. Any simulation error will only affect the robot once when it uses a hardwired control program, i.e. in perception. The control program is user-supplied and fixed, and therefore not affected by simulation error.

If, on the other hand, we used a *learning* controller, any problems due to simulation errors would be exacerbated, in that first the robot would learn a control strategy based on erroneous sensory perceptions, and then it would execute that erroneous control strategy, taking erroneous sensor readings as input. Simulation errors have a double impact in these situations, and experiments with learning controllers could therefore serve very well as a sensitive measure of how faithful the simulator really is.

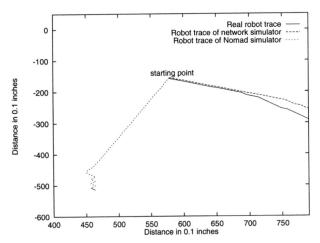

FIG. 6.10. SIMULATED AND REAL ROBOT TRAJECTORIES IN RESPONSE TO THE "FIND FREEST SPACE" PROGRAM. THE SIMPLE NUMERICAL MODEL PREDICTS THAT THE ROBOT WILL MOVE TO THE GEOMETRICAL CENTRE OF THE ROBOT'S ENVIRONMENT, WHICH IS AT (450, -450). THE NETWORK SIMULATOR PREDICTS A TRAJECTORY THAT IS MUCH CLOSER TO THE TRAJECTORY ACTUALLY TAKEN.

Experimental Setup We therefore conducted experiments with an instinct-rule based learning controller similar to the one described in case study 1 (p. 69), using a Pattern Associator. The control strategy, therefore, was encoded in terms of the Pattern Associator's network weights. The objective of the learning process was to acquire a wall following behaviour.

Learning took place in simulation, either in the simple numerical model, or in the trained network model. The weights of the trained networks were then taken and loaded into the Pattern Associator of the real robot to control the robot's movements.

The trajectory of the real robot was then plotted against the trajectory that the respective simulators predicted. These trajectories are shown in figure 6.11.

From figure 6.11 one can see that the network simulator performs better than the simple numerical robot simulator. However, one can also see that our assumption of a more sensitive experiment due to the double impact of any error is true: in comparison with figures 6.9 and 6.10 the predicted and simulated trajectory follow each other less closely here.

6.4.4 Case Study 9: Summary and Conclusions

Ultimately for every robotics research only an experiment with a real robot in its target environment will reveal whether the chosen control strategy works or not.

However, there are various reasons for looking at faithful models of robot-environment interaction:

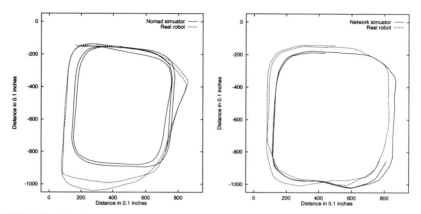

FIG. 6.11. *Left:* THE ROBOT TRACES PREDICTED BY THE NOMAD SIMULATOR AND THE REAL ROBOT USING THE WEIGHTS GENERATED BY THE NOMAD SIMULATOR. *Right:* THE NETWORK PREDICTED ROBOT TRACE IS SIMILAR TO THE REAL ONE USING THE WEIGHTS GENERATED BY THE NETWORK SIMULATOR.

- Low implementation cost.
- High speed.
- The possibility to repeat experiments under controlled conditions.
- The possibility to alter individual parameters in a controlled way.
- The possibility of obtaining a simpler model of robot-environment interaction, that is easier to comprehend and describe.

Experiments show that the largest source of error in simulating robots is in simulating their sensors, rather than simulating their actuators. Case study 9 looked at a method of *acquiring* models of a specific robot's sensory perception, rather than using pre-installed models, and to use the acquired model to predict the robot's behaviour in a target environment.

The results show that such modelling can indeed be achieved, and that an acquired model predicts the ultimate behaviour of the robot much more accurately than a simple numerical model. The downside of the approach taken in case study 9 is, of course, that one can only model a specific robot in a specific environment. I have argued before that sensing and acting are tightly coupled, and that the behaviour of a robot depends as much on the robot itself as it depends on the environment the robot is operating in. Given that premise, it is only logical to model one specific robot in one specific environment, and for faithful simulation we will not be able to avoid this restriction.

6.4.5   Case Study 9: Further Reading

- Ten Min Lee, Ulrich Nehmzow and Roger Hubbold, Mobile Robot Simulation by Means of Acquired Neural Network Models, *Proc. European Simulation Multiconference*, pp. 465-469, Manchester 1998. Available at http://www.cs.man.ac.uk/robotics/Simulation/simulation.html.

7 Analysis of Robot Behaviour

Summary. This chapter discusses the concept of a "science of mobile robotics" and presents methods by which the behaviour of a robot can be analysed quantitatively. Three case studies on quantitative analysis of robot navigation systems conclude the chapter.

7.1 Motivation

Mobile robotics deals with artefacts, i.e. designed machines that are made for a specific purpose. A typical *design process* looks something like this:

1. Build prototype;
2. Analyse behaviour;
3. Identify weaknesses;
4. Modify the original design accordingly;
5. Repeat the process.

Mobile robotics is an emerging new science, and robots are being used increasingly as tools for testing hypotheses about behaviour, reasoning, and intelligent interaction with the real world.

A typical scientific *research process* looks something like this:

1. Identify the question being asked;
2. Form a hypothesis about possible answers;
3. Identify a way of testing the hypothesis;
4. Conduct experiments;
5. Analyse the results;
6. Modify the hypothesis according to your interpretation of the results;
7. Repeat the process.

Both the design process and the scientific research process have one vitally important component in common: *analysis*.

Without analysis of results, all progress in science and design depends on fortuitous random changes, and can be unprincipled and ineffective. Powerful

167

analysis methods are therefore the essential tools for scientific and engineering investigation. This is the first strong motivation for developing methods of analysing robot performance.

There is a second reason. Science is not conducted in solitary confinement. In sciences like biochemistry, for instance, a result is only taken seriously by the research community if it has been replicated independently two or three times. A single publication of an observation, however important this observation appears to be, is not taken as an established fact yet, but as a hypothesis waiting for independent verification.

In order to replicate experiments, they need to be described accurately, with all relevant experimental parameters clearly identified, and stated unambiguously so that someone else can conduct the same experiment.

This is the second motivation for analysing robot behaviour quantitatively: the method of description is the tool that allows precise description of experiments, and thus independent replication.

The science of mobile robotics is relatively young. The majority of research results published in mobile robotics journals deals with "original" experiments, rather than with verification of other scientists' results. There is no culture yet in the mobile robotics community of verifying experimental observations independently.

There are several reasons for this fact. First, today's robots still differ so much from one another, that a comparison between them is very hard. The same is true for the environments in which the robots operate.

We said earlier in this book that the interaction of robot and environment is a close-knit relationship, which demands analysis of the entire robot-environment system. One way forward, therefore, is to develop models of robot-environment interaction. One such model was presented in chapter 6.

Secondly, we still lack the terminology to express the behaviour of our robots, as well as the characteristics of the environment in which they operate *precisely*. "Office-type environment", for example, is a qualitative description that does not facilitate precise independent replication of experiments.

There are two ways to address this problem. First of all, the community could agree on very simple standard environments, tasks and robots, so that identical conditions can be achieved ("benchmarks"). This approach is feasible, and occasionally used, but there are many problems with it: the environments tend to be so simplified that the robot's performance bears little relevance to a robot's behaviour in a realistic application scenario. Furthermore, benchmarks tend to focus people's research efforts so much that optimised behaviour for the specific benchmark in question is achieved, with little benefit for other applications.

A second way of addressing the "analysis terminology problem" is to, well, develop that missing analysis terminology ([Smithers 95], [Bicho & Schöner 97] and [Lemon & Nehmzow 98] provide examples). This is a slow process. However, as more scientists become interested in the problem of robot behaviour analysis, more and more methods of quantitative assessment of behaviour will become available, and be used for assessment of experimental results, as well as their independent replication.

This chapter will, first of all, present some mathematical tools to describe robot-environment interaction quantitatively. It concludes with three case studies of robot behaviour assessment. Other methods are conceivable, and the methods discussed here are not applicable to all mobile robot applications — the purpose of the case studies is to give examples, and pointers for more research.

7.2 Statistical Analysis of Robot Behaviour

Because of the complex interaction between robot and environment, governed by a multitude of factors, many of which are even unknown to us, no two experiments with robots are ever going to be identical. To make quantitative statements about robot behaviour we need to conduct experiments many times, and analyse the results using statistics.

The purpose of the following sections is to introduce some basic concepts of statistics that are useful to robotics. For a detailed introduction to statistics, see statistics textbooks like [Sachs 82].

7.2.1 Normal Distribution

Error Any measurement is subject to some error, which is usually "normal distributed" around a centre value, the "mean". The probability density of this normal distribution (also known as Gaussian distribution), $p(x)$, shown in figure 7.1, is defined by equation 7.1. In equation 7.1, μ denotes the mean value (equation 7.3), and σ the standard deviation (equation 7.4).

$$p(x) = \frac{1}{\sigma\sqrt{2\pi}} e^{\frac{-(x-\mu)^2}{2\sigma^2}} \qquad (7.1)$$

Each individual measurement is subject to an *absolute error* ϵ. This is given by equation 7.2.

$$\epsilon = a - x , \qquad (7.2)$$

with a being the measured value, and x the true (unknown) value.

Mean and Standard Deviation When a series of measurements of the same entity is conducted, the measurements will normally be distributed as shown in figure 7.1.

Assuming this normal distribution of errors, we can determine the expected value of our measurement – the mean μ – by using equation 7.3.

$$\mu = \frac{1}{n} \sum_{i=1}^{n} x_i \qquad (7.3)$$

where x_i is one individual measurement from the series of measurements, and n is the total number of measurements.

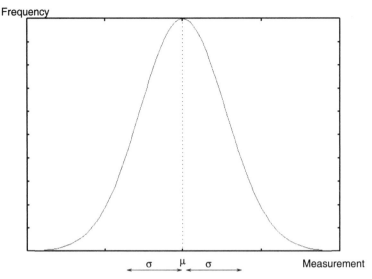

FIG. 7.1. NORMAL DISTRIBUTION. VALUES ARE CENTRED AROUND THE MEAN μ, WITH OUT-LIERS BECOMING LESS FREQUENT THE FURTHER FROM THE MEAN THEY ARE. 68.3% OF ALL MEASUREMENTS ARE IN THE INTERVAL $\mu \pm \sigma$.

Now that we have determined an expected value, we can also determine a mean error of the individual measurement. The mean error of the individual measurement is called *standard deviation*. It describes the mean deviation of the individual measurement from the mean of all measurements (equation 7.3). The standard deviation σ is defined as

$$\sigma = \sqrt{\frac{1}{n-1}\sum_{i=1}^{n}(x_i - \mu)^2} \, . \tag{7.4}$$

In a normal (Gaussian) distribution 68.3% of all measurements are in an interval of $\mu \pm \sigma$, 95.4% of all measurements are within $\mu \pm 2\sigma$, and 99.7% are within $\mu \pm 3\sigma$.

Increasing the number of measurements will improve our estimate of the mean μ, but not that of the standard deviation σ, the mean error of the individual measurement. This is because the accuracy of the individual measurement cannot be increased by increasing the number of measurements taken.

Example A robot's ability to track a light source is to be measured. The robot is equipped with a number of light sensors, and uses these to face the light source as accurately as possible.

The experiment is conducted as follows: the light source is moved to a fixed position, and the experimenter waits until the robot has stopped. The angular difference between true direction to the light source and the robot's vertical axis is then measured. After this measurement, the light source is moved again.

The following angular differences α are measured (nine measurements is a rather small sample, it is chosen here for the sake of simplicity):

Measurement No.	1	2	3	4	5	6	7	8	9
Difference α	-0.2	1.8	0.3	-2.1	-0.1	1.3	-0.7	0.8	-1.2

What is the expected angular difference, and what is the interval within which 68.3% of all measurements are?

Answer: using equation 7.3, we determine the mean as $\mu = -0.011$, and equation 7.4 yields $\sigma = 1.227$. This means that 68.3% of all measurements will lie in the interval -0.011 ± 1.227.

Standard Error The mean (equation 7.3) is also subject to error. We can determine the mean error of the mean $\overline{\sigma}$ as

$$\overline{\sigma} = \frac{\sigma}{\sqrt{n}} \ . \tag{7.5}$$

This *standard error* $\overline{\sigma}$ is a measure for the uncertainty of the mean, and $\mu \pm \overline{\sigma}$ denotes that interval within which the true mean lies with a certainty of 68.3%, $\mu \pm 2\overline{\sigma}$ the interval within the true mean lies with a certainty of 95.4% and $\mu \pm 3\overline{\sigma}$ is the 99.7% confidence interval.

As the number of measurements increases the standard error $\overline{\sigma}$ decreases. This means that the deviation of the mean μ from the true mean also decreases. However, as the standard error is proportional to the mean error of the individual measurement (equation 7.4) and inversely proportional to $\sqrt{n}$, it is not useful to increase the number of measurements arbitrarily to reduce uncertainty. If we want to reduce the measuring error, it is better to increase the measuring precision.

Exercise 4: Mean and Standard Deviation A robot is stationary in front of an obstacle, and obtains the following range readings from its sonar sensors (in cm): 60, 58, 58, 61, 63, 62, 60, 60, 59, 60, 62, 58.

What are the mean distance measured, and the standard deviation? Indicate the interval within which the true mean lies, and state the confidence of that measure. (Answers can be found in appendix 3.1 on p. 222).

7.2.2 Binomial Distribution

The binomial distribution is applicable to problems with the following underlying procedure: An experiment, whose outcome is either the event A or not the event A (e.g. giving a correct or incorrect answer to a classification question), is repeated n times. The experiments are independent from each other, meaning that the outcome of one experiment does not influence the outcome of subsequent experiments. The probability for A to happen is p, the probability for it not to happen is q. Obviously, $q = 1 - p$. Let X^n be the number of times A has happened in n experiments. Obviously, X^n will be a number between 0 and n.

The probability p_k^n that in n experiments event A happens k times (k lies between 0 and n) is given by equation 7.6.

$$p_k^n =: p(X^n = k) = \binom{n}{k} p^k q^{n-k} = \frac{n!}{(n-k)!k!} p^k q^{n-k}, \ k = 0, 1, \ldots n \ .$$

$$(7.6)$$

Example A robot has been programmed to go through a doorway. The probability p of the robot failing to go through the door has been determined through repeated experiments as $p = 0.03$. What is the probability that there will be one failure in 10 experiments?

Answer: Using equation 7.6, we can determine the probability as follows:
$p_1^{10} = \frac{10!}{(10-1)!1!} 0.03^1 (1 - 0.03)^{10-1} = 0.228$.

Mean, Standard Deviation and Standard Error
of the Binomial Distribution If the number n of experiments is sufficiently large (this is generally the case when $np > 4$ and $n(1 - p) > 4$) the mean μ_b and standard deviation σ_b of the binomial distribution can be determined by equations 7.7 and 7.8 respectively.

$$\mu_b = np \ . \tag{7.7}$$

$$\sigma_b = \sqrt{npq} = \sqrt{np(1 - p)} \ . \tag{7.8}$$

The mean μ_b indicates the expected number of times that event A happens in n experiments. The standard deviation σ_b indicates the spread of the distribution.

The standard error $\overline{\sigma}_b$ of the binomial distribution, i.e. the mean error of the mean, is defined similarly to the standard error of the normal distribution (equation 7.5), and given in equation 7.9.

$$\overline{\sigma}_b = \frac{\sigma_b}{\sqrt{n}} = \frac{\sqrt{np(1 - p)}}{\sqrt{n}} = \sqrt{p(1 - p)} \ . \tag{7.9}$$

Exercise 5: Application to Classification A mobile robot has been equipped with a fixed algorithm to detect doorways, using an on-board CCD camera. The probability of this system producing a correct answer is the same for each image.

The system is initially tested using 750 images, half of which contain a doorway, and half of which don't. The algorithm produces correct answers in 620 cases.

In a second series of experiments, 20 images are presented to the robot. What is the probability that there will be two classification errors, and which number of errors is to be expected in classifying those 20 images? (The answer is given in appendix 3.2 on page 222).

Poisson Distribution The Poisson distribution addresses the same underlying problem as the binomial distribution, the only difference being that n, the number of experiments, is very large, and p, the probability that an event A occurs, is very small. In other words, the Poisson distribution is like the binomial distribution for $n \to \infty$ and $p \to 0$. A further assumption is that $np = a$ is constant.

For the Poisson distribution, the probability Ψ_k^n of observing k times event A in n experiments is given by equation 7.10.

$$\Psi_k^n = \frac{a^k e^{-a}}{k!} \, , \tag{7.10}$$

with $np = a$.

The mean μ_p of the Poisson distribution is given by equation 7.11, the standard deviation σ_p by equation 7.12.

$$\mu_p = np = a \, , \tag{7.11}$$

$$\sigma_p = \sqrt{np} = \sqrt{a}. \tag{7.12}$$

7.2.3 Comparing the Means of Two Normal Distributions (T-Test)

It is often useful to have some measure of performance of a particular algorithm, control mechanism, etc. If, for example, two different control programs produced two different means of a particular result, it is necessary to decide whether there is a significant difference between these two means, in order to determine whether one of the two programs produces better results than the other.

The T-test is used to compare two means μ_x and μ_y from normally distributed values, whose standard deviations are (roughly) equal. The null hypothesis H_0 that is to be tested is $\mu_x = \mu_y$.

To establish whether the two means μ_x and μ_y are significantly different, the value T is computed as follows:

$$T = \frac{\mu_x - \mu_y}{\sqrt{(n_1 - 1)\sigma_x^2 + (n_2 - 1)\sigma_y^2}} \sqrt{\frac{n_1 n_2 (n_1 + n_2 - 2)}{n_1 + n_2}} \, , \tag{7.13}$$

with n_1 and n_2 being the number of data points in experiment 1 and experiment 2 respectively, μ_x and σ_x mean and standard deviation of experiment 1, and μ_y and σ_y mean and standard deviation of experiment 2.

The test is conducted as follows: the value of t_α is determined from table 7.1, with $k = n_1 + n_2 - 2$. If the inequality $|T| > t_\alpha$ holds, the null hypothesis H_0 is rejected, meaning that the two means differ significantly. The probability that the outcome of the T-test is wrong, i.e. that it indicates significance when there is none and vice versa, is dependent on the value of t_α. It is common to take take

k	1	2	3	4	5	6	7	8
t_α	12.706	4.303	3.182	2.776	2.571	2.447	2.365	2.306

k	9	10	14	16	18	20	30
t_α	2.262	2.228	2.145	2.12	2.101	2.086	2.042

Table 7.1. T-DISTRIBUTION, $p = 0.05$

the values for the 5% error level (p=0.05), as given in table 7.1, but tables for other error levels can be found in statistics textbooks.

Exercise 6: T-Test A robot control program is written to enable robots to withdraw from dead ends. In a first version of the program, the robot takes the following time in seconds to escape from a dead end:
$x = (10.2, 9.5, 9.7, 12.1, 8.7, 10.3, 9.7, 11.1, 11.7, 9.1)$.

After the program has been improved, a second set of experiments yields these results:
$y = (9.6, 10.1, 8.2, 7.5, 9.3, 8.4)$.

Do these results indicate that the second program performs significantly better? (The answer can be found in appendix 3.3 on p. 223).

7.2.4 Analysis of Categorical Data

Mean, standard deviation, T-test and many other statistical analysis methods can only be applied to continuous-valued data. In robotics experiments, however, there are many experiments in which results are obtained as "categories", for example in classification systems, whose task it is to allocate sensory data to one of several categories. In this section, we will look at methods of analysing such categorical data.

Contingency Tables *Nominal* variables are defined as variables that are members of an unordered set, such as for example "colour" or "taste". It is nominal variables that we consider here.

For the following considerations, we are interested in determining whether two nominal variables are associated or not. This question is relevant for example for classification tasks, where one variable is the input signal, and one the output. In this case, the question asked is "is the output of the classifier associated with the input signals?", in other words, "is the classifier doing a good job?".

Data of two variables can be displayed in a contingency table, which will allow us to perform a so-called crosstabulation analysis. For example, if there was a robot contest, in which three robots compete a number of times in three different disciplines, a contingency table which would state how often each robot won each contest could be built, and crosstabulation analysis could be used to determine whether there was a correlation between robot and discipline. This would establish whether any robot was particularly good at any specific discipline. Figure 7.2 shows the contingency table for this analysis.

	Contest A	Contest B	Contest C	
Robot X	$n_{A,X}$	$n_{B,X}$	$\cdots$	
Robot Y			$\cdots$	
Robot Z	$\cdots$	$\cdots$	$\cdots$	$N_{Z.}$
	$N_{.A}$	$N_{.B}$	$N_{.C}$	N

Table 7.2. EXAMPLE OF A CONTINGENCY TABLE. $n_{A,X}$ IS THE NUMBER OF TIMES ROBOT X WON CONTEST A, $N_{.A}$ THE TOTAL NUMBER OF WINNERS IN CONTEST A, $N_{Z.}$ THE TOTAL NUMBER OF WINS OF ROBOT Z, ETC.

Determining the Association Between two Variables: χ^2 Test One test to determine the significance of an association between two variables is the χ^2 test.

Let N_{ij} be the number of events where the variable x has value i and variable y has value j. Let N be the total number of events. Let $N_{i.}$ be the number of events where x has value i, regardless of y, and $N_{.j}$ the number of events where y has value j, regardless of the value of x.

$$N_{i.} = \sum_j N_{ij} \, ,$$
$$N_{.j} = \sum_i N_{ij} \, ,$$
$$N = \sum_i N_{i.} = \sum_j N_{.j} \, .$$

Deriving the Table of Expected Values The null hypothesis in the χ^2 test is that the two variables x and y have no significant correlation. In order to test this null hypothesis, "expected values" need to be determined, to express what values we expect to obtain if the null hypothesis were true. The expected values can either be derived from general considerations dependent on the application, or from the following reasoning.

In a table such as table 7.2, $\frac{n_{ij}}{N_{.j}}$ is an estimate of the probability that a certain event i happens, given j, i.e. $\frac{n_{ij}}{N_{.j}} = p(i|j)$. If the null hypothesis were true, the probability for a particular value of i, given a particular value of i should be exactly the same as the probability of that value of i regardless of j, i.e. $\frac{n_{ij}}{N_{.j}} = p(i|j) = p(i)$.

It is also true that $p(i) = \frac{N_{i.}}{N}$. Under the assumption that the null hypothesis is true we can therefore conclude:

$$\frac{n_{ij}}{N_{.j}} = \frac{N_{i.}}{N} \, , \tag{7.14}$$

which yields the table of expected values n_{ij}:

$$n_{ij} = \frac{N_{i.} N_{.j}}{N} \, . \tag{7.15}$$

χ^2 is defined in equation 7.16.

$$\chi^2 = \sum_{i,j} \frac{(N_{ij} - n_{ij})^2}{n_{ij}}. \tag{7.16}$$

The computed value for χ^2 (see equation 7.16) in conjunction with the $\chi^2_{0.5}$ probability function (table 7.3) can now be used to determine whether the association between variables i and j is significant or not. For a table of size I by J, the number of degrees of freedom m is

$$m = IJ - I - J + 1. \tag{7.17}$$

If $\chi^2 > \chi^2_{.05}$ (see table 7.3) there is a significant correlation between the variables i and j. The probability for this statement to be wrong is $p = 0.05$.

m	1	2	3	4	5	6	7	8	9	10
$\chi^2_{.05}$	3.8	6.0	7.8	9.5	11.1	12.6	14.1	15.5	16.9	18.3

Table 7.3. TABLE OF $\chi^2_{.05}$ VALUES

If m is greater than 30, significance can be tested by calculating $\sqrt{2\chi^2} - \sqrt{2m - 1}$. If this value exceeds 1.65, there is a significant correlation between i and j.

Practical Considerations Regarding the χ^2 Statistic In order for the χ^2 statistic to be valid, the data needs to be well conditioned. Two rules of thumb determine when this is the case:

1. In the n_{ij} table of expected values, no cell should have values below 1. In cases where $m \geq 8$ and $N \geq 40$ no values must be below 4 ([Sachs 82, p. 321]).
2. In the n_{ij} table of expected values, not more than 5% of all values should be below 5.

If either of the above conditions is violated, rows or columns of the contingency table can be combined to meet the two criteria given above.

Exercise 7: χ^2 Test A mobile robot is placed·in an environment that contains four prominent landmarks, A, B, C and D. The robot's landmark identification program produces four responses, α, β, γ and δ to the sensory stimuli received at these four locations. In an experiment totalling 200 visits to the various landmarks, contingency table 7.4 is obtained (numbers indicate the frequency of a particular map response obtained at a particular location).

Is the output of the classifier significantly associated with the location the robot is at? (The answer can be found in appendix 4.1 on p. 223).

	α	β	γ	δ	
A	19	10	8	3	$N_{A.} = 40$
B	7	40	9	4	$N_{B.} = 60$
C	8	20	23	19	$N_{C.} = 70$
D	0	8	12	10	$N_{D.} = 30$
	$N_{.\alpha} = 34$	$N_{.\beta} = 78$	$N_{.\gamma} = 52$	$N_{.\delta} = 36$	N=200

Table 7.4. CONTINGENCY TABLE OBTAINED FOR LANDMARK-IDENTIFICATION PROGRAM

Determining the Strength of an Association: Cramer's V The χ^2 test is a very general test in statistics, and as such has limited expressive power. In fact, provided the number of samples contained in a contingency table is large enough, the test will always indicate a significant correlation between the variables. This has to do with the "power" of the test, which will amplify even small correlations beyond the "significance" level, provided enough samples are available.

For this reason, it is better to re-parametrise χ^2 so that it becomes independent from the sample size. This will allow to assess the strength of an association, and to compare contingency tables with one another.

Cramer's V (or Phi Statistic) re-parametrises χ^2 to the interval $0 \leq V \leq 1$. $V = 0$ means that there exists no association between x and y, $V = 1$ means perfect association. V is given by equation 7.18,

$$V = \sqrt{\frac{\chi^2}{N min(I - 1, J - 1)}} , \qquad (7.18)$$

with N being the total number of samples in the contingency table of size $I \times J$, and $min(I - 1, J - 1)$ being the minimum of $I - 1$ and $J - 1$.

Exercise 8: Cramer's V Two different map-building paradigms are to be compared. Paradigm A yields a contingency table as given in table 7.5, paradigm B produces the table shown in figure 7.6. The question is: which of the two mechanisms produces a map with a stronger correlation between robot location and map response? (The answer is given in appendix 4.2 on p. 224).

	α	β	γ	δ	
A	29	13	5	7	$N_{A.} = 54$
B	18	4	27	3	$N_{B.} = 52$
C	8	32	6	10	$N_{C.} = 56$
D	2	7	18	25	$N_{D.} = 52$
	$N_{.\alpha} = 57$	$N_{.\beta} = 56$	$N_{.\gamma} = 56$	$N_{.\delta} = 45$	N=214

Table 7.5. RESULTS OF MAP-BUILDING MECHANISM 1

	α	β	γ	δ	ϵ	
A	40	18	20	5	7	$N_{A.} = 90$
B	11	20	35	10	3	$N_{B.} = 79$
C	5	16	10	39	5	$N_{C.} = 75$
D	2	42	16	18	9	$N_{D.} = 87$
E	6	11	21	9	38	$N_{D.} = 85$
	$N_{.\alpha} = 64$	$N_{.\beta} = 107$	$N_{.\gamma} = 102$	$N_{.\delta} = 81$	$N_{.\epsilon} = 62$	N=416

Table 7.6. RESULTS OF MAP-BUILDING MECHANISM 2

Determining the Strength of Association Using Entropy-Based Measures

The χ^2 analysis and Cramer's V allow us to determine whether or not there is a significant association between rows and columns of a contingency table.

However, what we would also like is some measure of the *strength* of the association. Two quantitative measures of the strength of an association will therefore be discussed below.

The particular scenario we have in mind here is this: a mobile robot explores its environment, constructs a map, and uses this map subsequently for localisation.

Whenever the robot is at some physical location L, therefore, its localisation system will generate a particular response R, indicating the robot's assumed position in the world. In a perfect localisation system, the association between L and R will be very strong, in a localisation system based on random guesswork the strength of the association between L and R will be non-existent, zero.

Entropy based measures, in particular the entropy H and the uncertainty coefficient U, can be used to measure the strength of this association. They are defined as follows.

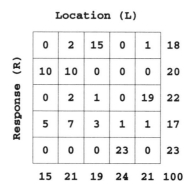

FIG. 7.2. EXAMPLE CONTINGENCY TABLE. THE ROWS CORRESPOND TO THE RESPONSE PRODUCED BY THE PARTICULAR LOCALISATION SYSTEM UNDER INVESTIGATION, AND THE COLUMNS TO THE "TRUE" LOCATION OF THE ROBOT AS MEASURED BY AN OBSERVER. THIS TABLE REPRESENTS 100 DATA POINTS, AND ALSO SHOWS THE TOTALS FOR EACH ROW AND COLUMN.

Using Entropy In the example given in figure 7.2, a sample consisting of 100 data points has been collected. Each data point has two attributes; one corresponding to the location predicted by the robot (the robot's *response*, R), and the other to the actual location of the robot measured by an observer (the robot's *true location*, L). For example, figure 7.2 shows one cell containing 19 data points where the robot's response was measured as row 3 and the location as column 5.

For contingency table analysis, first of all the row totals $N_{r.}$ for each response r , column totals $N_{.l}$ for each location l and the table total N are calculated according to equations 7.19, 7.20 and 7.21 respectively. N_{rl} is the number of data points contained in the cell at row r and column l.

$$N_{r.} = \sum_l N_{rl}, \tag{7.19}$$

$$N_{.l} = \sum_r N_{rl}, \tag{7.20}$$

$$N = \sum_{r,l} N_{rl}. \tag{7.21}$$

The row probability $p_{r.}$, column probability $p_{.l}$ and cell probability p_{rl} can then be calculated according to equations 7.22, 7.23 and 7.24.

$$p_{r.} = \frac{N_{r.}}{N}, \tag{7.22}$$

$$p_{.l} = \frac{N_{.l}}{N}, \tag{7.23}$$

$$p_{rl} = \frac{N_{rl}}{N}. \tag{7.24}$$

The entropy of L, $H(L)$, the entropy of R, $H(R)$ and the mutual entropy of L and R, $H(L, R)$ are given by equations 7.25, 7.26 and 7.27 respectively.

$$H(L) = -\sum_l p_{.l} \ln p_{.l}, \tag{7.25}$$

$$H(R) = -\sum_r p_{r.} \ln p_{r.}, \tag{7.26}$$

$$H(L, R) = -\sum_{r,l} p_{rl} \ln p_{rl}. \tag{7.27}$$

When applying equations 7.25, 7.26 and 7.27, bear in mind that $\lim_{p \to 0} p \ln p = 0$.

For the scenario described above, the most important question we would like to have an answer for is this: "Given a particular response R of the robot's localisation system, how certain can we be about the robot's current location L?" This is the entropy of L given R, $H(L \mid R)$. If, on the other hand, one particular location elicits different responses $R1$ and $R2$ on different visits, we don't care.

The important point for robot self-localisation is that each response R is strongly associated with exactly one location L.

$H(L \mid R)$ is obtained as follows:

$$H(L \mid R) = H(L, R) - H(R), \qquad (7.28)$$

where

$$0 \leq H(L \mid R) \leq H(L). \qquad (7.29)$$

This last property (equation 7.29) means that the range of values for $H(L \mid R)$ will be dependent on the size of the environment, because $H(L)$ increases as the number of location bins increases.

Using the Uncertainty Coefficient The entropy H is a number between 0 and $ln\ N$, where N is the number of data points. If H is 0, the association between L and R is perfect, i.e. each response R indicates exactly one location L in the world. The larger H becomes, the weaker is the association between L and R.

The uncertainty coefficient U provides yet another way of expressing the strength between row and column variables in a contingency table, and it has two very attractive properties: first of all, U always lies between 0 and 1, irrespective of the size of the contingency table. This allows comparisons between tables of different size. Secondly, the uncertainty coefficient is 0 for a nonexistent association, and 1 for a perfect association. This is intuitively the "right" way round (the stronger the association, the larger the number).

The uncertainty coefficient U of L given R, $U(L \mid R)$, is given as

$$U(L \mid R) \equiv \frac{H(L) - H(L \mid R)}{H(L)}. \qquad (7.30)$$

A value of $U(L \mid R) = 0$ means that R provides no useful information about L, and implies that the robot's response never predicts its true location. A value of $U(L \mid R) = 1$ means that R provides all the information required about L, and implies that the response always predicts the true location. It should also be noted that the ordering of the rows and columns in the contingency table makes no difference to the outcome of this calculation.

Exercise 9: Uncertainty Coefficient A robot localisation system produces the responses shown in figure 7.2. Is there a statistically significant correlation between the system's response, and the robot's location?

The answer is given in appendix 4.3 on p. 225.

7.2.5 Further Reading

- Edward Batschelet, *Circular Statistics in Biology*, Academic Press, New York, 1981.

- J.H. Zar, *Biostatistical Analysis*, Prentice Hall, New Jersey, 1984.
- Lothar Sachs, *Applied Statistics*, 2nd edition, Springer Verlag, Berlin, Heidelberg, New York, 1984.
- W. Press, S. Teukolsky, W. Vetterling and B. Flannery, *Numerical Recipes in C*, Cambridge University Press, Cambridge UK, 1992.

7.3 Case Studies of Performance Evaluation and Analysis

7.3.1 Case Study 10. Quantitative Comparison of Map-Building Systems

Case study 10 presents an episodic mapping mechanism used for the self-localisation of autonomous mobile robots, i.e. a mapping mechanism that uses a *sequence* of perceptions. A two-layer self organising neural network classifies perceptual and episodic information to identify "perceptual landmarks" (and thus the robot's position in the world) uniquely.

To assess the performance of the map-building system, a contingency table analysis using the entropy-based measures presented in the previous section is performed, and the episodic map-building system is compared with a static map-building algorithm that uses perceptual information only. The episodic map-building system is shown to perform better than the static paradigm.

Principal Idea For reasons discussed earlier in this book, we would like to anchor the robot's navigation system in exteroception, i.e. in the recognition of landmarks, rather than proprioception. The problem we have to deal with then is perceptual aliasing. One approach to achieve this is to use episodic mapping schemes.

The fundamental principle behind an episodic mapping mechanism is to take into account both the perceptual signature of the robot's current location, as well as a history of the robot's past perceptions. This allows the disambiguation of two locations with identical perceptual signatures, if the perceptions preceding those two locations differ. A localisation system based on this method was discussed in case study 7.

There are two main shortcomings to an episodic mapping mechanism: firstly, it is dependent upon robot motion along a fixed path (or a few fixed paths), because a unique and repeatable sequence of perceptions is required to identify a location. Secondly, localisation is affected by "freak perceptions" for a much longer time than in a navigation system based on one perception only, because the erroneous (freak) perception is retained for n time steps, where n is the number of past perceptions used for localisation. Such freak perceptions do not normally occur in computer simulations, but they occur frequently when a real robot interacts with the real world, because of idiosyncratic sensor properties (e.g. specular reflection of sonar signals), sensor noise, or electronic noise. The episodic mapping algorithm proposed here specifically addresses this question of how to cope with freak perceptions when using an episodic mapping mechanism.

The Static Mapping Mechanism The map-building component used in the static map-building paradigm was a two-dimensional self-organising feature map of $m \times m$ units ($m = 9$ or $m = 12$ in our experiments). The input to the SOFM consisted of the robot's 16 infrared sensor readings. Whenever the robot had moved more than 25 cm, a 16-element input vector to the first layer self-organising feature map was generated. This input vector contained the raw sensor readings from the robot's infrared sensors. The robot's turret maintained a constant orientation throughout the experiment to eliminate any influence of the robot's current orientation at a particular location, resulting in a unique sensory perception at each location, irrespective of the angle at which the robot approached that location. Note that the 16-element input vector does not actually convey much information about the current location of the robot. A coarse input vector such as this was deliberately chosen for these simulations to produce perceptual aliasing — the aim here was to find ways of achieving localisation even under very difficult circumstances.

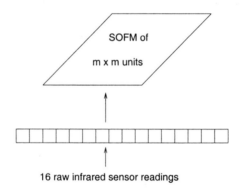

FIG. 7.3. THE STATIC MAPPING MECHANISM: THE SOFM CLUSTERS THE CURRENT SENSORY PERCEPTION AND THUS GENERATES THE STATIC MAPPING

As the robot moved through its environment, controlled by the operator, sensor readings were obtained and input vectors fed into the SOFM. The network clustered these perceptions according to their similarity and frequency of occurrence.

The Episodic Mapping Mechanism The episodic mapping paradigm used two layers of self-organising feature maps (see figure 7.4). Layer 1 was the layer described above.

Layer two was also a two-dimensional SOFM of $k \times k$ units ($k = 9$ or $k = 12$ in our experiments): it was trained using an input vector consisting of m^2 elements. All elements of this vector were set to "0", apart from the τ centres of excitation of layer 1 of the preceding τ time steps: they were set to "1". The value of the parameter τ was varied in our simulations, to determine whether there is an optimal value.

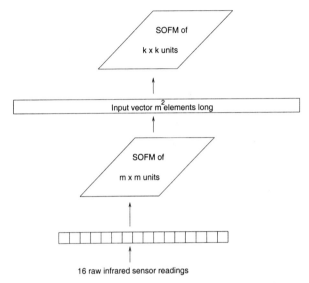

FIG. 7.4. THE EPISODIC MAP-BUILDING MECHANISM: THE FIRST LAYER SOFM CLUSTERS THE CURRENT SENSORY PERCEPTION, THE SECOND LAYER SOFM CLUSTERS THE LAST τ PERCEPTIONS AND THUS GENERATES THE EPISODIC MAPPING

Precedence relationships between these excitation centres are not encoded, as the input vector only contains information regarding the last τ excitation centres, but not the order in which they occurred. This means that the second layer of the dynamic map-builder — the output layer — uses information about the perceptual signature of the current location as well as temporal cues (in this case the robot's path through perceptual space before it arrived at the current location), but no precedence relationships between perceptions.

Resilience to Freak Perceptions The second layer SOFM performs a topological clustering on the last τ excitation centres observed in layer 1. As the output of layer 1 is a topological mapping of all 16 infrared sensor signals, and the output of layer 2 is again a topological map, the response of the episodic mapping system is far less sensitive to freak sensory perceptions than a mapping system that uses episodes of raw sensory data as input. This is a desirable property, because freak sensor signals occur regularly in real robotic systems, and mapping systems dependent on constant and reliable sensory perception would therefore be very brittle.

Quality Measures for Mappings To assess the quality of mappings achieved by the episodic mapping mechanism, and to quantify the influence of individual parameters, we used the entropy-based measure of performance described in section 7.2.4.

Evaluation of Results In general, we used the entropy $H(L \mid R)$ to determine the quality of a mapping: the lower the entropy $H(L \mid R)$, the higher the map quality. A "perfect" map has an entropy $H(L \mid R)$ of 0.

Throughout our experiments two fundamentally different mapping paradigms are compared: the "static mapping", using a single layer self-organising feature map, and the "episodic mapping", using a twin layer self-organising feature map (see section 7.3.1). The question is: does the episodic mapping paradigm produce maps with a better correlation between location and map response than the static mapping algorithm does?

Experimental Procedure The experimental procedure chosen must reflect the objectives of our research, which is threefold:

1. Identify the contribution of individual process parameters to the system's overall performance by altering one at a time under controlled conditions.
2. Compare different mapping paradigms under identical (not just similar) circumstances, so that spurious effects due to differences between experimental situations can be ruled out as causes of different performance.
3. Allow precise repetition of experiments for the validation of results.

These criteria cannot be fulfilled if "live" experimentation with a mobile robot is performed, because the inevitable variations between experiments remain unknown to the experimenter. Live experimentation makes it impossible to attribute the outcome of experiments to the experimental parameter in question — there are too many unobservable influences that affect robot-environment interaction.

One experimental setup that does not suffer from these unobservable influences would be that of using numerical models of robot-environment interaction. Such simulations produce identical results if set up in identical ways. Even if they contain stochastic elements the results they generate are reproducible, provided the random processes are initialised identically.

However, due to the fundamental limitations of computer simulations (see chapter 6), findings obtained through experiments using numerical modelling cannot be applied to mobile robotics directly. Instead, such results would have to be verified using real robot-environment interaction.

The experimental procedure adopted here, therefore, was to use *recorded* sensor data obtained by manually driving *FortyTwo* through the environment, and then to apply the different mapping schemes to the same data. This ensures that the input data to each mapping scheme is *identical* throughout all experiments.

Data was obtained in two different environments (A and B). In both environments, the robot was manually driven along a more or less fixed path, while sensor readings were recorded for later use by the static and by the episodic mapping mechanism.

Experiments in Environment A In the first experiment the robot was manually
driven along a (more or less) fixed path in an environment containing brick walls,
cloth screens and cardboard boxes. The 366 data points obtained in this environment contained the readings of the robot's 16 infrared sensors, and the locations
in (x, y) co-ordinates where readings were taken. The path of the robot and the
robot's perception of the environment are shown in figure 7.5.

Of the 366 data points, 120 were used for the initial training of the networks[1],
i.e. the map-building phase, and the remaining 246 data points were used to
establish the contingency tables.

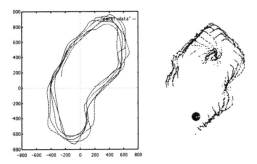

FIG. 7.5. ACTUAL TRAJECTORY TAKEN BY ROBOT IN ENVIRONMENT A, AND ACCUMULATED
INFRARED SENSOR READINGS (ENVIRONMENT A "AS THE ROBOT SEES IT"). DIMENSIONS IN
THE DIAGRAM ARE IN UNITS OF 2.5 MM. MAXIMUM EXTENT OF PATH: 2.87 M × 4.30 M.

To assess the influence of parameters such as the number of previous perceptions, size of the networks, or spatial resolution (bin size), three separate experiments were conducted using the same data. Figures 7.7, 7.8 and 7.9 show the
results obtained. In all experiments, the static mapping results (indicated by the
horizontal line) serve as a comparison, and the case of $\tau = 1$ (i.e. the episodic
mapping mechanism uses only the current perception for localisation) serves as
a control — the case $\tau = 1$ should produce mappings of similar quality to those
obtained in the static paradigm[2].

In the first experiment (figure 7.7) the physical space was partitioned into
15 bins, the 12×12 network of the second layer was partitioned into 16 bins
(see figure 7.6).

The results show that for history τ lengths between 2 and 7 previous perceptions ($1 < \tau < 8$) the episodic mapping mechanism performs better than the
static one. Once history length is too long, no benefits are obtained by considering temporal aspects, in fact including too many past perceptions reduces the
quality of the mapping. Our explanation for this observation is that beyond an

---

[1] The first layer network only was trained with the first 20 data points, the remaining 100 data points
were used to train both nets.

[2] "Similar", not "identical", because the episodic mapping mechanism produces a mapping of a
mapping, whereas the static paradigm maps raw sensor readings. "Similar" means that the episodic
mapping paradigm would be expected to perform neither significantly better nor significantly worse
than the static paradigm, an expectation that was confirmed in the experiments.

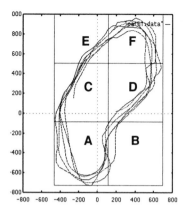
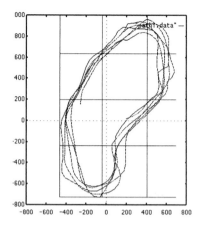
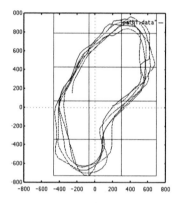

FIG. 7.6. PARTITIONING OF ENVIRONMENT A INTO 6, 12 AND 15 LOCATION BINS RESPECTIVELY. DIMENSIONS ARE GIVEN IN UNITS OF 2.5 MM.

optimal point the inclusion of further episodic information becomes a "confusing" influence due to noise. In other words: it is not sufficient to simply increase sensor resolution or temporal resolution to solve problems of perceptual aliasing.

If the same experiment is conducted, decreasing spatial resolution (i.e. dividing the physical space into larger bins, see figure 7.8), one would expect an increase in overall map quality, because there are fewer opportunities for "getting it wrong". This is indeed the observation: $H(L|R)$ decreases, indicating a stronger correlation between location and map response. Apart from that, experiment 2 shows similar results to experiment 1, indicating that up to a maximum length of $\tau = 7$ the performance of the episodic mapping mechanism is always better than that of the static one.

If both spatial resolution and map resolution are decreased, the episodic mapping mechanism always performs better than the static one (figure 7.9). The explanation for this observation is that the static mapping mechanism is dependent on perceptual resolution alone (if this decreases, the ability to localise decreases

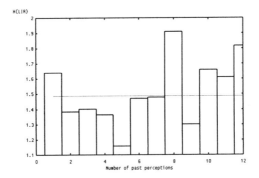

FIG. 7.7. EXPERIMENT 1. RESULTS OBTAINED IN ENVIRONMENT A, USING A 12×12 NET-WORK, PARTITIONED INTO 16 BINS. THE PHYSICAL SPACE OF 2.87M $\times$ 4.30M WAS DIVIDED INTO 15 BINS (SEE FIGURE 7.6). THE SINGLE LAYER NETWORK ACHIEVES H(L|R)=1.49 IN THIS EXPERIMENT (INDICATED BY HORIZONTAL LINE).

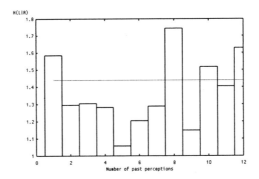

FIG. 7.8. EXPERIMENT 2. RESULTS OBTAINED IN ENVIRONMENT A, USING A 12×12 NET-WORK, PARTITIONED INTO 16 BINS. THE PHYSICAL SPACE OF 2.87M $\times$ 4.30M WAS DIVIDED INTO 12 BINS (SEE FIGURE 7.6). THE SINGLE LAYER NETWORK ACHIEVES H(L|R)=1.44 IN THIS EXPERIMENT (INDICATED BY HORIZONTAL LINE).

as well), whereas the episodic mapping mechanism can accumulate evidence by using past perceptions, and is therefore less affected by the decrease in perceptual resolution.

Experiments in Environment B For a second set of experiments, 456 data points were obtained by manually driving the robot through an environment containing cluttered furniture (desks, chairs), brick walls, and open space. Of these, 160 data points were used for training the networks[3], the remaining 296 data points were used to evaluate localisation performance.

Environment B was less structured than environment A, in that it contained a larger variety of perceptually distinct objects, and more clutter. It was also bigger, and the robot's path in it is longer than in environment A. Figure 7.10

---

[3] The first 20 data points were used for training the first layer network alone.

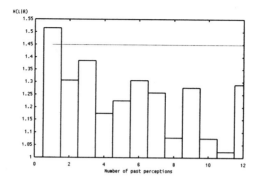

FIG. 7.9. EXPERIMENT 3. RESULTS OBTAINED IN ENVIRONMENT A, USING A 9×9 NETWORK, PARTITIONED INTO 9 BINS. THE PHYSICAL SPACE OF 2.87 M X 4.30 M WAS DIVIDED INTO 6 BINS (SEE FIGURE 7.6). THE SINGLE LAYER NETWORK ACHIEVES H(L|R)=1.45 IN THIS EXPERIMENT (INDICATED BY HORIZONTAL LINE).

shows the robot's path through this environment, and the robot's perception of it.

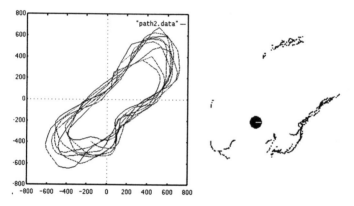

FIG. 7.10. ROBOT TRAJECTORY IN ENVIRONMENT B AND ACCUMULATED INFRARED SENSOR READINGS OBTAINED BY THE ROBOT IN ENVIRONMENT B (ENVIRONMENT B "AS THE ROBOT SEES IT"). DIMENSIONS ARE IN UNITS OF 2.5 MM, MAXIMUM EXTENT OF PATH: 3.37 M $\times$ 3.36 M.

In a first experiment, the output space of the 12×12 map was divided into 16 bins, the physical space was also divided into 16 bins (see figure 7.11).

Results are shown in figure 7.12. As before, the episodic mapping mechanism produces a better mapping than the static one, until a critical value of $\tau = 9$ is reached.

If the spatial resolution is decreased (figure 7.13) the overall map quality increases (as before), and the episodic mapping mechanism outperforms the static mapping mechanism for all values of τ.

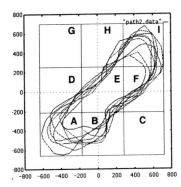 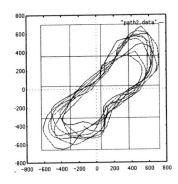

FIG. 7.11. PARTITIONING OF ENVIRONMENT B INTO 9 AND 16 LOCATION BINS RESPECTIVELY. DIMENSIONS ARE GIVEN IN UNITS OF 2.5 MM.

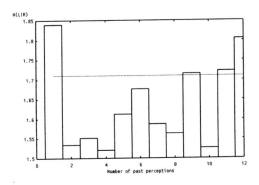

FIG. 7.12. EXPERIMENT 4. RESULTS OBTAINED IN ENVIRONMENT B, USING A 12×12 NET-WORK, PARTITIONED INTO 16 BINS. THE PHYSICAL SPACE OF 3.37 M $\times$ 3.36 M WAS DIVIDED INTO 16 BINS (SEE FIGURE 7.11). THE SINGLE LAYER NETWORK ACHIEVES H(L|R)=1.71 IN THIS EXPERIMENT (INDICATED BY HORIZONTAL LINE).

If both map resolution and spatial resolution are reduced (figure 7.14), the map quality decreases, but the episodic mapping paradigm again generates better maps than the static one, for all values of τ. These observations are similar to those made through the experiments conducted in environment A.

Related Work Related work addresses, on the one hand, implementations of topological map-building mechanisms on mobile robots, on the other hand the quantitative analysis of robot behaviour.

The mapping used here is similar in many ways to hippocampal mappings found in rats. In particular, place cells in the rat's hippocampus can be likened to activity patterns observed in the self-organising feature maps used here. There have been a number of implementations of robot navigation systems that simulate such place cells, notably the work of Burgess, Recce and O'Keefe ([Burgess & O'Keefe 96] and [Burgess *et al.* 93]), but also of others ([Mataric 91] and [Nehmzow & Smithers 91]).

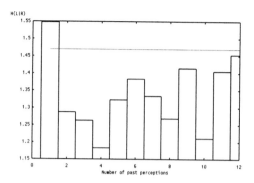

FIG. 7.13. EXPERIMENT 5. RESULTS OBTAINED IN ENVIRONMENT B, USING A 12×12 NET-WORK, PARTITIONED INTO 16 BINS. THE PHYSICAL SPACE OF 3.37 M $\times$ 3.36 M WAS DIVIDED INTO 9 BINS (SEE FIGURE 7.11). THE SINGLE LAYER NETWORK ACHIEVES H(L|R)=1.47 IN THIS EXPERIMENT (INDICATED BY HORIZONTAL LINE).

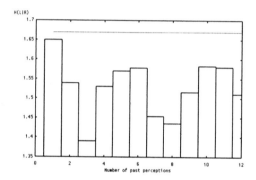

FIG. 7.14. EXPERIMENT 6. RESULTS OBTAINED IN ENVIRONMENT B, USING A 9×9 NET-WORK, PARTITIONED INTO 9 BINS. THE PHYSICAL SPACE OF 3.37 M $\times$ 3.36 M WAS DIVIDED INTO 9 BINS (SEE FIGURE 7.11). THE SINGLE LAYER NETWORK ACHIEVES H(L|R)=1.67 IN THIS EXPERIMENT (INDICATED BY HORIZONTAL LINE).

Self-organising mechanisms for static sensor signal clustering have been used for robot localisation before: see case study 5 and [Kurz 96] and [Zimmer 95], for instance. In these examples, the current sensory perception of a mobile robot is clustered through an unsupervised, self-organising artificial neural network, and the network's excitation pattern is then taken to indicate the robot's current position in perceptual space. If no perceptual aliasing were present, this would then also identify the robot's position in the world unambiguously. Contrary to work discussed here, however, no information about perception over time was encoded in these cases.

Regarding the use of episodic information as input to a self-organising struc-ture, this was also done in case study 5 (p. 116). The work discussed here differs from that approach, in that here we use a second layer Kohonen network that clusters the already clustered sensory information encoded in the first layer net-work, rather than using sequences of raw sensory data.

Regarding the quantitative analysis of robot behaviour, the work of Lee and Recce ([Lee 95]) is probably most relevant to the work presented here: using a quality metric (basically, a comparison between a map acquired by an exploring robot and a "precise" map supplied by the user) they evaluate different exploration strategies for mobile robots.

Case Study 10: Summary and Conclusions

This case study presents a localisation mechanism for autonomous mobile robots that uses spatial *and* episodic information to establish the robot's position in the world. Through a process of unsupervised, self-organising clustering, raw sensory perceptions of the robot are processed in the first stage of the process (static mapping), the last τ perceptions of this first layer are then clustered again to encode episodic information.

An entropy-based quality metric is used to compare the two localisation paradigms, and to determine the influence of individual process parameters upon the final map quality. For a suitably chosen history length τ the episodic mapping performs considerably better than the static one; the observation is that too long a history results in inferior performance.

The method of double topological mapping discussed here has the advantage of being less sensitive to freak sensor signals than an episodic mapping scheme that used raw sensor data. This is advantageous for actual robot localisation, because freak sensor signals are a common occurrence when real robots are used.

There are a number of unanswered questions, subject to future research. We have shown that a maximum useful episode length exists, beyond which episodic mapping produces worse results than static mapping. The information of what constitutes the optimal episode length τ is actually available to the algorithm through the uncertainty coefficient, it is therefore conceivable that the robot could determine the optimal episode length automatically. This may not be too critical a process, as in all experiments we observed that there was a broad range of values for τ that produced better performance than the static mapping mechanism. However, there is no experimental evidence yet that determining τ automatically will actually work in practice.

Also, although we use previous perceptions for the episodic mapping, we do not encode precedence relationships between those perceptions. Whether using this additional information would produce even better mappings again is subject to further research.

Case Study 10: Further Reading

- Ulrich Nehmzow, "Meaning" through Clustering by Self-Organisation of Spatial and Temporal Information. In C.L. Nehaniv (ed.), *Computation for Metaphors, Analogy & Agents*, Lecture Notes in Artificial Intelligence, Vol. 1562, pp. 209-229, Springer Verlag, Berlin, Heidelberg, New York, 1999.

7.3.2   Case Study 11. Assessment and Evaluation of a Route Learning System

Case study 11 analyses the results of experiments carried out with the route learning system discussed in case study 6. A performance metric is defined and used to measure the robot's ability to traverse the route.

Case study 6 presented a route learning system for a mobile robot that was based on self-organisation, used no *a priori* information, and worked in unmodified environments over routes of middle scale distance (beyond the sensor range of a "home" location). Here, we are interested to measure the system's performance quantitatively.

Experimental Setup   Again, *FortyTwo* (see section 3.3) was used in the experiments described here. The route learning system was the one discussed in case study 6 (p. 120).

The route from which the results were taken is shown in figure 7.15. This route is along the corridors of the first floor of the computer building at Manchester University, these corridors present a busy thoroughfare with access to both adjoining buildings and the departmental library.

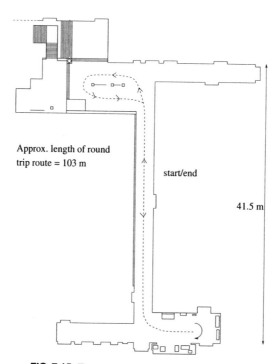

FIG. 7.15. THE ROUTE LEARNED BY THE ROBOT

Figure 7.16 shows a robot trace of the route using the robot's on-board odometry mechanism. The same effect is shown here that we saw earlier in figure 3.9: odometry drift.

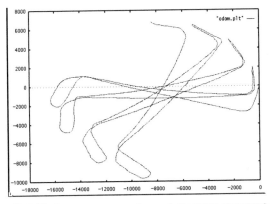

FIG. 7.16. ODOMETRY DRIFT (OVER 4 CIRCUITS OF ROUTE)

Since the system described here makes no use of metric information, there is no need to compensate for the accumulated error.

Experimental Results In our experiments the robot was trained in stages. For each stage the robot was led around the route by the operator for one complete circuit — this represents one training phase or round. At the end of each training round the robot is taken to the start point to traverse the route autonomously. The distance taken between each "failure point" (defined below) along the route is then recorded and the mean distance between failures ($MDBF$) calculated according to equation 7.31:

$$MDBF = \lim_{n \to \infty} \frac{1}{n} \sum_{i=1}^{n} DBF_i, \qquad (7.31)$$

with n being the number of readings taken, and DBF_i being the ith "distance between failure" reading. This metric gives us an indication of the robot's increasing (MDBF increasing) or decreasing (MDBF decreasing) ability to traverse the given route with each training round.

The definition of "failure" in the robot's route-following task is as follows:

- The robot touches an object (or wall);
  or
- The difference between required heading and observed heading is more than 90°.

Once a failure has occurred, the robot is returned to a position on the route just before the point of failure. The robot is then guided further along the route

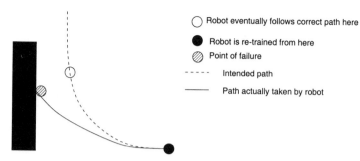

FIG. 7.17. AFTER A 'FAILURE', THE ROBOT IS MANUALLY DRIVEN BACK TO THE POSITION IT OCCUPIED JUST BEFORE THE FAILURE AND GUIDED MANUALLY PAST THE FAILURE POINT. IT RESUMES ITS PATH FROM A POSITION SLIGHTLY AFTER THE POINT OF FAILURE.

until it is able to pick up the route by itself, at which point the next reading commences (see figure 7.17).

In the experiments reported here, we collected 35 distances between failure ($n = 35$) before training the robot once again over a complete round. This figure was chosen as a compromise between the requirements for an expressive measurement and a reasonable time scale for collection of the data (bearing in mind the battery life of the robot). Once the robot was able to complete 15 rounds without a single failure it was deemed to have successfully learned the route and the experiment was terminated[4].

To achieve this, five training rounds were necessary in the environment given in figure 7.15. Figure 7.18 shows the MDBF in metres and the variation interval for each training round; as can be observed from the graph the robot does indeed improve in its route following capability with each successive training round.

Environmental Conditions Training of the robot was carried out in the evening between the hours of 6 pm and 3 am. Table 7.7 shows the number of people moving past the robot during the training and recall phases of the network training session detailed in section 7.3.2.

Training round	no. people passing	
	Training phase	Recall phase
1	3	3
2	2	6
3	2	5
4	4	4
5	2	9
Average	2.6	5.4

Table 7.7. SUMMARY OF ENVIRONMENTAL CONDITIONS

---

[4] Since one complete round of autonomous route following takes approximately 16 minutes, 15 rounds approximates to 4 hours running time - this is approaching the maximum running time for the robot on one set of batteries.

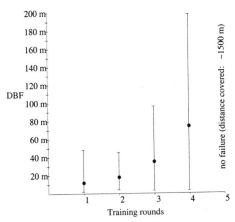

FIG. 7.18. MDBF RESULTS (THE DOT INDICATES THE MEAN, THE BARS INDICATE MINIMUM AND MAXIMUM READINGS)

Daytime Testing A further test was carried out with the fully trained network during the day when the corridors were much busier. In these conditions the robot was unable to complete 15 consecutive rounds without fail and an MDBF of 66.25 m was recorded.

During the course of taking these measurements it was noted that failure was caused by people sitting or standing within the environment rather than simply walking past the robot. This can be explained by the fact that objects in motion cause only temporary fluctuations to the environment and, if they pass quickly enough, the robot is able to re-gain the "correct" perceptual signature for its current location. Stationary people, on the other hand, may occasionally be identified as landmarks and cause confusion to the route follower. If, however, the change to the perceptual signature caused by stationary objects is small, then the generalisation properties of the network ensure that the same node or one of its neighbours will become active, generating correct behaviour despite the disturbance.

Perceptual Aliasing The size of the network used in these experiments was 1600 cells (a two-dimensional grid of 40 × 40 cells). The average number of cells involved in traversing one circuit of the route with the fully trained network was 258, taken over five consecutive circuits of the route[5]. Of these cells an average of 28 were involved in perceptual aliasing, which represents approximately 11% of those 258 cells (we define a cell as being involved in perceptual aliasing if it is repeated at a location, or locations, other than the one at which it was first encountered).

---

[5] The figure of 1600 cells was chosen to ensure a network of sufficient size for the given environment, as can be seen from the results this network was far too large (see below for discussion of this issue).

Roughly   following   Ballard   and   Whitehead's   definitions
([Ballard & Whitehead 92]) we can define two types of perceptual aliasing in
the context of our route following task:

1. Propitious aliasing: $(signatureA = signatureB) \wedge (actionA = actionB)$
2. Destructive aliasing: $(signatureA = signatureB) \wedge (actionA \neq actionB)$

Since the perceptual aliasing measured in our experiments does not interfere
with the robot's route following ability we can classify it as type 1. This type of
perceptual aliasing is obviously desirable in terms of network storage capacity.
An effect similar to destructive aliasing can be observed during the early stages
of training; here locations with signatures that are similar in some way but with
different actions can get confused until the network has been trained sufficiently
at the locations to pick up the differences between the signatures.

An example of this early interference is illustrated in figure 7.19. It was observed that, after the second round of training, some of the locations at which
the robot had performed the correct action for the first round were now failure
points. In the figure location A is an example of a location at which this phenomenon occurred.

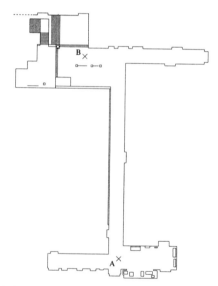

FIG. 7.19. LEARNING EXPERIENCES AT ONE POINT (E.G. B) CAN AFFECT ALREADY LEARNED
BEHAVIOUR AT ANOTHER LOCATION (A IN THIS CASE)

On inspection of the network it was found that the winning nodes for locations
A and B were within the same neighbourhood (i.e. the network had 'identified'
them as the same landmark). The effect of this was that training given at location
B on the second round, there being none required at A, had altered the trajectory
at A sufficiently to cause failure (in effect the nodes in this neighbourhood have
received twice as much training at B as at A). By the end of the third training

round the winning nodes for these locations were not contained within the same neighbourhood, i.e. destructive aliasing no longer occurred.

Case Study 11: Summary and Discussion This case study has analysed the route learning system presented earlier (p. 120). A mobile robot was trained to follow a route of just over 100 m in length and was able to follow it without error 15 times, at which point the experiment was terminated. The system uses perceptual landmarks and a map-building process based on self-organisation. Odometry was not used.

A metric (Mean Distance Between Failures) was introduced and used to measure the robot's route following performance; the results show a clear increase in navigational competence after each subsequent training session.

The route learning system was shown to cope with temporary changes to the environment (moving people). However, permanent changes (stationary people) could cause failure. As the map developed by the robot can be used for prediction of future perceptions, one way to solve this problem would be to detect deviations from expected perception and to use this information to decide an appropriate action.

Network capacity also needs to be considered. In these experiments the network size chosen was far larger than required for the given environment. However, it is not possible to determine, by simply observing the environment, what size of network would be optimal. Rather than using a fixed size of map, a better approach would be for the robot to autonomously determine the approximate size of map required according to the complexity of its surroundings. A rough guide could perhaps be achieved by counting the number of different input vectors gathered on one circuit of the route (difference being defined by a pre-determined similarity measure). An alternative approach might be to use growing networks such as Fritzke's neural gas network [Fritzke 95].

The system as it stands is restricted to following a canonical path (the information contained in the map is similar to "route knowledge" ([O'Keefe 89]) and as such is unsuitable for free navigation. However, the perceptual clustering mechanism can be augmented with relational information such as distance and direction to other locations to facilitate free navigation.

Case Study 11: Further Reading

- C. Owen and U. Nehmzow, Middle Scale Navigation — a Case Study, in N. Sharkey and U. Nehmzow (eds.), Spatial Reasoning in Mobile Robots and Animals, *Technical Report Series*, Report No. UMCS-97-4-1, Department of Computer Science, University of Manchester, Manchester 1997. Available at www.cs.man.ac.uk/cstechrep/titles97.html.

7.3.3   Case Study 12.
Evaluation of a Robot Localisation System

In case study 7 (p. 130) a self-organising system for robot self-localisation was presented. The system hypothesised the robot's current location by accumulating evidence over time ("evidence-based localisation", or EBL for short). In this 12th case study we will analyse this system, and determine how good its ability to localise is.

First of all, in order to assess the system's localisation performance, a performance measure has to be defined. In this case study, we use two methods. The first consists of determining the true position of the robot (for example by observation), and computing the mean difference in metres between the true and the assumed position.

The second method is based on entropy, and computes the strength of association between the robot's physical position in the world, and the localisation system responses obtained at the position. We start with the mean distance error method.

Computing the Mean Localisation Error   For the purpose of computing the mean localisation error, a number of computer simulations and experiments with *FortyTwo* have been carried out. The former are referred to as "simulation", the latter as "experiment" in the remainder of this section.

Simulations were conducted first, because they allow an evaluation under precisely defined and repeatable conditions, and the controlled introduction of specific errors. Experiments are then used to demonstrate that the system would actually serve its final purpose, i.e. to enable a mobile robot to self-localise.

In the experiments conducted with *FortyTwo*, the rotational and translational motors were controlled independently, and the turret left stationary, in order to provide a consistent "compass sense". In other words, the robot explores its environment with its sensors always facing in the same global direction rather than the direction of travel. Thus, the appearance of locations to the robot depends on the robot's position alone, not its orientation.

As discussed in section 5.4.4, the localisation system was implemented as hierarchy of behaviours, as shown in figure 5.35.

Two different exploration behaviours, wall following and wandering (both incorporating obstacle avoidance), were implemented in a Perceptron-like neural network, which was trained using instinct rules (see section 4.4 for details). After training, the controller is completely reactive, directly associating different perceptions from the sonar and infrared sensors with appropriate actions for the translational and rotational motors.

In each experiment or simulation, the localisation error is calculated as the difference between the actual position of the robot and the winning position estimate created by the localisation algorithm. Where two or more hypotheses share the same confidence level, the "worst case" error is taken from the hypothesis, i.e. the hypothesised location which lies furthest from the actual location.

Simulations

Exploration by Wall Following In each of the following simulations, the localisation error was recorded against time over 30 trials, and mean error curves were plotted. In addition, the time and number of iterations through the algorithm taken for the localisation error to fall below a distance threshold D ($D = 25$ cm) was also measured for each trial. A statistical analysis of these results is presented in table 7.8.

Simulated Error Condition	Steps Taken				Time Taken in sec.			
	Mean	Std. Dev.	Min	Max	Mean	Std. Dev.	Min	Max
No Error	3.6	1.1	1	6	169.6	67.7	22.5	313.5
10% Classification Err.	12.4	9.0	3	41	195.3	108.4	58.2	518.3
25% Drift Err	4.0	1.3	1	7	175.2	67.1	26.0	314.3
Both Errors	11.4	6.5	2	31	184.8	121.6	39.9	692.4

Table 7.8. COMPARISON OF LOCALISATION TIMES IN THE WALL FOLLOWING SIMULATIONS. HERE THE LOCALISATION TIME IS RECORDED AS THE TIME TAKEN FOR THE LOCALISATION ERROR TO FALL BELOW THE DISTANCE THRESHOLD D USED IN MAP-BUILDING. SIMILARLY, THE NUMBER OF ITERATIONS THROUGH THE ALGORITHM TAKEN ("STEPS") WERE RECORDED IN EACH TRIAL. THE RESULTS ARE TAKEN OVER THE 30 TRIALS CARRIED OUT FOR EACH SIMULATION.

The times used were taken from the UNIX system clock during the running of the simulation, and are considerably longer than those found on the real robot. The comparatively slow speed of execution was due to the fact that all four simulations described here were run concurrently, using a single simulated robot to provide the sensory input for each of the localisation programs. Thus, all results are based on the same sensor readings taken from the same simulated robot over the same time period, using the same exploration behaviour.

Control: No Errors Added A test environment was built on the simulator, as shown in figures 5.39 and 5.41. This was deliberately designed so that no single place had a unique perceptual signature, a "worst case scenario" for mobile robot localisation. Figure 7.20 shows the resulting localisation error, averaged over 30 trials. It can be seen that after about 250 seconds, the mean error curve falls below 25 cm, the distance threshold D used in the map-building process. Thus it can be seen that the algorithm will always localise to the nearest point in the map when no errors are present in the system.

Another important observation was made here. Referring to figure 5.41, imagine two wall following robots, one starting off around the origin, and the other on the far left of the map. Both would experience the same sequence of changes to the currently perceived ART category as they travelled clockwise around the enclosure, namely "0, 1, 2, 3, 0, 4, 5, 6, 0 ...". If the localisation algorithm really could only succeed after a unique sequence of ART categories had been covered, then it would only be at the next juncture, where the first robot would record a

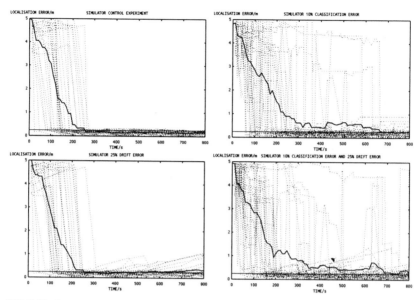

FIG. 7.20. SIMULATED WALL FOLLOWER WITH NO ERRORS ADDED (CONTROL, TOP LEFT), 10% CLASSIFICATION ERROR (TOP RIGHT), 25% DRIFT ERROR (BOTTOM LEFT) AND BOTH 10% CLASSIFICATION ERROR AND 25% DRIFT ERROR (BOTTOM RIGHT). THE THICK LINES SHOW THE MEAN ERROR TAKEN OVER 30 TRIALS. THE DOTTED LINES SHOW THE INDIVIDUAL TRIALS, AND THE HORIZONTAL LINE AT $y = 0.25$ DENOTES THE DISTANCE THRESHOLD D USED DURING MAP-BUILDING.

"4" and the second a "1", that their respective locations could be properly disambiguated. However, the simulation conducted here showed that this was not the case!

In fact, both simulated robots would find a winning location hypothesis emerging somewhere around "0, 1, 2, 3 ...", where the corresponding perceptual regions shown in figure 5.39 vary significantly in size. Thus it is not only the sequence of ART categories perceived which determines the robot's estimated position, but also the *size* of the corresponding regions in the map. Thus the robot continues to accumulate useful information even when no change is detected by the ART network. This aspect was never deliberately "programmed" into the system, rather it emerged from the use of relative odometry for comparing successive hypotheses in the localisation algorithm.

Introducing a Classification Error In a further simulation, a 10% classification error was added to the ART network. Every time the current ART category was sampled, a 1 in 10 chance of misclassification was introduced, where one of the other possible categories was randomly selected. This is a very pessimistic scenario. In practice, the classification error rate is much lower than this on *FortyTwo*.

Results are shown in figure 7.20. Although the downward trend is prevalent once again, the mean error curve takes around 650 seconds to reach the 25 cm level. However, this is a worst case average, taking into account a steadily declining number of "rogue" values, where a bad hypothesis has made a temporary rise in confidence over the eventual winner. The rogue values are gradually suppressed as the best hypothesis picks up enough "momentum" due to the gain term used in the algorithm.

Clearly, the balance between the gain and decay terms used in the algorithm is important here; if the overall gain is too low then the good hypotheses may never emerge, but if it is too high then the rogue hypotheses may take a long time to be overtaken. A separate set of simulations showed that an appropriate level for the gain factor is around $1.5 \leq GAIN \leq 8$, with a decay factor of around $0.6 \leq DECAY \leq 0.8$, given that hypotheses are deleted when their confidence falls below a minimum level $MIN = 0.5$.

Table 7.8 shows that although the mean time taken to localise was only a bit higher than in the control, it took a lot more steps through the algorithm. This is because each time the localiser looks at the current ART category, there is a 1 in 10 chance that a misclassification will trigger another iteration (in fact a 2 in 10 chance, because the algorithm will be triggered again when the correct classification is obtained once more.)

Introducing a Drift Error   Here, an artificial global drift in odometry was deliberately introduced. This was done by integrating the distance travelled by the robot, and then adding the required percentage of this to the absolute odometry readings in a drift direction randomly chosen at the start of each trial.

In a separate set of simulations, it was found that even with a drift error of up to 20%, the performance of the localisation algorithm was almost indistinguishable from the control. Introducing a 25% drift error had some impact on performance, as shown in figure 7.20. Here it can be seen that some of the winning hypothesis became corrupted by drift and took a while to decay before being replaced by another correct hypothesis. The distance threshold D used in the matching part of localisation algorithm becomes critical here; if it is too low the matching process will fail, if it is too high the algorithm will never discriminate between good and bad hypotheses. A value of $2D$, twice the distance threshold used in map-building, was found to be sufficient for normal operation.

However, it should be noted that the resilience to drift error is not particularly surprising given that these simulations have used a "perfect" map and that the algorithm only uses relative odometry. As far as the localiser is concerned, the metric information contained in the map is only used as a rough measure of proximity, so local distortions in the map should not be a problem. A big problem yet to be addressed is how to cope with drift error during map-building, i.e. how to make sure that the map will be globally consistent. For example, with a drift in odometry, the same location could be represented twice because one of the criteria for adding locations to the map is a sufficiently distinct position in Cartesian space to other, already mapped locations. This criterion would obviously be met if locations are indeed distinct, but also if they appear to be distinct due to drift error.

Introducing Both Classification and Drift Error   A fourth simulation revealed a particularly interesting synergy arising from the combination of two different error effects. Both the 10% classification error and the 25% drift error were applied. Figure 7.20 shows both the rogue classification and drift effects discussed previously. However, what is unusual about these results is the relative comparison with the other simulations in table 7.8, particularly against the 10% classification error on its own. It can be seen that adding the drift error actually made the algorithm localise in fewer steps and less time!

This can be explained as follows: the 10% classification error results in rogue hypotheses gaining confidence as described before. Under certain circumstances, they will gain in confidence when the misclassifications (and classifications) of the ART network produce more overall evidence in their favour than against. Given that the evidence accumulation step of the algorithm favours hypotheses which stay within the bounds of the distance threshold D, the rogue hypotheses can therefore expect to be maintained longer if they can keep position during the steps where their confidence is being decreased. Therefore, accurate dead reckoning will actually allow the rogue hypotheses to survive longer than less accurate dead reckoning. Introducing the 25% drift error means that the rogue hypotheses decay faster than in the simulation with 10% classification error, in this case more than offsetting the negative impact of the drift effect.

Apart from this interesting anomaly, figure 7.24 (which gives a comparison of the influence of all introduced errors on the robot's ability to localise) shows that there is little to separate the overall performance of the algorithm in the different simulations, showing a graceful degradation in performance with respect to error. The localisation algorithm is robust with respect to drift error, but this will need to be investigated on a bigger scale to evaluate the problem during map-building. Classification errors do not seem to affect the performance against time too much, but the algorithm has to work harder to achieve this.

Exploration by Wandering In the previous sections, the wall follower was used for exploration. In contrast to this one-dimensional strategy, a variable "two-dimensional" strategy was used here (see figure 7.21), where the same locations may be visited from many different directions. (Maintaining a steady turret orientation made recognition by ART2 possible here, as discussed before.)

Sonar was used for input to the ART2 network, as it was found that much of the space away from the walls of the enclosure contained no features discernible by infrared (an interesting feature of ART2 is that "flatline" patterns, i.e. those with no obvious features detectable above the accepted level of background noise, cannot be classified in any category). Again, no single area of the environment was uniquely defined in perceptual space (see figure 7.22).

The wandering behaviour used was based on learned smooth, continuous obstacle avoidance. To prevent the robot from getting stuck in loops around one part of the environment, random noise was added to the output vector of the neural controller. In addition, to cover different areas of the environment using this exploration strategy, and also to make the behaviour unpredictable, the sensitivity of the obstacle avoiding behaviour was changed at random intervals by adjusting a gain term applied to the rotational "motor neuron". Thus, this simula-

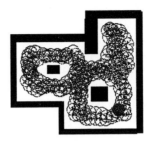

FIG. 7.21. SIMULATOR TEST ENVIRONMENT FOR "TWO-DIMENSIONAL" LOCALISATION. THE TRACE TAKEN FROM THE SIMULATOR SHOWS THAT THE WANDERING ROBOT MAY APPROACH LOCATIONS FROM ARBITRARY DIRECTIONS.

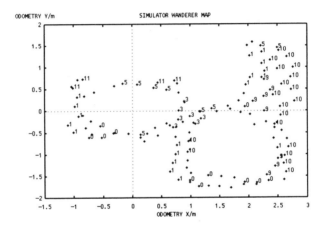

FIG. 7.22. LOCATION POINTS CREATED BY SIMULATED WANDERING ROBOT. FOR CLARITY, NOT ALL OF THE ART CATEGORIES ARE SHOWN HERE.

tion made a good test of the robot's ability to localise without relying on visiting the same sequence of locations each time.

Even with the above extensions, the wandering robot could take a very long time to build a complete map in a small enclosure like the test environment. This is hardly surprising, as the exploration strategy chosen basically relies on blind chance and "the law of averages" to eventually steer the robot towards uncharted areas of the map.

This was also reflected in the results obtained (see figure 7.23). While the robot never failed to localise eventually, it could take a long time before it was able to find a perceptually unique path through the enclosure. The mean number of steps taken was 10.2, but there was a lot of variation around this level (standard deviation 7.5 steps), depending on the luck of the localiser in being party to a good piece of exploration by the wandering behaviour.

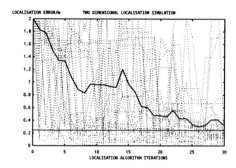

FIG. 7.23. LOCALISATION ERROR FOR WANDERING SIMULATION (MEAN ERROR TAKEN OVER 30 TRIALS)

Despite the limitations discussed above, the wandering simulation does seem to verify the underlying principles of the localisation algorithm, providing a good existence proof of the ability to localise without following a rigid sequence of "landmarks". However, significantly better results were achieved in both map-building and localisation when using the wall follower, indicating a big advantage in exploration using canonical paths over random movement (see also [Nehmzow 95b] for a more detailed discussion of this aspect). In particular, map-building is far more efficient, using much fewer location points in a similar sized area. A map constructed from a single tour of the environment can contain all of the information needed by the lost robot to re-localise using the same exploration strategy. Localisation was also found to be much easier when following the same path as before.

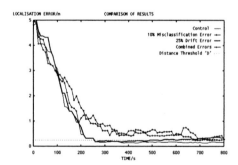

FIG. 7.24. COMPARISON OF THE DIFFERENT WALL FOLLOWING SIMULATIONS. MEAN ERRORS TAKEN OVER 30 TRIALS EACH. AN IDENTICAL WALL FOLLOWING BEHAVIOUR WAS USED THROUGHOUT. THE TIMES TAKEN FROM THE SIMULATOR ARE THE RESULT OF THE SPEED OF THE OPERATING SYSTEM USED, AND SHOULD NOT BE TAKEN AS "REAL TIME"; THEY ARE PROVIDED FOR RELATIVE COMPARISON OF THE RESULTS ONLY.

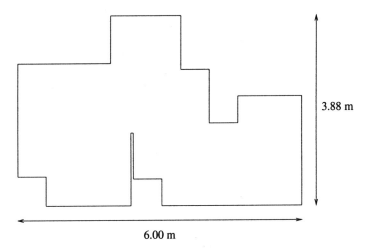

FIG. 7.25. WORLD USED FOR REAL ROBOT TESTS. A CLOCKWISE WALL FOLLOWER WAS USED FOR EXPLORATION, AND THE ROBOT'S INFRARED SENSORS WERE USED FOR INPUT TO THE ART2 NETWORK.

Experiments with a Real Robot   After having completed these simulations, the system was then tested on *FortyTwo* in the Robotics Laboratory at Manchester University. The wall following behaviour was used for exploration, and the ART2 network configured to receive input from the robot's 16 infrared sensors. Map-building was carried out during a single circuit of an enclosure made from walls and boxes, which is shown in figure 7.25. This was purposely designed to contain areas of perceptual aliasing, as shown in the map (figure 7.26). The average forward speed of the robot travelling around this enclosure was $0.10 \, ms^{-1}$.

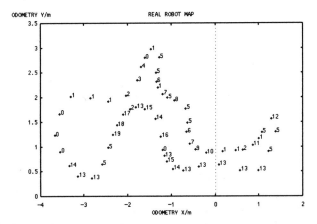

FIG. 7.26. MAP CREATED BY REAL ROBOT. THE LOCATION POINTS FOLLOW THE PATH OF THE WALL FOLLOWING ROBOT AROUND THE ENCLOSURE SHOWN IN FIGURE 7.25.

The algorithm was run for 20 iterations per trial for 30 trials. The results given in figure 7.27 show a steady downward trend in the mean localisation error over time. The "actual" position of the robot had to be taken from global odometry, because no external means of recording *FortyTwo's* real position was available. The results shown will therefore only be as accurate as the drift in odometry will allow.

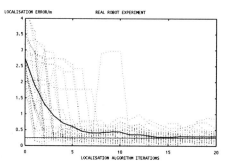

FIG. 7.27. LOCALISATION ERROR ON REAL ROBOT. THE THICK LINE SHOWS THE MEAN ERROR TAKEN OVER 30 TRIALS. THE DOTTED LINES SHOW THE INDIVIDUAL TRIALS, AND THE HORIZONTAL LINE AT $y = 0.25$ DENOTES THE DISTANCE THRESHOLD D USED DURING MAP-BUILDING.

In addition, the time and number of iterations through the algorithm taken for the localisation error to fall below the distance threshold D was measured in each trial. The mean number of steps was 7.0, with a standard deviation of 5.6. The mean time taken was 27.3 seconds, with a standard deviation of 21.9 seconds (the average curve shown in figure 7.27 takes longer than this to reach the D level because this calculation takes into account the worst case localisation errors as explained previously).

Inspection of individual localisation attempts showed that the algorithm was able to localise successfully once the robot had travelled through a unique sequence of perceptions along the perimeter of the enclosure. For example, following the route taken by the robot clockwise in figure 7.26, the sequence "0, 1, 5" of ART2 categories uniquely identifies the point at (-1.3, 2.8). However, the sequence "0, 1" would be ambiguous, because there are two possible places in the route where this occurs.

In the results shown, the localisation error is calculated as the difference between the "actual" position of the robot obtained from the wheel encoders and the winning position estimate created by the localisation algorithm. Where two or more hypotheses share the same confidence level, the error is taken from the hypothesis which lies furthest from the actual location. As the system localises to the stored place in the map which lies closest to the actual position of the robot, the theoretically best possible result should be a localisation error of between 0 and D, the distance threshold used in map-building.

As before, further analysis of the results showed that it is not only the sequence of ART categories perceived which determines the robot's estimated position, but also the *size* of the corresponding regions in Cartesian space (i.e. the number of neighbouring places sharing the same perceptual category). Thus, the robot continues to accumulate useful information even when no change is detected by the ART network. This aspect was never deliberately "programmed" into the system, rather it emerges from the use of relative odometry in the localisation algorithm.

The experiment was also repeated on the robot using an anti clockwise wall following behaviour for re-localisation, rather than the standard clockwise wall follower used for map-building. This showed the same level of performance as before, demonstrating the ability to re-localise independently of a fixed temporal sequence of landmarks as in previous work, e.g. case study 5 on page 110.

Evaluating Performance Using Entropy-Based Measures So far, we have evaluated localisation performance by determining a localisation error in metres, and observing changes to the error as the experiment progresses.

A second method of assessing performance is to use the entropy-based measures introduced in section 7.2.4, which determine the strength of association between the robot's physical position and the internal response of its localisation system.

Using the experimental procedure described above, we can quantify the performance of our localisation system over the distance travelled by the robot. However, for the results to be meaningful, we need to be able to compare the performance of our system (quantitatively) against that of other localisation systems. In these experiments, we therefore decided to compare our system with two "base-line" localisation strategies; localisation using dead-reckoning and localisation using only currently observable landmarks.

Description	Route Location in m	No. of Bins	Trials	Places in EBL Map
A Drinks-machine area	60	24	298	88
B T-shaped hallway	54	14	263	71
C L-shaped corridor	146	40	474	185
D Small empty room	23	8	232	33
E Single corridor	51	14	248	61
F E plus moving people	51	14	249	61

Table 7.9. CHARACTERISATION OF THE SIX DIFFERENT ENVIRONMENTS IN WHICH ENTROPY-BASED PERFORMANCE MEASURES WERE APPLIED TO THE ROBOT'S EVIDENCE-BASED LOCALISATION (EBL) SYSTEM

The experimental procedure described above was repeated in six different environments around Manchester University's Computer Building, which are summarised in table 7.9. In each experiment, the first lap of the recorded robot data was used for map-building if required, and the remaining data was used for testing. In each case, the number of trials was carefully chosen so that each part of the environment was equally represented in the data.

Environments A to E remained unchanged throughout the experiments. To assess the impact of changes in an environment on the different systems, we added moving people to environment E to obtain a "dynamic" environment F. We left this environment unchanged during map-building. However, during the recording of the data used for testing, 29 persons walked past the robot (in-between the robot and the wall it was following in 11 of the cases). A further nine persons stood in the corridor or in doorways as the robot went past, thus adding extra landmarks not present in the map. In addition, on four occasions, fire-doors in the immediate vicinity of the robot were left open for several seconds, thus removing landmarks present in the map (although we were careful not to allow the robot to escape into uncharted territory here).

Uncorrected Dead Reckoning Here, the robot was allowed to use only its raw odometer readings to localise. At the start of each trial, the robot's uncorrected odometry (see figure 3.9) was initialised to the "correct" position and orientation taken from the corrected odometer trace shown in figure 3.11. The recorded robot data was then played back, using dead reckoning to produce (x, y) co-ordinates over time.

To obtain the response R, the (x, y) co-ordinates produced by the dead reckoning strategy were coarse-coded into bins, using the dotted grid shown in figure 3.11. To maintain a finite number of possible responses, whenever the position estimate occupied one of the bins not occupied by the corrected odometer trace, the response was classified as being "outside" the environment and was assigned to a separate bin number for the rest of that trial.

Perceptual Landmarks Only Here, the robot was allowed to use only its current sonar and infrared readings to localise, i.e. currently observable landmarks. In this system, the current sensory input is classified according to its nearest neighbour amongst a set of stored prototypes. Each stored prototype consists of a normalised sonar signature and a normalised infrared signature. Classification is decided by normalising the current sonar and infrared readings, and using equation 7.32 (as in the evidence-based localiser) to determine the nearest neighbour.

$$d_k = ||\vec{S}_c - \vec{S}_k|| + ||\vec{I}_c - \vec{I}_k|| \qquad (7.32)$$

where d_k is the current sensor difference for place k, $\vec{S}_k$ and $\vec{I}_k$ are the normalised sonar and infrared readings respectively for location k, and $\vec{S}_c$ and $\vec{I}_c$ are the normalised current sonar and infrared readings respectively (in these experiments, $D = 0.375\,m$, $T = 1.5$, see table 5.1).

To facilitate direct comparison with the evidence-based localiser, we used exactly the same stored prototypes created by the map-building component of that system. During testing, the output class (i.e. the nearest neighbour) was taken as the robot's response R.

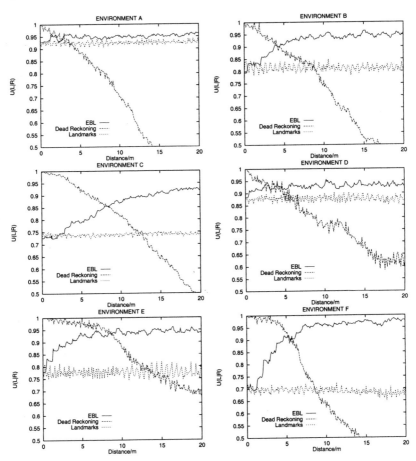

FIG. 7.28. RESULTS IN THE SIX DIFFERENT ENVIRONMENTS. IT IS TRUE FOR ALL ENVIRON-MENTS THAT DEAD RECKONING PERFORMANCE DETERIORATES WITH INCREASING TRAVEL DISTANCE, WHILE EVIDENCE-BASED LOCALISATION (EBL) IMPROVES. LOCALISATION BASED PURELY ON LANDMARK RECOGNITION IS NOT AFFECTED BY DISTANCE TRAVELLED.

	EBL Dist./m for $U(L\mid R) = 0.9$	Landmark Classifier $\overline{U(L\mid R)}$	Landmark Classifier $\overline{H(L\mid R)}$	Dead Reckoning $\overline{U(L\mid R)}$	Dead Reckoning $\overline{H(L\mid R)}$
A	0.0	0.925	0.227	0.663	1.013
B	3.8	0.814	0.487	0.724	0.719
C	13.6	0.739	0.980	0.785	0.807
D	0.5	0.878	0.236	0.786	0.413
E	3.0	0.776	0.585	0.864	0.355
F	4.7	0.690	0.808	0.686	0.819

Table 7.10. SUMMARY OF RESULTS FOR EVIDENCE-BASED LOCALISATION, LOCALISATION BY PERCEPTUAL LANDMARKS, AND LOCALISATION BY UNCORRECTED DEAD RECKONING (CF. FIGURE 7.28). $\overline{U(L\mid R)}$ AND $\overline{H(L\mid R)}$ ARE THE MEAN UNCERTAINTY COEFFICIENTS AND THE MEAN ENTROPIES RESPECTIVELY.

Results As we would expect, the results in figure 7.28 show that the performance of
dead reckoning worsens over time, while the system using only currently observable landmarks performs at a roughly constant level and the performance of the
evidence-based system improves over time. The evidence-based localiser took
longer to localise in the dynamic environment, but still eventually achieved the
same overall level of performance. The performance of both the landmark-based
localiser and dead reckoning worsened in the dynamic environment (avoiding
the people meant more turns, and thus more accumulated rotational drift in the
robot's odometry).

The measures obtained in the different experiments are also summarised in
table 7.10. Here, the mean values of $U(L \mid R)$ (equation 7.30) for the landmark-
based system and dead reckoning reflect respectively the overall levels of perceptual aliasing and odometer drift which occurred in the different environments.

7.3.4   Case Study 12: Further Reading

- Tom Duckett and Ulrich Nehmzow, A Robust, Perception-Based Local-
  isation Method for a Mobile Robot, *Technical Report Series*, Report No.
  UMCS-96-11-1, Dept. of Computer Science, University of Manchester,
  Manchester, 1996.
- Tom Duckett and Ulrich Nehmzow, Mobile Robot Self-Localization and
  Measurement of Performance in Middle Scale Environments, *Journal of
  Robotics and Autonomous Systems*, No. 24, Vols. 1-2, pp. 57-69, 1998.

7.4   Summary

Analysis lies at the heart of scientific research. The outcome of an experiment
has to be assessed with respect to some performance criterion, and related to
initial predictions made by some hypothesis. Analysis will reveal whether the
robot performs well or badly, and whether a certain hypothesis regarding robot-
environment interaction makes predictions that can be confirmed experimentally,
or not.

The simplest method of analysis is some qualitative description. This includes
verbal descriptions of the robot's performance, indicating whether the robot ac-
complishes some task or not, and how well it does in the opinion of the observer.
Qualitative descriptions also include plots of trajectories, photographs etc. The
problem with qualitative descriptions is that they are subjective, and therefore
badly suited for guiding the design process, or independent verification of experiments.

Quantitative descriptions, i.e. measurable performance indicators, provide a
more precise tool for analysis. They can be used to alter system parameters in
a systematic manner, to achieve better performance. They can also be used in
independent replication of the experiments by others, a central procedure in science. The difficulty is to find quantitative descriptions that are meaningful with
respect to the robot's task.

Section 7.2 introduced some statistical methods that can be used to analyse robot behaviour, and the three case studies gave examples of how this can be done in practice.

For robot tasks that involve localisation, the association between the robot's true position and the assumed position can be established using contingency table analysis. Entropy and Uncertainty Coefficient (see section 7.2.4) give a quantitative evaluation of how strong this association is. Case studies 10 and 12 used them to evaluate robot map-building and localisation systems.

In case study 11 the objective was to measure how quickly and how successfully a robot learned to follow a route indicated by the operator. This was achieved by defining an error condition, and measuring the mean distance between failures (i.e. situations in which the error condition was encountered). This mean distance between failures gave a statistical description of the relationship between training time and failure rate in following the prescribed route.

In conclusion, the main point of this chapter is that it is desirable to have quantitative measures of the robot's behaviour and performance with respect to some goal. Such measures allow the controlled modification of the system parameters, and the replication of the work by other research groups. The case studies present examples of how this can be done.

8 Outlook

Summary. The final chapter looks back at the successes of mobile robotics, the reasons for them, and identifies challenges in mobile robotics research that lie ahead.

8.1 Achievements

Since *SHAKEY* and its companions in the late 1960s and early 1970s mobile robotics has come a long way. Operation in the early days was unreliable and marred by undependable hardware and crude sensors. Most ambitious plans either could not be achieved at all (such as building a robot that would assemble a Heathkit television set) or performance was disappointingly poor (e.g. robots that could only complete parts of a sequence of actions, or took a very long time to plan their moves).

Robot hardware was so unreliable then, and computing hardware so slow that research into intelligent mobile robotics moved away from actually building robots, and focused on simulation and theoretical control issues instead. Now, robot hardware — sensors, actuators and batteries in particular — has improved so much that automated guided vehicles are in common use in factories.

We have also benefited from the enormous improvements of computing hardware, which have made the implementation of sophisticated control software possible. For example, we can now analyse camera images at frame rate to guide cars on motorways, or interpret large amounts of sensory data in real time. As a consequence, we have been able to send mobile exploration robots to Mars[1] or down volcanoes[2], and are beginning to see commercially available household robots in such unstructured and changeable environments as our living rooms and gardens[3]. Autonomous mobile robots are now able to self-localise and navigate in unmodified environments, using the naturally occurring landmarks they

---

[1] The mobile robot *SOJOURNER* was used to explore Mars (http://mpfwww.jpl.nasa.gov/rover/sojourner.html).

[2] The mobile robot *DANTE* explored volcanoes in Antarctica in 1994 (http://volcano.und.nodak.edu/vwdocs/vw_news/dante.html).

[3] Autonomous lawn mowers are already available, and autonomous vacuum cleaners will soon arrive in the shops.

perceive, and they will be increasingly used in industrial applications for transportation tasks. Autonomous robots will also play a more and more important role in exploration and inspection tasks.

The largest commercial impact of mobile robotics, however, will probably be in intelligent toys. Entertainment robots with a large repertoire of possible actions and complex control structures are now available commercially, and will become more and more part of our life.

8.2 Reasons for Success

What lay behind these successes? Obviously, the technological advances in both robot hardware and computing hardware were one fundamental component, but there were other factors.

One of the most important steps forward was probably the realisation that hardware and software are inseparable. The idea of building "intelligent controllers" and to stick them onto robot platforms once those platforms were available, did not work. It did not work because hardware and software depend on each other. The signals from a sensor (hardware) form the basis of the control process (software). The control process then drives an actuator (hardware) to accomplish some task.

The realisation of this interdependency resulted in a revised view of how mobile robotics research should be conducted: much more with real robots, and much less with simplified numerical models. The use of "embedded, situated agents" was one major contributing factor to the advances in mobile robotics.

There was further confirmation that using real robots would lead to results that could not be achieved otherwise: the interaction between robot and environment produced unpredictable effects ("emergent phenomena"), such as obstacles being shifted through contact, or people moving out of the robot's way (the easy way of obstacle avoidance: the obstacle avoiding the robot). Once real robots were available in sufficient numbers and used for research (this was the case from the late 1980s onwards), research produced more reliable and successful robots.

Another contributing factor to the successes was the trend towards distributed control structures composed of simple components ("behaviours"), interacting with each other and generating the robot's overall behaviour through synergy. Such controllers tend to be less brittle than monolithic controllers.

In summary, the advances of technology paved the way, because they made new approaches to control possible. The resulting shift in research paradigm, increasingly concentrating on research with real robots operating in their target environment, led to further advances towards reliable, robust and task-achieving robots.

8.3 Challenges

And yet, we haven't got widespread applications of "intelligent robots" yet. What are the outstanding problems?

As I see it, there are three major areas of challenges in mobile robotics research: technological, control and methodological challenges.

8.3.1 Technological Challenges

Any control algorithm is only as good as the information it is provided with. There are challenges to develop new sensor modalities (recent examples of such new sensor modalities include global positioning systems and laser radar), and sensors that preprocess their raw data and thus provide more meaningful information to the controller. An example for the latter are commercially available cameras that automatically track a coloured object and provide information about the object's position to the controller.

We will have to move towards continuous operation of robots if mobile robots are to have a wider impact on industry and society. Ultimately, mobile robots will have to operate virtually without supervision, performing some specified task continuously without the need of operator attendance (apart from maintenance). Currently, the supply of power to mobile robots is the bottleneck here, and new technologies in batteries, fuel cells, solar power or internal combustion engines will be needed. Hand in hand with this goes the need for self-charging robots that are able to connect to charging stations without external guidance. The first laboratory models are already available.

8.3.2 Control Challenges

I think that one of the major goals of mobile robotics research must be to achieve greater autonomy in robots, ultimately to lead to continuous operation in unstructured and partially unpredictable environments. The longer the periods of operation and the less structured the environment, however, the higher the probability that the robot will encounter situations that have not been anticipated by the designer.

Learning, in a wide sense of the word, constitutes one of the biggest challenges in the control of mobile robots. We have achieved learning of direct input-output associations, learning of reward functions that can be used for decision making, and the acquisition of internal representations of the robot's environment.

However, the problem of common sense — guiding the reasoning process by experience to avoid considering silly possibilities — is as pressing as ever. It is a central problem in intelligent mobile robotics. A further fundamental open problem is that of generating generalised internal representations, to construct concepts, and to detect novelty. These are different aspects of the same broad question of how to make sense from perception. Generalisation and concept formation, on the one hand, reduce the amount of memory needed — important to continuous operation — but more importantly, they provide the yardstick against which the robot's sensory perceptions can be assessed. Novelty detection, on the other hand, is essential for many tasks of mobile robots, including inspection, surveillance, navigation and learning of fundamental sensor-motor competences.

8.3.3   Methodological Challenges

I see three major challenges regarding the methods of mobile robotics research: terminology, design, and procedure.

Terminology The objectives of research, the description of the method, the results and their interpretation all depend crucially on the terminology we use. Mobile robotics by nature invites hyperbole. A robot may be evaluating a cost function and turn as a result, but is this "thinking"? Robots will carry out increasingly more tasks, most of them mundane and repetitive, because that is what robots are good at. But this doesn't mean that they "take over".

I see a twofold challenge in our use of terminology: on the one hand, imprecise language makes it hard for scientists to understand what actually was done in an experiment, and what precisely the results were. On the other hand, hyperbole raises hopes in the public that can not be fulfilled, and thus can lead to a similar disillusionment as happened to AI in the 1970s.

Design Versus Evolution Controllers for mobile robots can be designed, or evolved through genetic algorithms. The latter is an attractive option, as it promises to lead to solutions that have not been found by other means. However, that promise has to be fulfilled yet. Up to now there are no solutions to mobile robot control through simulated evolution that have not been found through design as well. Design is still our strongest tool to obtain controllers for mobile robots.

The challenge here is therefore to develop the tool of design further, and to refine the design process. Currently, many control parameters and even entire control structures are determined by trial and error. There are few design tools for mobile robot controllers, and the usual method is to implement a controller on a robot and to "try it out". Unlike in other design tasks (for example designing an electronic circuit), there is no established design methodology in mobile robotics that will lead to the controller in a deterministic way.

Design has to do with experimental procedure, which is the last methodological challenge I will mention.

Procedure As discussed in chapter 7, evaluation of robot behaviour to a large degree still depends on *qualitative* measures. In order to guide the design process, it is necessary to use more and more *quantitative* evaluations of the robot's performance. The challenge here is to develop these measures.

But there is also a twofold challenge to the research community as a whole: first, to adopt such measures and therefore to allow quantitative assessment of results, and second, to establish a research practice of independent verification of experiments. Currently such replication of experiments is usually impossible (apart from specialised cases), because we haven't got uniquely identifying descriptions of robots, tasks and environments. The challenge is to find these descriptions, and to use them in independent verification of experimental results.

8.4   The Beginning

This book has presented a glimpse of the fascinating research area of artificial intelligence in mobile robotics. Case studies have given examples of learning and navigating robots, of quantitative performance measures and robot simulation through model learning. But this is only the beginning! This book is intended to be a springboard for your own ideas about intelligent, autonomous mobile robots that move without supervision, learn through trial and error, adapt to a changeable world, and become better and better at their tasks. *Viel Erfolg!*

8.5   Further Reading

On Mobile Robotics in General

- Ronald C. Arkin, *Behavior-Based Robotics*, MIT Press, Cambridge MA, 1998.
- Phillip McKerrow, *Introduction to Robotics*, Addison-Wesley, Sydney, 1991.
- Johann Borenstein, H.R. Everett and Liqiang Feng, *Navigating Mobile Robots*, AK Peters, Wellesley MA, 1996.

On AI and Cognitive Science in Robotics

- Valentino Braitenberg, *Vehicles : Experiments in Synthetic Psychology*, MIT Press, Cambridge MA, 1984.
- Rolf Pfeifer and Christian Scheier, *Understanding Intelligence*, MIT Press, Cambridge MA, 1999.
- Raymond Kurzweil, *The Age of Intelligent Machines*, MIT Press, Cambridge MA, 1990.
- Michael A. Arbib (ed.), *The Handbook of Brain Theory and Neural Networks*, MIT Press, Cambridge MA, 1995.
- C.R. Gallistel, *The Organisation of Learning*, MIT Press, Cambridge MA, 1990.

Answers to Exercises

Summary. This appendix contains the answers to the exercises given in the book.

1 Sonar Sensors

The following observations can be made looking at the sonar reading of figure 3.5. First of all, the side looking sonar reveals that the robot was driven at a more or less constant distance of ca. 60 cm to the wall. Four doors are also clearly visible on the lower sonar line.

Each door is preceded by two peaks on the front-facing sonar, namely when the first door post is detected ("A" in figure 1), and when the second door post appears ("B" in figure 1).

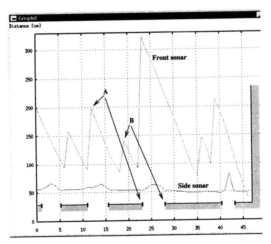

FIG. 1. INTERPRETATION OF SONAR SENSOR READINGS

Even the width of the doors can be estimated. As the first door post ("A") is detected in time step 12, and lost in time step 19, the robot has detected the door post for six time steps. In the particular example given here a measurement was taken every 20 cm, so that the width of the doors would be roughly 1.20 m. Not an unreasonable measurement!

That the robot is moving towards a wall at the end of the run can be deduced from the fact that the distance readings of the front sensor are decreasing constantly after time step 40.

Whether or not the doors were open in the experiment is not quite so easy to decide. The depth of the doors is measured at about 10 cm, which indicates they were closed. However, the beam of the side-looking sonar may not be narrow enough to pass through the doorway, and therefore detect the door posts, even if the door itself is open.

2 Robot Learning

2.1 Full Obstacle Avoidance, using McCulloch and Pitts Neurons

The truth table to be implemented is shown in table 1.

LW	RW	LM	RM
0	0	1	1
0	1	-1	1
1	0	1	-1
1	1	-1	-1

Table 1. TRUTH TABLE FOR FULL OBSTACLE AVOIDANCE

Line one of this truth table indicates that the threshold Θ must be below zero. As before, we choose $\Theta = -0.01$. We determine the weights w_{LW} and w_{RW} for the left motor neuron here. The weights for the right motor neuron are found analogously.

Lines two, three and four of the truth table translate into the following three inequalities:

$$w_{RW} < \Theta$$
$$w_{LW} > \Theta$$
$$w_{LW} + w_{RW} < \Theta$$

These three inequalities can be satisfied with, for example, $w_{LW} = 0.3$ and $w_{RW} = -0.5$.

2.2 A Target Following, Obstacle Avoiding Robot

The truth table for the target seeking, obstacle avoiding robot described in section 4.5 is given in table 2. This robot will obviously never execute a forward movement, because the beacon sensor either indicates "steer left" or "steer right", which will be executed as a turn. Therefore, we can restrict the truth table to the

LW	RW	BS	LM
0	0	-1	-1
0	0	1	1
0	1	-1	-1
0	1	1	-1
1	0	-1	1
1	0	1	1
1	1	-1	don't care
1	1	1	don't care

Table 2. TRUTH TABLE FOR TARGET SEEKING AND OBSTACLE AVOIDANCE

function of the left motor, and later implement the exact opposite function of the left motor for the right motor.

We will now attempt to implement this truth table using one McCulloch and Pitts neuron per motor — again looking at the left motor only. The structure of this network is shown in figure 2.

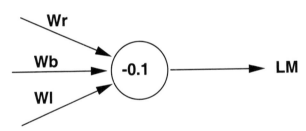

FIG. 2. STRUCTURE OF THE REQUIRED NEURON FOR THE LEFT MOTOR

Lines 1 and 2 of the truth table yield $w_B > \Theta$ (with an arbitrary selection of $\Theta = -0.01$ here).

Line 5 of the truth table yields $w_L - w_B > \Theta$, and from line 4 of the truth table we can determine the inequality $w_R + w_B < \Theta$.

This allows us to select three weights that satisfy the requirements, for example $w_L = 5$, $w_B = 3$ and $w_R = -5$. Going through all lines of the truth table confirms that these weights would implement the required function.

The final network structure is shown in figure 3. Weights for the right motor are the mirror image of those for the left motor (taking into account, of course, that the beacon sensor has a "+1/-1" encoding for direction).

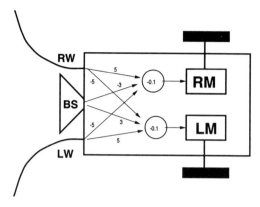

FIG. 3. A TARGET SEEKING MOBILE ROBOT THAT AVOIDS OBSTACLES, USING MCCULLOCH
AND PITTS NEURONS.

3 Error Calculations
and Contingency Table Analysis

3.1 Mean and Standard Deviation

A robot is stationary in front of an obstacle, and obtains the following range
readings from its sonar sensors (in cm): 60, 58, 58, 61, 63, 62, 60, 60, 59, 60,
62, 58.

Using equation 7.3, we can compute the mean distance measured as
$\mu = \frac{721}{12} = 60.08$ cm. Equation 7.4 can be used to compute the standard deviation as $\sigma = \sqrt{\frac{1}{11} 30.92} = 1.68$. This means that 68.3% of all range values lie
in an interval of (60.08 ± 1.68) cm.

The standard error is $\bar{\sigma} = 0.48$ (equation 7.5), indicating that with a certainty
of 68.3% the true mean lies in the interval 60.08 cm $\pm$ 0.48 cm.

3.2 Classifier System

A mobile robot has been equipped with a fixed algorithm to detect doorways, using an on-board CCD camera. The probability of this system producing a correct
answer is the same for each image.

The system is initially tested using 750 images, half of which contain a doorway, and half of which don't. The algorithm produces correct answers in 620
cases.

In a second series of experiments, 20 images are presented to the robot. What
is the probability that there will be two classification errors, and which number
of errors is to be expected in classifying those 20 images?

Answer: If a classifier system is used in n independent trials to classify data,
it will produce n answers, each of which is either correct or incorrect. This is a
binomial distribution.

We define p as the probability of producing an incorrect answer. In this case $p = 1 - \frac{620}{750} = 0.173$.

The probability p_2^{20} of making 2 mistakes in twenty classifications can be determined using equation 7.6: $p_2^{20} = \frac{20!}{(20-2)!2!} 0.173^2 (1 - 0.173)^{20-2} = 0.186$.

The number of errors μ_b to be expected in 20 experiments is given by equation 7.7 as $\mu_b = np = 20 \cdot (1 - \frac{620}{750}) = 3.47$.

3.3 T-Test

A robot control program is written to enable robots to withdraw from dead ends. In a first version of the program, the robot takes the following time in seconds to escape from a dead end: x=(10.2, 9.5, 9.7, 12.1, 8.7, 10.3, 9.7, 11.1, 11.7, 9.1). After the program has been improved, a second set of experiments yields these results: y=(9.6, 10.1, 8.2, 7.5, 9.3, 8.4).

Do these results indicate that the second program performs significantly better?

Answer: Assuming that the outcome of the experiments has a normal (Gaussian) distribution, we can apply the T-test to answer this question.

$\mu_x = 10.21, \sigma_x = 1.112, \mu_y = 8.85, \sigma_y = 0.977$.

Applying equation 7.13 yields:

$$T = \frac{10.21 - 8.85}{\sqrt{(10-1)1.112^2 + (6-1)0.997^2}} \sqrt{\frac{10*6(10+6-2)}{10+6}} = 2.456 .$$

As $k = 10 + 6 - 2$, $t_\alpha = 2.145$ (from table 7.1). The inequality $|2.456| > 2.145$ holds, the hypothesis H_0 (i.e. $\mu_x = \mu_y$) is rejected, which means that the second program performs significantly better than the first one, the probability for this statement to be erroneous is 0.05.

4 Analysis of Categorical Data

4.1 χ^2 Analysis

A mobile robot is placed in an environment that contains four prominent landmarks, A, B, C and D. The robot's landmark identification program produces four responses, α, β, γ and δ to the sensory stimuli received at these four locations. In an experiment totalling 200 visits to the various landmarks, the following contingency table is obtained (numbers indicate the frequency of a particular map response obtained at a particular location):

Is the output of the classifier significantly associated with the location the robot is at?

Answer: Following equation 7.15 $n_{A\alpha} = \frac{40*34}{200} = 6.8, n_{A\beta} = \frac{40*78}{200} = 15.6$, and so on (the table of expected values is table 4).

	α	β	γ	δ	
A	19	10	8	3	$N_{A.} = 40$
B	7	40	9	4	$N_{B.} = 60$
C	8	20	23	19	$N_{C.} = 70$
D	0	8	12	10	$N_{D.} = 30$
	$N_{.\alpha} = 34$	$N_{.\beta} = 78$	$N_{.\gamma} = 52$	$N_{.\delta} = 36$	$N = 200$

Table 3. CONTINGENCY TABLE FOR LANDMARK IDENTIFICATION PROGRAM

	α	β	γ	δ
A	6.8	15.6	10.4	7.2
B	10.2	23.4	15.6	10.8
C	11.9	27.3	18.2	12.6
D	5.1	11.7	7.8	5.4

Table 4. TABLE OF EXPECTED VALUES FOR LANDMARK IDENTIFICATION PROGRAM

The table of expected values is well conditioned for the χ^2 analysis, no values are below 4.

Following equation 7.16, $\chi^2 = \frac{(19-6.8)^2}{6.8} + \frac{(10-15.6)^2}{15.6} + \ldots = 66.9$. The system has $16 - 4 - 4 + 1 = 9$ degrees of freedom (equation 7.17). $\chi^2_{0.05} = 16.9$, according to table 7.3. The inequality

$$\chi^2 = 66.9 > \chi^2_{0.05} = 16.9 \tag{1}$$

holds, therefore there *is* a significant association between robot location and output of the location identification system.

4.2 Cramer's V

Two different map-building paradigms are to be compared. Paradigm A yields a contingency table as given in table 5, paradigm B produces the table shown in figure 7. The question is: which of the two mechanisms produces a map with a stronger correlation between robot location and map response?

We use Cramer's V to answer that question.

	α	β	γ	δ	
A	29	13	5	7	$N_{A.} = 54$
B	18	4	27	3	$N_{B.} = 52$
C	8	32	6	10	$N_{C.} = 56$
D	2	7	18	25	$N_{D.} = 52$
	$N_{.\alpha} = 57$	$N_{.\beta} = 56$	$N_{.\gamma} = 56$	$N_{.\delta} = 45$	$N=214$

Table 5. RESULTS OF MAP-BUILDING MECHANISM 1

	α	β	γ	δ
A	14.4	14.1	14.1	11.4
B	13.9	13.6	13.6	10.9
C	14.9	14.7	14.7	11.8
D	13.9	13.6	13.6	10.9

Table 6. EXPECTED VALUES FOR MAP-BUILDING MECHANISM 1

The tables of expected values are given in tables 6 and 8. Looking at both tables of expected values, one can see that the data is well conditioned and meets the criteria listed in section 7.2.4.

In the case of map-building mechanism 1, we determine $\chi^2 = 111$ and $V = 0.42$, in the case of mechanism 2 we obtain $\chi^2 = 229$ and $V = 0.37$. Map 1 has the stronger correlation between map response and location. Both experiments are subject to some random variation, however, so that it is necessary to run each experiment a number of times, to eliminate the influence of random noise.

	α	β	γ	δ	ϵ	
A	40	18	20	5	7	$N_{A.} = 90$
B	11	20	35	10	3	$N_{B.} = 79$
C	5	16	10	39	5	$N_{C.} = 75$
D	2	42	16	18	9	$N_{D.} = 87$
E	6	11	21	9	38	$N_{D.} = 85$
	$N_{.\alpha} = 64$	$N_{.\beta} = 107$	$N_{.\gamma} = 102$	$N_{.\delta} = 81$	$N_{.\epsilon} = 62$	N=416

Table 7. RESULTS OF MAP-BUILDING MECHANISM 2

	α	β	γ	δ	ϵ
A	13.8	23.1	22.1	17.5	13.4
B	12.2	20.3	19.4	15.4	11.8
C	11.5	19.3	18.4	14.6	11.2
D	13.4	22.4	21.3	16.9	13
E	13.1	21.9	20.8	16.6	12.7

Table 8. EXPECTED VALUES FOR MAP-BUILDING MECHANISM 2

4.3 Analysis of a Robot Localisation System, Using the Uncertainty Coefficient

A robot localisation system produces the responses shown in figure 7.2. Is there a statistically significant correlation between the system's response, and the robot's location?

In order to answer this question, we compute the uncertainty coefficient $U(L \mid R)$, according to equation 7.30. To do this, we need to compute $H(L)$, $H(R)$ and $H(L \mid R)$.

By applying equations 7.25, 7.26, 7.27 and 7.30 we obtain

$$H(L) = -(\tfrac{15}{100} ln \tfrac{15}{100} + \tfrac{21}{100} ln \tfrac{21}{100} + \ldots + \tfrac{21}{100} ln \tfrac{21}{100}) = 1.598,$$

$$H(R) = -(\tfrac{18}{100} ln \tfrac{18}{100} + \tfrac{20}{100} ln \tfrac{20}{100} + \ldots + \tfrac{23}{100} ln \tfrac{23}{100}) = 1.603,$$

$$H(L, R) = -(0 + \tfrac{2}{100} ln \tfrac{2}{100} + \tfrac{15}{100} ln \tfrac{15}{100} + \ldots + \tfrac{23}{100} ln \tfrac{23}{100} + 0) = 2.180,$$

$$H(L \mid R) = 2.180 - 1.603 = 0.577, \text{ and}$$

$$U(L \mid R) = \tfrac{1.598 - 0.577}{1.598} = 0.639.$$

This is an uncertainty coefficient that indicates a fairly strong correlation between the the robot's location and the localisation system's response.

List of Exercises and Case Studies

Exercises

Case Studies

References

[Allman 77] John Allman, Evolution of the Visual System in Early Primates, *Progress in Psychobiology and Physiological Psychology*, Vol. 7, pp. 1-53, Academic Press, New York, 1977.

[Arbib 95] M. Arbib (ed.), *The Handbook of Brain Theory and Neural Networks*, MIT Press, Cambridge MA, 1995.

[Arkin 98] Ronald Arkin, *Behavior-Based Robotics*, MIT Press, Cambridge MA, 1998.

[Atiya & Hager 93] S. Atiya and G.D. Hager, Real-Time Vision-Based Robot Localization, *IEEE Transactions on Robotics and Automation*, Vol. 9, No. 6, pp. 785-800, 1993.

[Ballard & Whitehead 92] D.H. Ballard and S.D. Whitehead, Learning Visual Behaviours, in H. Wechsler, *Neural Networks for Perception*, Vol. 2, pp 8-39, Academic Press, New York, 1992.

[Ballard 97] D. H. Ballard, *An Introduction to Natural Computation*, MIT Press, Cambridge MA, 1997.

[Barto 90] Andrew G. Barto, *Connectionist Learning for Control*, in [Miller *et al.* 90] pp. 5-58.

[Barto 95] Andrew G. Barto, *Reinforcement Learning*, in [Arbib 95, pp. 804-809].

[Batschelet 81] Edward Batschelet, *Circular Statistics in Biology*, Academic Press, New York, 1981.

[Beale & Jackson 90] R. Beale and T. Jackson, *Neural Computing: An Introduction*, Adam Hilger, Bristol, Philadelphia and New York, 1990.

[Bennett 96] A. Bennett, Do Animals Have Cognitive Maps?, *Journal of Experimental Biology*, Vol. 199, pp. 219-224, The Company of Biologists Limited, Cambridge UK, 1996.

[Bicho & Schöner 97] Estela Bicho and Gregor Schöner, The dynamic approach to autonomous robotics demonstrated on a low-level vehicle platform, *Journal of Robotics and Autonomous Systems*, Vol. 21, Issue 1, pp. 23-35, 1997. Available at http://www.elsevier.nl/locate/robot.

[Bishop 95] Christopher Bishop, *Neural Networks for Pattern Recognition*, Oxford University Press, Oxford, 1995.

[Borenstein *et al.* 96] Johann Borenstein, H. R. Everett and Liqiang Feng, *Navigating Mobile Robots*, AK Peters, Wellesley MA, 1996.

[Braitenberg 84] Valentino Braitenberg, *Vehicles : Experiments in Synthetic Psychology*, MIT Press, Cambridge MA, 1984.

[Brooks 85] Rodney Brooks: A Robust Layered Control System for a Mobile Robot, *MIT AI Memo*, No. 864, Cambridge MA, 1985. Available at http://www.ai.mit.edu/publications/pubsDB/pubsDB/onlinehtml.

[Brooks 86a] Rodney Brooks, Achieving Artificial Intelligence through Building Robots, *MIT AI Memo*, No. 899, Cambridge MA, May 1986. Available at http://www.ai.mit.edu/publications/pubsDB/pubsDB/onlinehtml.

[Brooks 90] R. Brooks, Elephants Don't Play Chess, in P. Maes (ed.), *Designing Autonomous Agents: Theory and Practice from Biology to Engineering and Back*, MIT Press, Cambridge MA, 1990.

[Brooks 91a] Rodney Brooks, Artificial Life and Real Robots, in F. Varela and P. Bourgine (eds), *Toward a Practice of Autonomous Systems*, pp. 3-10, MIT Press, Cambridge MA, 1991.

[Brooks 91b] Rodney Brooks, Intelligence without Reason, *Proc. IJCAI 91*, Vol. 1, pp. 569-595, Morgan Kaufmann, San Mateo CA, 1991. Available at http://www.ai.mit.edu/publications/pubsDB/pubsDB/onlinehtml.

[Broomhead & Lowe 88] D.S. Broomhead and D. Lowe, Multivariable functional interpolation and adaptive networks, *Complex Systems*, Vol. 2, pp. 321-355, 1988.

[Bühlmeier *et al.* 96] A. Bühlmeier, H. Dürer, J. Monnerjahn, M. Nölte and U. Nehmzow, Learning by Tuition, Experiments with the Manchester 'FortyTwo', *Technical Report* , Report No. UMCS-96-1-2, Dept. of Computer Science, University of Manchester, Manchester, 1996.

[Burgess & O'Keefe 96] N. Burgess and J. O'Keefe, Neuronal Computations Underlying the Firing of Place Cells and their Role in Navigation, *Hippocampus*, Vol. 7, pp. 749-762, 1996.

[Burgess *et al.* 93] N. Burgess, J. O'Keefe and M. Recce, Using Hippocampal 'Place Cells' for Navigation, Exploiting Phase Coding, in Hanson, Giles and Cowan (eds.), *Advances in Neural Information Processing Systems*, Vol. 5, pp. 929-936, Morgan Kaufmann, San Mateo CA, 1993.

[Calter & Berridge 95] Paul Calter and Debbie Berridge, *Technical Mathematics*, 3rd edition, John Wiley and Sons, New York, 1995.

[Carpenter & Grossberg 87] G. Carpenter and S. Grossberg, ART2: Self-Organization of Stable Category Recognition Codes for Analog Input Patterns, *Applied Optics*, Vol. 26, No. 23, pp. 4919-4930, 1987.

[Cartwright & Collett 83] B.A. Cartwright and T.S. Collett, Landmark Learning in Bees, *Journal of Comparative Physiology*, Vol. 151, pp. 521-543, 1983.

[Churchland 86] Patricia Smith Churchland, *Neurophilosophy*, MIT Press, Cambridge MA, 1986.

[Clark *et al.* 88] Sharon A. Clark, Terry Allard, William M. Jenkins and Michael M. Merzenich, Receptive Fields in the Body Surface Map in Adult Cortex Defined by Temporally Correlated Inputs, *Nature*, Vol. 332, Issue 31, pp. 444-445, March 1988.

[Colombetti & Dorigo 93] M. Colombetti & M. Dorigo, Robot Shaping: Developing Situated Agents through Learning, *Technical Report*, Report Number 40, International Computer Science Institute, Berkeley CA, April 1993.

[Connell & Mahadevan 93] J. Connell and S. Mahadevan (eds.), *Robot Learning*, Kluwer, Boston MA, 1993.

[Cosens 93] Derek Cosens, personal communication, Department of Zoology, Edinburgh University, Edinburgh, 1993.

[Crevier 93] D. Crevier, *AI: The Tumultuous History of the Search for Artificial Intelligence*, Basic Books (Harper Collins), New York, 1993.

[Critchlow 85] Arthur Critchlow, *Introduction to Robotics*, Macmillan, New York, 1985.

[Daskalakis 91] Nikolas Daskalakis, *Learning Sensor-Action Coupling in Lego Robots*, MSc Thesis, Department of Artificial Intelligence, Edinburgh University, Edinburgh, 1991.

[Duckett & Nehmzow 96] T. Duckett and U. Nehmzow, A Robust, Perception-Based Localisation Method for a Mobile Robot, *Technical Report*, Report Number UMCS-96-11-1, Dept. of Computer Science, University of Manchester, Manchester, 1996.

[Duckett & Nehmzow 97] Tom Duckett and Ulrich Nehmzow, Experiments in Evidence Based Localisation for a Mobile Robot, in Proc. AISB workshop on "Spatial Reasoning in Animals and Robots", *Technical Report*, Report Number UMCS-97-4-1, ISSN 1361-6153, Dept. of Computer Science, University of Manchester, Manchester 1997.

[Duckett & Nehmzow 98] Tom Duckett and Ulrich Nehmzow, Mobile Robot Self-Localization and Measurement of Performance in Middle Scale Environments, *Journal of Robotics and Autonomous Systems*, No. 24, Vols. 1-2, pp. 57-69, 1998. Available at http://www.elsevier.nl/locate/robot.

[Duckett & Nehmzow 99] Tom Duckett and Ulrich Nehmzow, Knowing Your Place in Real World Environments, *Proc. Eurobot 99*, IEEE Computer Society, 1999.

[Edlinger & Weiss 95] T. Edlinger and G. Weiss, Exploration, Navigation and Self-Localization in an Autonomous Mobile Robot, *Autonome Mobile Systeme '95*, Karlsruhe, Germany, Nov 30 - Dec 1 1995.

[Elfes 87] Alberto Elfes, Sonar-Based Real-World Mapping and Navigation, *IEEE Journal of Robotics and Automation*, RA Vol. 3, Issue 3, pp. 249-265, June 1987.

[Emlen 75] S.T. Emlen, Migration: Orientation and Navigation, in D.S. Farner, J.R. King and K.C. Parkes (eds.), *Avian Biology*, Vol. V, pp. 129-219, Academic Press, New York, 1975.

[Franz *et al.* 98] Matthias Franz, Bernhard Schölkopf, Hanspeter Mallot and Heinrich Bülthoff, Learning View Graphs for Robot Navigation, *Autonomous Robots*, Vol. 5, pp. 111-125, 1998.

[Fritzke 93] B. Fritzke, Growing Cell Structures — a Self-Organizing Network for Unsupervised and Supervised Learning, *Technical Report*, Report Number 93-026, International Computer Science Institute, Berkeley CA, 1993.

[Fritzke 94] B. Fritzke, Growing Cell Structures - a Self-Organizing Network for Unsupervised and Supervised Learning, *Neural Networks*, Vol. 7, No. 9, pp. 1441-1460, 1994.

[Fritzke 95] Bernd Fritzke, A Growing Neural Gas Network Learns Topologies, in G. Tesauro, D. S. Touretzky, and T. K. Leen (eds.), *Advances in Neural Information Processing Systems 7*, pp. 625-632. MIT Press, Cambridge MA, 1995.

[Gallistel 90] C.R. Gallistel, *The Organisation of Learning*, MIT Press, Cambridge MA, 1990.

[Giralt *et al.* 79] G. Giralt, R. Sobek and R. Chatila, A Multi-Level Planning and Navigation System for a Mobile Robot — A First Approach to HILARE, *Proc. IJCAI*, Tokyo, 1979.

[Gladwin 70] Thomas Gladwin, *East is a Big Bird*, Harvard University Press, Cambridge MA, 1970.

[Gould & Gould 88] James L. Gould and Carol Grant Gould, *The Honey Bee*, Scientific American Library, New York, 1988.

[Grossberg 88] S. Grossberg, *Neural Networks and Natural Intelligence*, MIT Press, Cambridge MA, 1988.

[Harnad 90] Stevan Harnad, The Symbol Grounding Problem, *Physica D*, Vol. 42, pp. 225-346, 1990.

[Heikkonen 94] J. Heikkonen, *Subsymbolic Representations, Self-Organising Maps, and Object Motion Learning*, PhD Thesis, Lappeenranta University of Technology, Lappeenranta, Finland, 1994.

[Hertz *et al.* 91] John Hertz, Anders Krogh, Richard G. Palmer, *Introduction to the Theory of Neural Computation*, Addison-Wesley, Redwood City CA, 1991.

[Horn & Schmidt 95] J. Horn and G. Schmidt, Continuous Localization of a Mobile Robot Based on 3D Laser Range Data, Predicted Sensor Images, and Dead-Reckoning, *Journal of Robotics and Autonomous Systems*, Vol. 14, No. 2-3, pp. 99-118, 1995. Available at http://www.elsevier.nl/locate/robot.

[Hubel 79] David H. Hubel, The Visual Cortex of Normal and Deprived Monkeys, *American Scientist*, Vol. 67, No. 5, pp. 532-543, 1979.

[Jones & Flynn 93] Joseph L. Jones and Anita M. Flynn, *Mobile Robots: Inspiration to Implementation*, A K Peters, Wellesley MA, 1993.

[Kaelbling 90] Leslie Pack Kaelbling, Learning in Embedded Systems, PhD Thesis, *Stanford Technical Report*, Report Number TR-90-04, June 1990. Published under the same title, MIT Press, Cambridge MA, 1993.

[Kaelbling 92] Leslie Kaelbling, An Adaptable Mobile Robot, in F. Varela and P. Bourgine (eds), *Toward a Practice of Autonomous Systems*, pp. 41-47, MIT Press, Cambridge MA, 1992.

[Kanade *et al.* 89] T. Kanade, F. C. A. Groen and L. O. Hertzberger (eds.), *Intelligent Autonomous Systems 2*, Proceedings of IAS 2, ISBN 90-800410-1-7, Amsterdam, 1989.

[Kampmann & Schmidt 91] Peter Kampmann and Günther Schmidt, Indoor Navigation of Mobile Robots by Use of Learned Maps, in [Schmidt 91], pp. 151-169.

[Kleijnen & Groenendaal 92] J. Kleijnen and W. van Groenendaal, *Simulation — A Statistical Perspective*, John Wiley and Sons, New York, 1992.

[Knieriemen & v.Puttkamer 91] T. Knieriemen and E. von Puttkamer, Real-Time Control in an Autonomous Mobile Robot, in [Schmidt 91], pp. 187-200.

[Knieriemen 91] T. Knieriemen, *Autonome Mobile Roboter*, BI Wissenschaftsverlag, Mannheim, 1991.

[Knudsen 82] E.I. Knudsen, Auditory and Visual Maps of Space in the Optic Tectum of the Owl, *Journal of Neuroscience*, Vol. 2, 1177-1194 (after [Gallistel 90]).

[Kohonen 88] Teuvo Kohonen, *Self Organization and Associative Memory*, Springer Verlag, Berlin, Heidelberg, New York, 2nd edition, 1988.

[Kohonen 95] Teuvo Kohonen, Learning Vector Quantization, in [Arbib 95, pp. 537-540].

[Kuipers & Byun 88]   B. J. Kuipers and Y.-T. Byun, A Robust, Qualitative Method for Robot Spatial Learning, *Proc. AAAI*, pp. 774-779, Morgan Kaufman, San Mateo CA, 1988.

[Kurz 94]   A. Kurz, *Lernende Steuerung eines autonomen mobilen Roboters*, VDI Fortschrittsberichte, VDI Verlag, Düsseldorf, 1994.

[Kurz 96]   A. Kurz, Constructing Maps for Mobile Robot Navigation Based on Ultrasonic Range Data, *IEEE Transactions on Systems, Man and Cybernetics, Part B: Cybernetics*, Vol. 26, No. 2, pp. 233-242, 1996.

[Kurzweil 90]   Raymond Kurzweil, *The Age of Intelligent Machines*, MIT Press, Cambridge MA, 1990.

[Kyselka 87]   Will Kyselka, *An Ocean in Mind*, University of Hawaii Press, Honolulu, 1987.

[Lee 95]   David Charles Lee, *The Map-Building and Exploration Strategies of a Simple Sonar-Equipped Mobile Robot; an Experimental Quantitative Evaluation*, PhD Thesis, University College London, London, 1995.

[Lee *et al.* 98]   Ten-min Lee, Ulrich Nehmzow and Roger Hubbold, Mobile Robot Simulation by Means of Acquired Neural Network Models, *Proc. European Simulation Multiconference*, pp. 465-469, Manchester, 1998.

[Lemon & Nehmzow 98]   Oliver Lemon and Ulrich Nehmzow, The Scientific Status of Mobile Robotics: Multi-Resolution Mapbuilding as a Case Study, *Journal of Robotics and Autonomous Systems*, No. 24, Vols 1-2, pp. 5-15, 1998. Available at http://www.elsevier.nl/locate/robot.

[Leonard *et al.* 90]   J. Leonard, H. Durrant-Whyte and I. Cox, Dynamic Mapbuilding for an Autonomous Mobile Robot, *Proc. IEEE IROS*, pp. 89-96, 1990.

[Lewis 72]   D. Lewis, *We, the Navigators*, University of Hawaii Press, Honolulu, 1972.

[Lowe & Tipping 96]   D. Lowe and M. Tipping, "Feed-Forward Neural Networks and Topographic Mappings for Exploratory Data Analysis", *Neural Computing and Applications*, Vol. 4, pp. 83-95, 1996.

[Lynch 60]   Kevin Lynch, *The Image of the City*, MIT Press, Cambridge MA, 1960.

[Maes & Brooks 90]   Pattie Maes and Rodney Brooks, Learning to Coordinate Behaviors, *Proc. AAAI 1990*, pp. 796-802, Morgan Kaufman, San Mateo CA, 1990.

[Maeyama *et al.* 95]   S. Maeyama, A. Ohya, S. Yuta, Non-stop Outdoor Navigation of a Mobile Robot, *Proc. International Conference on Intelligent Robots and Systems (IROS) 95*, pp. 130-135, Pittsburgh PA, 1995.

[Mahadevan & Connell 91]   Sridhar Mahadevan and Jonathan Connell, Automatic Programming of Behavior-based Robots using Reinforcement Learning, *Proc. 9th National Conference on Artificial Intelligence, AAAI 1991*, pp. 768-773, Morgan Kaufman, San Mateo CA, 1991.

[Martin & Nehmzow 95]   P. Martin and U. Nehmzow, "Programming" by Teaching: Neural Network Control in the Manchester Mobile Robot, *Conference on Intelligent Autonomous Vehicles IAV 95*, pp. 297-302, 1995.

[Mataric 91]   Maja Mataric, Navigating with a Rat Brain: A Neurobiologically-Inspired Model for Robot Spatial Representation, in [SAB 91], pp. 169-175.

[Mataric 92]   M. J. Mataric, Integration of Representation Into Goal-Driven Behaviour-Based Robots, *IEEE Transactions on Robotics and Automation*, Vol. 8, No. 3, pp. 304-312, June 1992.

[McCulloch & Pitts 43]   W. S. McCulloch and W. Pitts, A Logical Calculus of Ideas Immanent in Nervous Activity, *Bulletin of Mathematical Biophysics*, Vol. 5, pp. 115-133, 1943.

[McKerrow 91]   Phillip McKerrow, *Introduction to Robotics*, Addison-Wesley, Sydney, 1991.

[Miller *et al.* 90]   W. Thomas Miller, Richard S. Sutton and Paul J. Werbos (eds.), *Neural Networks for Control*, MIT Press, Cambridge MA, 1990.

[Mitchell 97]   T. Mitchell, *Machine Learning*, McGraw-Hill, New York, 1997.

[Moody & Darken 89]   J. Moody and C. Darken, Fast Learning in Networks of Locally Tuned Processing Units, *Neural Computation*, Vol. 1, pp. 281-294, 1989.

[Moravec 83]   H. Moravec: The Stanford Cart and the CMU Rover, *Proceedings of the IEEE*, Vol. 71, No. 7, 1983.

[Moravec 88]   Hans P. Moravec: Sensor Fusion in Certainty Grids for Mobile Robots, *AI Magazine Summer 1988*, pp. 61-74, 1988.

[Nehmzow *et al.* 89] U. Nehmzow, J. Hallam and T. Smithers, Really Useful Robots, in [Kanade *et al.* 89] Vol. 1, pp. 284-293.

[Nehmzow & Smithers 91] Ulrich Nehmzow and Tim Smithers, Mapbuilding Using Self-Organising Networks, in [SAB 91] pp. 152-159.

[Nehmzow *et al.* 91] Ulrich Nehmzow, Tim Smithers and John Hallam, Location Recognition in a Mobile Robot Using Self-Organising Feature Maps, in G. Schmidt (ed.), *Information Processing in Autonomous Mobile Robots*, pp. 267-277, Springer Verlag, Berlin, Heidelberg, New York, 1991.

[Nehmzow & Smithers 92] Ulrich Nehmzow and Tim Smithers, Using Motor Actions for Location Recognition, in F. Varela and P. Bourgine (eds.), *Toward a Practice of Autonomous Systems*, pp. 96-104, MIT Press, Cambridge MA, 1992.

[Nehmzow 92] U. Nehmzow, *Experiments in Competence Acquisition for Autonomous Mobile Robots*, PhD Thesis, University of Edinburgh, Edinburgh, 1992.

[Nehmzow 94] U. Nehmzow, Autonomous Acquisition of Sensor-Motor Couplings in Robots, *Technical Report*, Report Number UMCS-94-11-1, Dept. of Computer Science, University of Manchester, Manchester, 1994.

[Nehmzow & McGonigle 94] Ulrich Nehmzow & Brendan McGonigle, Achieving Rapid Adaptations in Robots by Means of External Tuition, in D. Cliff, P. Husbands, J. A. Meyer and S. Wilson (eds.), *From Animals to Animats 3*, pp. 301-308, MIT Press, Cambridge MA, 1994.

[Nehmzow 95a] U. Nehmzow, Flexible Control of Mobile Robots through Autonomous Competence Acquisition, *Measurement and Control*, Vol. 28, pp. 48-54, March 1995.

[Nehmzow 95b] U. Nehmzow, Animal and Robot Navigation, *Robotics and Autonomous Systems*, Vol. 15, No. 1-2, pp. 71-81, 1995. Available at http://www.elsevier.nl/locate/robot.

[Nehmzow & Mitchell 95] Ulrich Nehmzow and Tom Mitchell, The Prospective Student's Introduction to the Robot Learning Problem, *Technical Report*, Report Number UMCS-95-12-6, Department of Computer Science, Manchester University, Manchester, 1995.

[Nehmzow *et al.* 96] Ulrich Nehmzow, Andreas Bühlmeier, Holger Dürer and Manfred Nölte, Remote Control of Mobile Robot via Internet, *Technical Report*, Report Number UMCS-96-2-3, Dept. of Computer Science, Manchester University, Manchester, 1996.

[Nehmzow *et al.* 98] Ulrich Nehmzow, Toshihiro Matsui and Hideki Asoh, "Virtual Coordinates": Perception-based Localisation and Spatial Reasoning in Mobile Robots, *Proc. Intelligent Autonomous Systems 5 (IAS 5)*, Sapporo, 1998. Reprinted in *Robotics Today*, Vol. 12, No. 3, Society of Manufacturing Engineers, Dearborn MI, 1999.

[Nehmzow 99a] Ulrich Nehmzow, Vision Processing for Robot Learning, *Industrial Robot*, Vol. 26, No 2, pp. 121-130, 1999, ISSN 0143-991X.

[Nehmzow 99b] U. Nehmzow, "Meaning" through Clustering by Self-Organisation of Spatial and Temporal Information, in C. Nehaniv (ed.), *Computation for Metaphors, Analogy and Agents*, Lecture Notes in Artificial Intelligence 1562, pp. 209-229, Springer Verlag, Heidelberg, London, New York, 1999.

[Nehmzow 99c] U. Nehmzow, Acquisition of Smooth, Continuous Obstacle Avoidance in Mobile Robots, in H. Ritter, H. Cruse and J. Dean (eds.), *Prerational Intelligence: Adaptive Behavior and Intelligent Systems without Symbols and Logic*, Vol. 2, pp. 489-501, Kluwer Acad. Publ., Dordrecht, 1999.

[Newell & Simon 76] A. Newell and H. Simon, Computer Science as Empirical Enquiry: Symbols and Search, *Communications of the ACM*, Vol. 19, Issue 3, pp. 113-126, 1976.

[Nilsson 69] N. Nilsson, A Mobile Automation: An Application of Artificial Intelligence Techniques, *First International Joint Conference on Artificial Intelligence*, pp. 509-520, Washington DC, 1969.

[Nomad 93] *Nomad 200 User's Guide*, Nomadic Technologies, Mountain View CA, December 1993.

[O'Keefe & Nadel 78] J. O'Keefe and L. Nadel, *The Hippocampus as a Cognitive Map*, Oxford University Press, Oxford, 1978.

[O'Keefe 89] J. O'Keefe, Computations the Hippocampus Might Perform, in L. Nadel, L. A. Cooper, P. Culicover and R. M. Harnish (eds.), *Neural Connections, Mental Computation*, MIT Press, Cambridge MA, 1989.

[Oreskes *et al.* 94] N. Oreskes, K. Shrader-Frechette and K. Belitz, Verification, Validation, and Confirmation of Numerical Models in the Earth Sciences, *Science*, Vol. 263, pp. 641-646, 4th Feb. 1994.

[O'Sullivan *et al.* 95] J. O'Sullivan, T. Mitchell and S. Thrun, Explanation Based Learning for Mobile Robot Perception, in K. Ikeuchi and M. Veloso (eds.), *Symbolic Visual Learning*, ch. 11, Oxford University Press, Oxford, 1995.

[Owen 95] C. Owen, *Landmarks, Topological Maps and Robot Navigation*, MSc Thesis, Manchester University, Manchester, 1995.

[Owen & Nehmzow 96] Carl Owen and Ulrich Nehmzow, Route Learning in Mobile Robots through Self-Organisation, *Proc. Eurobot 96*, pp. 126-133, IEEE Computer Society, 1996.

[Owen & Nehmzow 98] Carl Owen and Ulrich Nehmzow, Map Interpretation in Dynamic Environments, *Proc. 8th International Workshop on Advanced Motion Control*, IEEE Press, ISBN 0-7803-4484-7, 1998.

[Pfeifer & Scheier 99] Rolf Pfeifer and Christian Scheier, *Understanding Intelligence*, MIT Press, Cambridge MA, 1999.

[Pomerleau 93] D. Pomerleau, Knowledge-Based Training of Artificial Neural Networks for Autonomous Robot Driving, in [Connell & Mahadevan 93] pp. 19-43.

[Prescott & Mayhew 92] Tony Prescott and John Mayhew, Obstacle Avoidance through Reinforcement Learning, in J. E. Moody, S. J. Hanson and R. P. Lippman (eds.), *Advances in Neural Information Processing Systems 4*, pp. 523-530, Morgan Kaufman, San Mateo CA, 1992.

[Press *et al.* 92] W. Press, S. Teukolsky, W. Vetterling and B. Flannery, *Numerical Recipes in C*, Cambridge University Press, Cambridge UK, 1992.

[Puterman 94] Martin Puterman, *Markov Decision Processes — Discrete Stochastic Dynamic Programming*, John Wiley and Sons, New York, 1994.

[Ramakers 93] Wilfried Ramakers, *Investigation of a Competence Acquiring Controller for a Mobile Robot*, Licentiate Thesis, Vrije Universiteit Brussel, 1993.

[Recce & Harris 96] M. Recce and K. D. Harris, Memory for Places: A Navigational Model in Support of Marr's Theory of Hippocampal Function, *Hippocampus*, Vol. 6, pp. 735-748, 1996.

[Reilly *et al.* 82] D. L. Reilly, L. N. Cooper and C. Erlbaum, A Neural Model for Category Learning. *Biological Cybernetics*, Vol. 45, pp. 35-41, 1982.

[Rosenblatt 62] Frank Rosenblatt: *Principles of Neurodynamics: Perceptrons and the Theory of Brain Mechanisms*, Spartan, Washington DC, 1962.

[Rumelhart & McClelland 86] David E. Rumelhart, James L. McClelland and the PDP Research Group, *Parallel Distributed Processing*, Vol. 1 "Foundations", MIT Press, Cambridge MA, 1986.

[Rumelhart *et al.* 86] D. E. Rumelhart, G. Hinton, and R. J. Williams, Learning Internal Representations by Error Propagation, in D. Rumelhart and J. McClelland (eds), *Parallel Distributed Processing*, Vol. 1, pp. 318-362, MIT Press, Cambridge MA, 1986.

[SAB 91] Jean-Arcady Meyer and Stewart Wilson (eds.), *From Animals to Animats*, Proc. 1st Intern. Conference on Simulation of Adaptive Behaviour, MIT Press, Cambridge MA, 1991.

[Sachs 82] Lothar Sachs, *Applied Statistics*, Springer Verlag, Berlin, Heidelberg, New York, 1982.

[St. Paul 82] Ursula von Saint Paul, Do Geese Use Path Integration for Walking Home?, in F. Papi and H.G. Wallraff (eds.), *Avian Navigation*, pp. 298-307, Springer Verlag, Berlin, Heidelberg, New York, 1982.

[Shepanski & Macy 87] J. F. Shepanski and S. A. Macy, Teaching Artificial Neural Networks to Drive: Manual Training Techniques of Autonomous Systems Based on Artificial Neural Networks, *Proceedings of the 1987 Neural Information Processing Systems Conference* pp. 693-700, American Institute of Physics, New York, 1987.

[Schmidt 91] G. Schmidt (ed.), *Information Processing in Autonomous Mobile Robots*, Springer Verlag, Berlin, Heidelberg, New York, 1991.

[Schmidt 95] Dietmar Schmidt, Roboter als Werkzeuge für die Werkstatt, *Spektrum der Wissenschaft*, pp. 96-100, ISSN 0170-2971, March 1995.

[Shubik 60] Martin Shubik, Simulation of the Industry and the Firm, *American Economic Review*, L, No. 5, pp. 908-919, 1960.

[Smithers 95] T. Smithers, On Quantitative Performance Measures of Robot Behaviour, *Journal of Robotics and Autonomous Systems*, Vol. 15, pp. 107-133, 1995. Available at http://www.elsevier.nl/locate/robot.

[Sonka *et al.* 93] M. Sonka, V. Hlavac, and R. Boyle, *Image Processing, Analysis and Machine Vision*, Chapman and Hall, London, 1993.

[Sparks & Nelson 87] D. L. Sparks and J. S. Nelson, Sensory and motor maps in the mammalian superior colliculus, *Trends in Neuroscience*, Vol. 10, pp. 312-317, 1987 (after [Gallistel 90]).

[Spektrum 95] *Spektrum der Wissenschaft*, pp. 96-115, ISSN 0170-2971, March 1995.

[Stelarc] Stelarc. http://www.stelarc.va.com.au.

[Stevens *et al.* 95] A. Stevens, M. Stevens and H. Durrant-Whyte, 'OxNav': Reliable Autonomous Navigation, *Proc. IEEE International Conference on Robotics and Automation*, Vol. 3, pp. 2607-2612, Piscataway NJ, 1995.

[Sutton 84] R. Sutton, *Temporal Credit Assignment in Reinforcement Learning*, PhD Thesis, University of Massachusetts, Amherst MA, 1984.

[Sutton 88] R. Sutton, Learning to Predict by the Method of Temporal Differences, *Machine Learning*, Vol. 3, pp. 9-44, 1988.

[Sutton 90] R. Sutton, Integrated Architectures for Learning, Planning and Reacting Based on Approximating Dynamic Programming, *Proceedings of the 7th International Conference on Machine Learning*, pp. 216-224, Morgan Kaufman, San Mateo CA, 1990.

[Sutton 91] Richard S. Sutton, Reinforcement Learning Architectures for Animats, in [SAB 91] pp. 288-296.

[Tani & Fukumura 94] J. Tani and N. Fukumara, Learning Goal-Directed Sensory-Based Navigation of a Mobile Robot, *Neural Networks*, Vol. 7, No. 3, pp. 553-563, 1994.

[Tolman 48] E. C. Tolman, Cognitive Maps in Rats and Men, *Psychol. Rev.*, Vol. 55, pp. 189-208, 1948.

[Torras 91] Carme Torras i Genís, Neural Learning Algorithms and their Applications in Robotics, in Agnessa Babloyantz (ed.), *Self-Organization, Emerging Properties and Learning*, pp. 161-176, Plenum Press, New York, 1991.

[Walcott & Schmidt-Koenig] C. Walcott and K. Schmidt-Koenig, The effect on homing of anaesthesia during displacement, *Auk 90*, pp. 281-286, 1990.

[Walter 50] W. Grey Walter, An Imitation of Life, *Scientific American*, Vol. 182, Issue 5, pp. 42-45, 1950; and A Machine that Learns, *Scientific American*, Vol. 51, pp. 60-63, 1951.

[Waterman 89] Talbot H. Waterman, *Animal Navigation*, Scientific American Library, New York, 1989.

[Watkins 89] Christopher J.C.H. Watkins, *Learning from Delayed Rewards*, PhD Thesis, King's College, Cambridge, 1989.

[Webster 81] *Webster's Third New International Dictionary*, Encyclopaedia Britannica Inc., Chicago, 1981. See also http://www.m-w.com/cgi-bin/dictionary.

[Wehner & Räber 79] R. Wehner and F. Räber, Visual Spatial Memory in Desert Ants *Cataglyphis bicolor*, *Experientia*, Vol. 35, pp. 1569-1571, 1979.

[Wehner & Srinivasan 81] R. Wehner and M. V. Srinivasan, *Searching Behaviour of Desert Ants, Genus* Cataglyphis (Formicidae, *Hymenoptera)*, *Journal of Comparative Physiology*, Vol. 142, pp. 315-338, 1981, after [Gallistel 90].

[Wehner *et al.* 96] R. Wehner, B. Michel and P. Antonsen, Visual Navigation in Insects: Coupling Egocentric and Geocentric Information, *Journal of Experimental Biology*, Vol. 199, pp. 129-140, The Company of Biologists Limited, Cambridge UK, 1996.

[Weiss & v.Puttkamer 95] G. Weiss and E. v. Puttkamer, A Map Based on Laserscans Without Geometric Interpretation, *Intelligent Autonomous Systems 4* (IAS 4), pp. 403-407, Karlsruhe, Germany, March 1995.

[Whitehead & Ballard 90] Steven Whitehead and Dana Ballard, Active Perception and Reinforcement Learning, *Neural Computation*, Vol. 2, pp. 409-419, 1990.

[Wichert 97] Georg von Wichert, Ein Beitrag zum Erlernen der Wahrnehmung: Grundlagen und Konsequenzen für die Architektur autonomer, mobiler Roboter, *PhD Thesis*, Technical University of Darmstadt, Darmstadt, 1997.

[Wiltschko & Wiltschko 95] R. Wiltschko and W. Wiltschko, *Magnetic Orientation in Animals*, Springer Verlag, Berlin, Heidelberg, New York, 1995.

[Wiltschko & Wiltschko 98] W. Wiltschko and R. Wiltschko, The Navigation System in Birds and its Development, in R. P. Balda, I. M. Pepperberg and A. C. Kamil (eds.), *Animal Cognition in Nature*, pp. 155-200, Academic Press, 1998.

[Yamauchi & Beer 96] B. Yamauchi and R. Beer, Spatial Learning for Navigation in Dynamic Environments, *IEEE Transactions on Systems, Man and Cybernetics, Part B: Cybernetics*, Vol. 26, No.3, pp. 496-505, 1996.

[Yamauchi & Langley 96] B. Yamauchi and P. Langley, Place Recognition in Dynamic Environments, *Journal of of Robotics Systems*, Special Issue on Mobile Robots, Vol. 14, No. 2, pp. 107-120, 1996.

[Zimmer 95] U. Zimmer, Self-Localization in Dynamic Environments, *IEEE/SOFT International workshop BIES 95*, Tokyo, 1995.

Index